O God, there is a dark and lonesome gulf in worship, a cavern of the awesome into which we rarely go. We prefer catchy tunes, bright vestments, and holiday prayers. We would rather exchange fellowship than touch holiness. Enable us in this precious time to venture into the depths of worship which can never be found totally in individual spirituality but which open slowly before the shared pain, struggle, and love of the communion of the saints. Amen.

# TOUCH HOLINESS

*Edited by*
**Ruth C. Duck**
*and*
**Maren C. Tirabassi**

**THE PILGRIM PRESS**
New York

Biblical quotations, unless otherwise noted, are from the Revised Standard Version of the Bible, copyright 1946, 1952, © 1971, 1973 by the Division of Christian Education of the National Council of the Churches of Christ in the U.S.A., and are used by permission.

Excerpts cited as (Phillips) reprinted with permission of Macmillan Publishing Company from *New Testament in Modern English* (Revised Edition) by J. B. Phillips. Copyright © 1958, 1960, 1972 by J. B. Phillips.

Psalm 42:1–2 adapted and reprinted from *Psalms Now,* Copyright © 1973 Concordia Publishing House (3558 S. Jefferson Ave., St. Louis, Mo 63118. Phone: 800-325-3391; item 15-2125). Adapted and reprinted by permission from CPH. James 2:9 adapted and reprinted from *Epistles Now,* Copyright © 1974, 1976 Concordia Publishing House (item 15-2166). Adapted and reprinted by permission from CPH. Matthew 25:40 adapted and reprinted from *Jesus Now,* Copyright © 1973 Concordia Publishing House (item 15-2714). Adapted and reprinted by permission from CPH.

Scripture taken from the *Holy Bible: New International Version* (NIV). Copyright 1973, 1978, 1984 by the International Bible Society. Used by permission of Zondervan Bible Publishers.

Excerpts from the *New English Bible* (NEB) © The Delegates of the Oxford University Press and The Syndics of the Cambridge University Press, 1961, 1970.

Excerpts from the *Good News Bible,* the Today's English Version of the New Testament (TEV). Copyright © 1966, 1971, 1976 by the American Bible Society.

Excerpt on p. 51 from *True Prayer* by Kenneth Leech. Copyright © 1980 by Kenneth Leech. Reprinted by permission of Harper & Row, Publishers, Inc.

Excerpts on pp. 159–62 from the *Book of Worship—United Church of Christ* (New York: United Church of Christ Office for Church Life and Leadership, 1986). Adapted and reprinted by permission.

Excerpts on p. 161 from the *Book of Worship* of the Evangelical and Reformed Church. Used by permission of United Church Press.

The image "Bakerwoman God" on p. 120 comes from the poem of that name in *Womanpriest: A Personal Odyssey,* 2d ed., Lura Media, 1988, by Alla Renee Bozarth (Alla Bozarth-Campbell).

Designed by Publishers' WorkGroup

**Library of Congress Cataloging-in-Publication Data**

Touch holiness : resources for worship / edited by Ruth C. Duck and
   Maren C. Tirabassi.
      p.    cm.
   ISBN 0–8298–0809–4
    1. Public worship—Handbooks, manuals, etc.  2. Worship programs.
I. Duck, Ruth C.,   .  II. Tirabassi, Maren C.
BV25.T68    1989                        89–39435
264—dc20

The Pilgrim Press, 475 Riverside Drive, New York, NY 10115

# Contents

# *Preface*

This book is an offering to all who prepare worship services. That preparation entails great responsibility. Those who come to worship bring joys, fears, doubts, and hopes. Struggles and blessings crowd their minds, fill their hearts, bind their spirits. In worship they long to express their feelings, release their worries, and experience renewal and challenge. Printed shared worship words can be empowering, illuminating, or tedious. This book is an offering to all who prepare worship services and occasionally have days when images are fuzzy, metaphors are stale, and the Spirit is not blowing where we will.

We have collected these written resources from more than sixty gifted contributors. The resources reflect faith and vision shared originally in congregations and college chapels, on retreats, and at denominational meetings. Some are formal and some casual; some are elegant, some conversational. They are shaped as poetry or prose; they are long or short; they spring from a variety of theological and liturgical perspectives.

There was a time in the process of compiling this book when we were overwhelmed by the dissimilarities and dissonances, the confusion of so many styles. But out of that variety itself, that beautiful variety, a composite of greater strength emerged. All those worship words—the collect for the third Sunday in Lent, the call to worship for the twentyfourth Sunday after Pentecost, the seventeenth invocation from general resources using images from Hawaii, the prayer accompanying the presentation of a rose on the occasion of the birth of twins, the Order of Christian Dying into Life—all those worship words became worship. We too were drawn into the lonesome place, the precious time, and the shared pain, struggle, and love through which we touch holiness.

## THE STRUCTURE OF THE BOOK

We have organized the material into three parts. The first part contains material coordinated according to times of the church year; the second part contains resources for the sacraments and the rites of the church; and the third part, resources that may be used at any time during the year.

Part 1, Resources Based on the Lectionary and the Liturgical Year, provides calls to

worship, invocations, prayers of confession, and collects or unison prayers for every
Sunday of the church year. Additional materials, such as Advent Candlelighting Rituals,
appear at the end of each section.

Many churches today use the three-year Roman Lectionary of 1969 or an adaptation
of it, such as the *Common Lectionary*. Our authors wrote many of these resources to
coordinate with specific Sundays or scriptures in the lectionary. To assist the reader, we
identify the Sunday and/or scripture for which a specific resource was written or might
be used. Some of the resources were written for a Sunday in Year A, others for Year B,
and others for Year C. When only the year in the cycle is identified, the author wrote
the material in response to the scriptures for that day, without actually quoting or
paraphrasing any one of the texts. When a scripture reference is given without indicating
the year, the text is quoted or paraphrased in the prayer, although it may not be the
lectionary text for the day. When both scripture reference and year are given, that
usually means the resource was written for a specific Sunday and the scriptures listed
were quoted or paraphrased. We used the *Common Lectionary* to identify where a text
comes in the lectionary. However, individual references occasionally do not conform
exactly to the *Common Lectionary*. When no scripture reference or year is given, the call
to worship or prayer is appropriate for the season yet not tied to the lectionary readings.
Readers may also discover that a prayer coordinated to a particular Sunday or year will
be appropriate for another Sunday or year in the same season.

Readers who follow the system that names Sundays after Pentecost by Proper
numbers will be able to select the resources they need by adding two to the Sunday
number; for example, the twelfth Sunday after Pentecost is Proper 14. Those who do not
use the lectionary may find it useful to identify resources for a given Sunday by
consulting the scripture index, looking through resources for the entire season, or
selecting materials from Part 3 (General Resources).

Besides offering resources written to correspond to the church year and lectionary as
they presently exist, we offer two proposals for reform of the lectionary. First, we
suggest the celebration of Epiphany on January 6, and with a greater emphasis on the
incarnation and the baptism of Jesus than on the coming of the magi. Second, we offer
alternative lectionary readings for the purpose of doing greater justice to women, by
remembering women of faith and highlighting feminine images of God in scripture.

Part 2, Sacraments and Rites of the Church, provides a variety of resources for use in
services when baptism or holy communion is celebrated. A service of rededication to
Christian life is also offered, as is A Service of Thanksgiving for Christian Dying into
Life, an innovative ritual for use by those who are experiencing new life after a time of
loss. Resources for confirmation and marriage are also included in this section.

Part 3, General Resources, includes resources which might be used any Sunday during
the church year: calls to worship, invocations, prayers of confession, unison prayers,
prayers of intercession, and benedictions. Another section includes sung service
materials, including new texts for the doxology and sung benediction responses.
Resources for use at special times in the lives of congregations are also included. For

example, from Barneveld, Wisconsin, devastated by a tornado in 1984, comes a Service of Thanksgiving and Dedication of a Church (Rebuilt after Natural Disaster). The Order for Commissioning a Search Committee is another resource which some churches will find useful.

Scripture was used by our authors in various ways. Some directly quoted scripture; others paraphrased; still others alluded to particular passages or scripture images. Please consult the passage referenced to discover how a scripture was used in a specific resource. Scriptures were quoted or adapted from the Revised Standard Version of the Bible unless otherwise noted.

Words in italics or enclosed in brackets are instructions for worship leaders and are not meant to be read aloud during worship.

The support, advice, and work of many people went into producing this book. We want to express thanks to the authors who shared their creative work and who graciously responded to our editorial suggestions.

We are also grateful to several people at The Pilgrim Press. Marion Meyer, who was Senior Book Editor at Pilgrim, guided the development of the book in its beginning stages. Stephanie Egnotovich, who became Senior Book Editor after Meyer retired, has ably guided the completion of the book with many excellent suggestions for its improvement. Larry Kalp, Secretary for Publication at the United Church Board for Homeland Ministries, encouraged our work during the transition period. Thanks to Desiree Lindsay, Rose Amodeo, and Donna Miner, who were responsible for word processing. Lindsay and Amodeo were theological students at the time when they worked on the book, and they also offered helpful suggestions about its content. Thanks also to Barbara Rogers, who developed the scripture index.

We are grateful to Horace Allen and Marjorie Procter-Smith, liturgical scholars who served as consultants to us in the matter of lectionary reform. Allen, who also guided Ruth Duck in the writing of her doctoral dissertation at Boston University School of Theology, serves on the Consultation on Common Texts which produced the *Common Lectionary*. Procter-Smith, Assistant Professor of Worship at Perkins School of Theology, has advised the Consultation on Common Texts concerning lectionary reform for the purpose of justice to women.

Maren Tirabassi and Ruth Duck are both clergy associated with the Massachusetts Conference of the United Church of Christ. They met while serving on the committee that plans worship for the Conference Annual Meeting. The idea of working together on this book originated with Susannah Baker, Associate Conference Minister for Policy and Administration. The Metrical Service Music (General Resources) was gathered by the Massachusetts Conference Committee on Worship and by Allen Happe.

Editing this book has been time-consuming and has met with many delays. Thus, Maren's husband, Don Tirabassi, who has assisted with various tasks in the book, has dubbed it "The Never-Ending Story," after a film that Ruth's husband, John Stoppels, also loves. Thanks to both, and to Maren's children, for their support and help during the three years it has taken to develop this book.

Now we offer these worship resources to you. We hope that on the lips and in the hearts of those who come together longing to touch holiness, these words become worship. Worship is a living joy and an aching wonder even for clergy and lay leaders . . . and even for compilers of resource books. It is found among the communion of saints and in the shelter of God's hand.

RUTH C. DUCK
MAREN C. TIRABASSI

# RESOURCES BASED ON THE LECTIONARY AND THE LITURGICAL YEAR

# *Resources for Advent*

## CALLS TO WORSHIP

### FIRST SUNDAY OF ADVENT (YEAR A, ISA. 2:3–4)

Hear the invitation of the prophet Isaiah:
Come, let us go up to God's holy mountain,
that we may learn to walk in all God's ways.
For God will judge between the nations,
and shall decide for many peoples,
and they shall beat their swords into plowshares,
and their spears into pruning hooks.
Nation shall not lift up sword against nation,
neither shall they learn war any more.
Let us come before God and learn God's ways of peace. (RCD)

Or

To stand watch—
over a sick child or a rising loaf,
at the gate of a factory,
upon the ramparts of a walled city
or on the craggy top of a mountain—
calls for alert senses and sensitivities.
Standing watch demands an awareness of surroundings, for even when it seems as though there is nothing out there to watch for, you must be ready for anything. Standing watch builds anticipation.

In this season we seek to watch with eagerness for the promised but always surprising arrival of Christ. God comes to be with us, ready or not. May our worship this morning and in days ahead be times of looking forward with perceptive and receptive watchfulness. (GER)

3

## SECOND SUNDAY OF ADVENT (MATT. 1:23; ISA. 7:14, ADAPTED)

LEADER:   A tiny jewel of light
dances on the edge of the horizon:
a solitary star before sunrise
glimmers a promise of dawn
at the end of the world's blight.

PEOPLE:   It is the light of the World,
"Emmanuel" (God-with-us),
the Promised One.
Come to us, Emmanuel!
We have seen your light
and gather here
awaiting the day of your coming.                    (JWH)

## THIRD SUNDAY OF ADVENT (1 JOHN 4:9–12)

God's love has been made known among us,
for God has sent Christ into the world
that all people might live.
My friends, if God so loved us,
we also ought to love one another.
No one has ever seen God,
but if we love one another,
God abides in us.
Let us worship God
and seek to love as God has loved us.                    (RCD)

## FOURTH SUNDAY OF ADVENT (YEAR C, LUKE 1)

Let us rejoice in God our Savior,
who has done great things for us,
who fills the hungry with good things!
Let us open ourselves to the Spirit of life and new birth!
Let us worship God!                    (RCD)

# INVOCATIONS

## FIRST SUNDAY OF ADVENT (YEAR A, ISA. 2:1–5)

Compassionate God, greet us with your grace this day, for we need you. We cannot save ourselves. Though we may be frantic with activity, our efforts do not yield peace, peace as you can give. Today we would be quiet enough to hear your voice. Today we would be still enough to feel your touch. Help us to find that place where we can receive as well as give, wait as well as act, and listen as well as speak. Our whole world needs your peace. Let us come before you and learn your ways, laying down our weapons and feeding the hungry. Come to us now, through Jesus the Christ. Amen. (RCD)

## SECOND SUNDAY OF ADVENT (ISA. 40:3–4)

Gracious God, we hear the promise of the coming of Jesus into a manger and into our hearts and homes. Bless our Advent waiting; fill our worship with anticipation of your love; and dedicate us to prepare your way by lifting up the valleys in our lives and making smooth the rough places of others. For we pray in the name of Emmanuel—God with us. Amen. (MCT)

## THIRD SUNDAY OF ADVENT

Eternal Creator, with you each moment of life is full of wonder and surprise. We pray you to make us watchful as we await the coming of Christ. Grant that we may not be found sleeping in sin, but awake and rejoicing in your newness of life. Through the same Jesus Christ our Savior. Amen. (MGMG)

## FOURTH SUNDAY OF ADVENT

As Christmas trees are lighted,
as people rush to shop and send their cards,
as Christmas songs are heard everywhere,
keep us close to you,
that the one whose coming we celebrate—
Jesus Christ—may be honored by all we do.

May all that we do in this season
shine forth with your love.
We are your people.
Love through us.
Let Christ be seen in us;
for we pray in Christ's name. Amen. (RCD)

# PRAYERS OF CONFESSION

## FIRST SUNDAY OF ADVENT (YEAR A, ISA. 2:4; MIC. 4:3)

We confess, O God, that we do not take seriously your coming into our lives. We do not believe that salvation is near; we do not act uprightly, loving you, our neighbors, or ourselves; nor do we bend our swords and spears. Forgive us, we pray, that we might once again walk in your light, choosing for the world of our Christ. Amen.          (JWR)

## SECOND SUNDAY OF ADVENT

Silent Word, Creative Act, Hidden Truth, Revealed Love: we wait for you. To be precise, we are impatient for you to come and set things right. We are insecure with our world, fearful of crime in the streets, and anxious about ourselves. We refuse your guidance, but we often wish you would act according to our plans. We seldom pause to consider that you are waiting for us: waiting for some genuine act of contrition; waiting for us to repent and change; waiting for us to listen and respond with a burning passion to your truth, your justice, and your mercy. Furnish us with humble hearts and willing spirits to receive you as you come to us through all the experiences of our lives. Amen.

(APH)

OR

## (Year C, Mal. 3:1–2)

*Call to Confession*

How can we stand in the presence of God? Let us confess those places where we need to grow to prepare for Christ to come to our lives.

*Prayer of Confession*

God of the loving heart, we confess before you those places in our hearts where we have refused you entrance: people we have refused to love; habits we never get around to changing; good things we have left undone; and ways in which we hurt you, ourselves, and others. Come to us in the light of your Christ. Shine on those places we have hidden from you. Show us new ways to live. Sweep clean the rooms of our hearts, that Christ may find a home among us. Be known among us now and forever! Amen.   (RCD)

*Words of Assurance*

This is the good news in Jesus Christ.
We can stand before God,
not through our own goodness,
but through God's great kindness to us.
Rejoice and be glad, for God comes to you!                    (RCD)

## THIRD SUNDAY OF ADVENT

O Holy God, our very waiting in Advent is itself a confession: If we are waiting for Emmanuel, we are not yet with you; if we are waiting for Jesus, we need a Savior; if we are waiting for a Messiah, the proud are still powerful, the mighty are still exalted, the hungry stand unheard at the door; if we are waiting for your incarnation in human form, we confess that we have not known you in our sister, we have not loved you in our brother, we have not served you in our neighbor. In this time of great meaning, in the stillness of Advent love and light, hear our deepest confession; heal us and make us new through the good tidings of your presence in our lives. Amen.

(MCT)

## FOURTH SUNDAY OF ADVENT

We sing, "O come all ye faithful," God, but we confess that we are not always faithful. We could have shown love this past week, but we kept ourselves busy with other things. We spoke without thinking and hurt someone. We treated the gifts and greetings and meals as chores, leaving out the most important ingredient—caring. We are sorry. Please forgive us, and accept our worship.

Amid the bright colors that surround us this season—the red, the green, the gold—send the light of your Christ, that all that is good may be revealed more clearly and all that is wrong may be exposed and changed.

We pray in the name of Jesus who was born in Bethlehem, who lived and died for our sakes, and who lives and reigns with you and the Holy Spirit, now and forever. Amen.

(RCD)

# UNISON PRAYERS/COLLECTS

## FIRST SUNDAY OF ADVENT

God without beginning and without end, your promise comes to us, bringing hope. May we in turn come to your mountain, bending our swords and spears, seeking instruction, and walking in your light; in the name of Jesus the Christ, the light of the world. Amen.

(JWR)

## SECOND SUNDAY OF ADVENT

Wonderful Counselor, Mighty God, O Promised One. Once again we come to this time of Advent and await your presence.

Give us the patience to seek the meaning of these busy days.

Give us the courage to wait in times of pain and trouble.

Give us the compassion to wait for one another.

Give us the faith to wait for the Messiah when we are threatened by the Herods of this world.

Give us the hope to wait for the Savior even when we cannot hear the angels singing.

Give us the love that does not wait when it meets Christ in our neighbor. Amen.

(MCT)

## THIRD SUNDAY OF ADVENT

In your Christ, O God, we discover salvation coming to all who need. Our past has been made new, our futures restored, the earth rejoices with your spiral of beauty—grant, we pray, that our lives be fulfilled in this your fulfillment for us; through Christ Jesus. Amen.

(JWR)

## FOURTH SUNDAY OF ADVENT

O God, at this time each year, we remind ourselves that you have come and continue coming into our lives. You shatter reasoned expectations, give wonder and awe, and fulfill promises little understood. Watching and waiting, we pray, hasten the day! Amen.

(AKJ)

# LITANIES

## FIRST SUNDAY OF ADVENT

LEADER:    We've seen the star in the East, and again we begin our journey to worship the ruler of the Jews. On the advent road, the star lights our anticipation of family gathering, of loving friendship, of saving holiness.

PEOPLE:    On the advent road, the star gleams in Rachel's tears for loved ones gone, for times of pain, for times remembered that will be no more.

LEADER:    On the advent road, the starlight dances with joyous celebration, winter play, carol singing, yuletide spirit, Christmas giving.

PEOPLE:    On the advent road, the star leads us by Herods of greed and need, haste and waste, neglect and death.

ALL:    On the advent road, hand in hand, we follow the star, with shepherds' fear and angels' joy, that we might see the newborn child.    (AKJ)

## SECOND SUNDAY OF ADVENT (YEAR A, ISA. 11:1–10)

LEADER:    Wonder of wonders—the wolf shall dwell with the lamb.

PEOPLE:    No one shall hurt or destroy in God's holy mountain.

LEADER:    Wonder of wonders—the leopard shall lie down with the kid.

PEOPLE:    The earth shall be full of the knowledge of God as the waters cover the sea.

LEADER:    Wonder of wonders—calf and lion together shall be led by a little child.

PEOPLE:    No one shall hurt or destroy in God's holy mountain.

LEADER:    Wonder of wonders—cow and bear, lion and ox shall share their dinner in peace.

PEOPLE:    The earth shall be full of the knowledge of God as the waters cover the sea.

LEADER:    Wonder of wonders—the nursing baby will play with the serpent, and a child will sit unharmed by the venomous snake.

PEOPLE:    No one shall hurt or destroy in God's holy mountain.

LEADER:    Wonder of wonders—the Messiah shall judge for the world's poor, for the meek, the lowly, and the little of the earth.

PEOPLE:    The earth shall be full of the knowledge of God as the waters cover the sea.

LEADER:    This is how you shall know the Messiah—by a spirit of wisdom and understanding, of counsel and might, of knowledge and fear of God.

PEOPLE:    Wonder beyond wonders, grace upon grace, joy at the heart of joy.    (MCT)

## THIRD SUNDAY OF ADVENT—LITANY FOR HEALING
## (YEAR A, MATT. 11:1–11, 28)

LEADER:    God of love and power, we come to you for healing. Where relationships are full of stress and unkind words shatter the spirit,

PEOPLE:   Grant reconciliation and renewal.

LEADER:   When the load seems too heavy and our backs are tight with pressure,

PEOPLE:   Place on us your yoke, which is easy, and your burden, which is light.

LEADER:   When change comes too fast and too painfully, and our lives are all in pieces,

PEOPLE:   Help us shape ourselves anew out of the fragments.

LEADER:   Hear our silent prayers for healing: [*Silence*]

LEADER:   We pray also for healing in our world.

PEOPLE:   May divided factions grow to understand one another and seek the good of all.

LEADER:   We pray for peacemakers:

PEOPLE:   Give your wisdom to those who seek to limit the use of nuclear weapons and who labor for peace in any way.

LEADER:   In wounded places of our globe—South Africa, Central America, the Middle East, and elsewhere,

PEOPLE:   God, heal as you know how; lead your people as they seek justice and peace.

LEADER:   Hear our silent prayers for the healing of nations: [*Silence*]

ALL:   God of love and power, you are the healer who came to us in Jesus Christ. We know you are near when people are healed and the poor hear good news. Be known among us in healing power, for we pray in the name of Jesus Christ, who was and is, and is to come. Amen.     (RCD)

OR

### (Year A, Isa. 35:1–3, 5–7a, 9–10)

LEADER:   Let the wilderness and dry lands exult,
          let the wasteland rejoice and bloom.

PEOPLE:   Let it bring forth flowers like the jonquil,
          let it rejoice and sing for joy.

LEADER:   The glory of Lebanon is bestowed upon it,
          the splendor of Carmel and Sharon.

PEOPLE:   They shall see the glory of God,
          the splendor of our God.

LEADER:   Strengthen all weary hands,
          steady all trembling knees.

PEOPLE:   The eyes of those blind shall be opened,
          the ears of those deaf unsealed,
          then those lame shall leap like a deer,
          and the tongues of the dumb sing for joy.

LEADER:   For water gushes in the desert, streams in the wasteland.

PEOPLE:   The scorched earth becomes a lake,
          the parched land springs of water.

LEADER:  No lion will be there,
         nor any fierce beast roam about it,
         but the redeemed will walk there,
         for those whom God has ransomed shall return.
ALL:     They will come to Zion shouting for joy—
         everlasting joy on their faces—
         joy and gladness will go with them,
         and sorrow and lament be ended.

                                                                          (JWR)

## FOURTH SUNDAY OF ADVENT
## (YEAR A, PS. 24:1–2, 7–10, ADAPTED)

LEADER:  The earth is God's and all that is in it,
         the world and all who dwell therein;
PEOPLE:  For it is God who founded it upon the seas,
         and made it firm upon the rivers of the deep.
LEADER:  Lift your heads, O gates!
         Lift them high, O everlasting doors,
         and the ruler of glory shall come in.
PEOPLE:  Who is this ruler of glory?
LEADER:  God, strong and mighty,
         God, mighty in battle!
PEOPLE:  Lift your heads, O gates!
         Lift them high, O everlasting doors,
         and the ruler of glory shall come in.
LEADER:  Who is this ruler of glory?
ALL:     The God of hosts!
         This is the ruler of glory!

*Silent prayer*

*Collect (paraphrases "O Little Town of Bethlehem")*

We stand at the doors to your great temple, O God, and we open wide our hearts awaiting the one who deals with our sin. May Emmanuel descend to us, we pray, casting out our sin and entering in; may Christ be born in us each day; we pray through Christ's name. Amen.

                                                                          (JWR)

# OTHER ADVENT RESOURCES

1. All praise to you, Emmanuel, God-promised, and God with us; all praise to you in the silence and the singing of this sacred season of Advent. Because of you, stars shine in our lives and our poor manger places become holy straw. May the good tidings of peace on earth and good will to the people of the earth be on our lips, as with the shepherds and the angels. We give you thanks, Emmanuel, for becoming human—weak and poor and cold and lonely. We become more human for knowing you—more able to lift our burdens and open our doors to strangers. We give you thanks, Emmanuel, for choosing the low and the rejected and the broken; so we find mercy in our struggles and courage in the rough places and crooked paths, even in the shadow of death. All praise to you, Emmanuel, God-promised and God-with-us, for your advent candle burns brightly in our lives. Amen.          (MCT)

2. Holy Center of this most holy season, Jesus, child and ruler, all our stars point to your birth; all our wanderings come home to you; all our griefs and delights find a place in the stable where you choose to transform poverty and pain and loneliness and rejection. Your light shines in our lives; your peace embraces our anger, sorrow, and loss; your life opens us to new discovery of our most intimate selves and of our neighbors, however we may find them—as poor as shepherds, as foreign as magi, as thoughtless as innkeepers, as helpless as infants. In your humble birth we discover your everlasting majesty and grace. We welcome you and offer you our thanks and praise, in your glorious name. Amen.          (MCT)

3. Call to Worship and Invocation Based on Ps. 96

*Call to Worship*

O sing a new song!
O sing to God, all the earth!
Let the heavens be glad,
let the earth rejoice,
let the sea roar, and all that fills it;
let the field exult, and everything in it!
Then shall all the trees of the wood sing for joy
before God, for God comes to judge the earth.
God will judge the world with righteousness,
and the peoples with truth.          (RCD)

*Invocation*

God, we rejoice when you come to us, for you bring justice and peace; you rule with grace and truth. Now in this season we rejoice in your coming in Jesus Christ. Come, reign among us in the power of the Holy Spirit. Amen.          (RCD)

4.  In the advent seasons,
    when the past has fled, unasked, away
    and there is nothing left to do but wait,
    God, shelter us.

    Be our surrounding darkness;
    be fertile soil
    out of which hope springs
    in due time.

    In uncertain times,
    help us to greet the dawn
    and labor on, love on,
    in faith awaiting your purpose
    hid in you
    waiting to be born
    in due time.

                                                                                    (RCD)

# ADVENT CANDLELIGHTING RITUAL I

## FIRST SUNDAY—THE PROPHETS' CANDLE

Today we begin the season of Advent by lighting the first of five candles in our Advent wreath. This candle we shall name the prophets' candle. From ancient and modern prophets we hear of the coming of a Savior. Sometimes prophetic words are hard to believe. We are uncertain of their truth. We must wait and be patient. In honor of all the prophets, we light this candle.

*Light one purple candle.*

*Prayer*

Dear God of the Prophets, give us this day the prophetic word of hope, that in the moments of despair we might look to you for comfort. We give you thanks for all the prophets past and present. Amen.

## SECOND SUNDAY—THE BETHLEHEM CANDLE

Today we light the second Advent candle, the Bethlehem candle. This candle is offered in honor of the birthplace of Jesus as well as of the many places where Christ is born in the hearts of believers. While Bethlehem was so busy with commerce that it had only a stable to offer Jesus, let our Bethlehems be places of warmth and welcome. In honor of Bethlehem we light this candle.

*Light another purple candle.*

*Prayer*

Dear God, who comes to us through Jesus at Bethlehem, enable us to open our hearts so that we might have Christ in us. We give you thanks for the places where we meet the Christ. Amen.

## THIRD SUNDAY—THE SHEPHERDS' CANDLE

Today we light the third Advent candle, the shepherds' candle. This candle is offered in honor of the shepherds whose love and care for their sheep become the example of God's love for us. We remember that the shepherds were the first witnesses of our Savior's birth. In honor of all good shepherds and, especially, Jesus the Christ, we light this candle.

*Light the last purple candle.*

*Prayer*

Dear God, our Good Shepherd, empower our lives to be filled with love, that in loving others we might bear witness to your love for us. We give you thanks for shepherds, especially Jesus. Amen.

## FOURTH SUNDAY—THE ANGELS' CANDLE

Today we light the fourth Advent candle, the angels' candle. This candle is offered in honor of the angels who told the good news to the shepherds, "Glory be to God in the highest and on earth, peace and goodwill toward all." The angels sang with joy so that all who could hear were filled with joy. In honor of all the angels who continue to proclaim the good news of joy, we light this candle.

*Light the fourth candle.*

*Prayer*

Dear God, you surround us with your angel of love so that we are able to live a life filled with joy. Thank you for these angels, and help us to become angels of love for others. Amen.

## CHRISTMAS EVE—THE CHRIST CANDLE

Tonight is the night for which we have been waiting. The Advent wreath is completed with the Christ candle in the center. "For unto us a child is given, unto us a Savior is born and the order of the world will be upon his shoulders." With the birth of Christ our lives are centered, focused, turned toward God. We light this candle because Christ is the center of our lives.

*Light the white candle in the center.*

*Prayer*

Dear God, who comes to us in Jesus, on this night as we celebrate the birth of Jesus, let the power of Christ come into our hearts that we might find peace with you forever. Amen.

(CCC)

# ADVENT CANDLELIGHTING RITUAL II

## FIRST SUNDAY IN ADVENT

READER 1: This is the first Sunday in Advent, the time of preparing for the coming of Christ our Savior. Today our word is *wait*. God does not come at our command. We wait on God, scripture says. Advent is a time to wait, to wonder what God has in store for us.

READER 2: [*Isa. 63:15—64:5a*]

READER 1: As we light* the first Advent candle, we wait—we wait for God's new age; we wait for Christ to be reborn in our hearts; we wait for our prayers to be answered.

READER 2: Let us pray together. Christ, you know how hard it is for us to wait. We want everything right now. Help us to use our time well as we wait for Christ. Amen.

## SECOND SUNDAY IN ADVENT

READER 1: This is the second Sunday in Advent, the time of preparing for the coming of Christ our Savior. Today our word is *prepare*. Not only do we wait for our Savior, but we use this time of waiting creatively. We prepare for Christmas with gift purchases, tree trimming, home decorating, card mailing. We prepare for Christ with prayer, quiet contemplation, resolutions to be better people than we are now.

READER 2: [*Isa. 40:1–5, 9–11*]

READER 1: We light* the first Advent candle, remembering that we wait for Christ. We also light* today's candle, remembering that we must *prepare* our hearts for Christ's coming.

READER 2: Let us pray. Gracious God, help us to prepare not only our homes but also our hearts and lives for the coming of Emmanuel. Let us make our way straight, that Christ may come to us in the fullness of time, as we wait and prepare a place in our lives. Amen.

## THIRD SUNDAY IN ADVENT

READER 1: This is the third Sunday in Advent, the time of preparation for the coming of Christ our Savior. Today our word is *witness*. We do more than wait for our Savior or prepare ourselves. We are also called to witness. We should not keep news to ourselves, but rather share it with others. When the news is good news, our hearts overflow to tell others about the love we have found.

*Candles are lit where the asterisks appear.

READER 2: [*Isa. 61:1–4, 8–11*]

READER 1: We relight* our first Advent candle, which reminds us to wait on Christ. We also relight* last week's candle, remembering that we prepare as we wait. Now we light* today's candle, which reminds us to witness to the light that is coming into our world.

READER 2: Let us pray. Holy God, we find it difficult to tell the good news, and yet the world is yearning to hear it. Help us witness to the truth of our Savior, that others may come to the light and also be saved by grace. Let these candles remind us to wait, to prepare and to witness to Christ's coming. Amen.

## FOURTH SUNDAY IN ADVENT

READER 1: This is the fourth Sunday in Advent, the time of preparing for the coming of Christ our Savior. Today our words are *Let it be.* We remember that we are to wait, prepare, and witness. Now, as Christ's arrival nears, we are reminded of Mary's words, "Let it be." It is not up to us to dictate to God how Christ will come into our world and lives, for God continually surprises us. Let God's will be done in each of us.

READER 2: [*2 Sam. 7:8–16*]

READER 1: We relight our candles which remind us to wait,* to prepare,* to witness.* Now we complete our circle, lighting the candle which proclaims, "Let it be."* Christ is the light of our world, and we have only to open ourselves and he will come to us.

READER 2: Let us pray. Gracious God, our time of waiting is almost over. We pray that we have prepared well, that we have proclaimed and witnessed to Christ's coming, and that we are now willing to let Christ enter our hearts and lives. Amen.

## CHRISTMAS

READER 1: Our time to wait is over. Christmas is here. Our days of preparation are completed. What has not been done will now have to be left undone. We have witnessed to this very hour, this very night, and we hope that the world has heard the good news which we have spoken. We have decided to "Let it be," to do things God's way rather than our own, and to be satisfied with God's will.

READER 2: [*Isa. 52:7–10*]

READER 1: Our circle of Advent candles is lit; now tonight/today we light* the central candle, reminding us that Christ is the light of the world, the center of our lives, the shining beacon of hope for all the universe. Christ is born. Praise God!

READER 2:   Let us pray. O Holy God, thank you that the time of waiting and
            preparing is over and that the light of Christ shines so very clearly tonight.
            May our joy be full and our hearts rejoice for the world shall never be the
            same again. Truth and justice and righteousness have come to free all from
            the bondage of sin. Thank you, God, for this holy night of nights! Amen.

                                                                            (RLA)

# CHRISTMAS EVE CANDLELIGHTING SERVICE
## (2 Cor. 4:6; Gen. 1:1–3; 1 John 1:1–2, 5, 7; 4:7a; Matt. 5:16)

[Congregations have various opinions about using lighted candles on Christmas Eve. When a congregation decides the beauty of candlelighting is important enough to undertake the safety risks, a number of things can be done to reduce the risk. People can be seated while the candles are lit; water can be available in a number of locations in the sanctuary; only as many candles can be distributed as adults are present, so that when children hold the candles, an adult with no candle can supervise; the use of hymnals can be avoided; and sturdy candle holders can be made.

It can be quite effective simply to distribute candles during the last few minutes of the service, light them from the Christ candle, and sing. The candles may be extinguished before people leave the church.

What follows is an order for doing this.]

*Sentences Before Distribution of Candles:*

The God who said,
"Let there be light,"
has caused light to shine in our hearts.
That light is the glory of God
reflected in the face of Jesus Christ.
As our candles are a sea of light
lit from the one light of Christ,
so may the church reflect Christ's light and love in the world.

*Scripture Readings During the Distribution of Candles:*

In the beginning, God created the heavens and earth.
The earth was without form and void,
and darkness was on the face of the deep;
and the Spirit of God was moving over the waters.
And God said, "Let there be light";
and there was light.

A leader of the church of Ephesus wrote:

That which was from the beginning, which we have seen with our eyes, which we have looked upon and touched with our hands, concerning the word of life . . . we proclaim to you: God is light! If we walk in the light, as God is in the light, we have communion with one another . . . Friends, let us love one another, for love is of God.

*After all the candles have been lit, Christmas carols are sung, one stanza only, without using hymnals. Remain seated. During the last hymn, all may raise their candles.*

In a few moments, I will blow out my candle, and when I do, I ask that you do so as well. Carry the light of Christ in your hearts now and always.

### The Charge

Jesus said:
"You are the light of the world."
Let your light so shine
that people around you
will be moved by the good things you do
to glorify God in heaven.
Go in peace; God is with you. Amen. (RCD)


*Extinguish candles.*

# *Resources for Christmastide*

## CALLS TO WORSHIP

### CHRISTMAS EVE

LEADER: Tonight old dreams die
and new dreams come to life.
The Promise is fulfilled!

PEOPLE: Glory to God in the highest,
and on earth, peace.

LEADER: Hope gives way to joy
and prayer to proclamation.

PEOPLE: Glory to God in the highest,
and on earth, peace.

LEADER: Our candles illuminate our story.
Dawn invades midnight.
The Light of the World has come.

PEOPLE: Glory to God in the highest,
and on earth, peace.

LEADER: And this light is a light for all;
igniting a flame within the soul,
warming us from within,
radiating love,
lighting our lives
with the presence of God-come-alive
in human flesh
within us and among us
now and always.

PEOPLE: Glory to God in the highest,
and on earth, peace, goodwill to all.

(JWH)

### CHRISTMAS DAY (YEAR C, ISA. 52:7, 9)

LEADER:  How beautiful upon the mountains are the feet of one who brings good tidings.

PEOPLE:  We receive good tidings of joy, words of peace, a message of salvation.

LEADER:  Break forth into singing, for God has comforted the people, brought bloom to the wasteland, shown strength in all the nations.

PEOPLE:  Word of the infant born in Bethlehem is our good news.

LEADER:  Christ is born. The prophet's hopes are made flesh and all our longings are made human in joy.

PEOPLE:  Rejoice and be glad, for Christ is born today!                    (MCT)


### FIRST SUNDAY IN CHRISTMASTIDE
### (YEAR B, LUKE 2:25–38; ALLUDES TO LUKE 1)

LEADER:  Some people say that Christmas is for children.

PEOPLE:  Christmas is also for people of age and experience.

LEADER:  Elizabeth, Mary's cousin, and Zechariah, the priest, accepted new birth breaking into all their familiar patterns.

PEOPLE:  Simeon the singer and Anna the prophet hoped for many years to see the Messiah and then recognized the Messiah in a poor couple's baby.

LEADER:  How then shall we respond to Christ's promised coming?

PEOPLE:  With willingness for change, with patience in long waiting, with silence and singing, with the ability to see Christ in the least likely of our brothers and sisters.                    (MCT)


### SECOND SUNDAY IN CHRISTMASTIDE
### (YEAR A, JOHN 1:1–5, 9–14)

LEADER:  In the beginning was the Word and the Word was with God and the Word was God.

PEOPLE:  We understand that Christ was creative, speaking within all the universe.

LEADER:  John says that in Christ was life, life that was light which could not be overcome.

PEOPLE:  John's image portrays impossible possibility—that good shall not be overwhelmed by evil.

LEADER:  The human being who was preexistent Word and true light was also rejected by the world and ill-received by his own neighbors.

PEOPLE:  We worship the Son of God and the man of Nazareth—Jesus, who gives us power to become children of God.                    (MCT)

# INVOCATIONS

## CHRISTMAS EVE

*Unison Invocation*

O Holy God, we hear the story of shepherds and magi, of maiden and carpenter, of prophets and angels, and we too come to Bethlehem for a blessing. You are born in our hearts because you have chosen the weakness of our bodies for your birth. We are filled with love because you have taken upon yourself our humanity; we are filled with hope because you have offered us your Spirit, your life and your light; we are filled with faith because all that is meek and lowly and humble in us and in creation becomes holy this night. Our salvation has come into this holy time and we say together, "Glory to God in the highest, and on earth, peace and goodwill to all." Amen. (MCT)

*Responsive Invocation*

LEADER: Emmanuel: God, you are with us.
PEOPLE: We have heard the promise of the prophets;
LEADER: We have caught the notes of an angel's song;
PEOPLE: We have seen a star in the heavens, and we have believed.
LEADER: Tonight we have come to be with you because you have come to be with us.
PEOPLE: We seek an innocent, helpless baby in a crude manger;
LEADER: We seek a Messiah who will reign with justice;
PEOPLE: And you, who are the weakest and the strongest, the most humble and the most mighty, have found us.
LEADER: Now we may find ourselves.
PEOPLE: Now we may love each other, now we may truly worship you,
ALL: Crying aloud with the heavenly host: "Glory to God in the highest! Peace on earth and goodwill among all people." Amen. (MCT)

## CHRISTMAS DAY

O Jesus, Christ and Redeemer, we greet your morning with joy. We lift our spirits with thanksgiving for all your mercies to us that your sharing of our human situation brings. We thank you for Christmas joy—for toys and for friendship renewed and for hearts warmed by the love of dear ones and the greeting of strangers. We thank you for this Christian community which has become Bethlehem for us this morning. Even as we greet this morning with joy, we ask you to transform our joy into new lives as we find ourselves and each other in the new life of Christ Jesus. Amen. (MCT)

## A SUNDAY IN CHRISTMASTIDE

Giver of gifts, amid the tall tinseled trees your light breaks through to the world. We hear that you have come to us in love and in flesh. Speak to us anew of that eternal love which reaches out to us in the birth of Jesus. Amen.                    (CAT)

## SUNDAY CLOSEST TO NEW YEAR'S DAY (PS. 100)

Creative God, you make all things new in heaven and on earth.
We come to you in a new year with new desires and old fears,
new decisions and old controversies,
new dreams and old weaknesses.
Because you are a God of hope, we know that you create all the possibilities of the future.
Because you are a God of love, we know that you accept all the mistakes of the past.
Because you are the God of our faith, we enter your gates with thanksgiving and praise,
we come into your presence with gladness and a joyful noise,
and we serve and bless you, praying the prayer of our Savior Jesus Christ.                    (MCT)

# PRAYERS OF CONFESSION

## CHRISTMAS EVE

Gracious God, who promised to send a Redeemer to your people, we confess that we have not trusted your promise, but have busied ourselves with activities which obstruct its fulfillment.

We give presents, but fail to be present with one another.

We socialize with friends, but fail to welcome the stranger in our midst.

We create commotion, and refuse to receive your peace.

Forgive us, God, for our busyness and our lack of trust. Teach us to wait with expectant patience for the fulfillment of your promise to us. Amen.                    (MSH)


## CHRISTMAS DAY

O God, the prophet proclaims, the angels announce, the star lights the way, and we still ask, "Where?" Like children, we stand first on one foot and then the other, waiting impatiently for a parade, so eager for the bands and floats that we miss it while telling a friend what's coming.

We want a circus God.

We want ringmasters and acrobats, tigers and elephants, beautiful bareback riders—not some straw-strewn hovel with a swaybacked donkey and a tired woman with dark skin.

God, keep us willing and alert, that when you reveal yourself, we may be aware. Amen.                    (JHD)


## FIRST SUNDAY IN CHRISTMASTIDE

Gracious God, we have sought you in high and holy places; we are ill-prepared to acknowledge your presence among the lowly and poor. We believe you are profound but we overlook your obvious truths. We are anxious about the unknown but we hardly consider the realities immediately in front of us. Turn us, incarnate God, by the simple wonders of your love, to a rebirth of faith and hope and joy. Amen.                    (APH)


## SECOND SUNDAY IN CHRISTMASTIDE

Jesus Christ, God with us, you came that we may have life and have it more abundantly. We have not always lived up to your expectations for us. We confess that too often we are

—Impoverished of spirit. Grant us the fullness of your grace.

—Wrapped up in ourselves. Open us to others.

—Slow to learn. Teach us of your ever-expanding truth.

—Proud over little. Whet our hunger and thirst for justice.

—Scattered like grains of the field. Gather us into a single loaf.

—Distracted of mind. Direct us to what is most important: your love for us, your will for our lives, and your sustaining Presence in every circumstance. Amen.     (APH)

# UNISON PRAYERS

## CHRISTMAS EVE OR DAY

Emmanuel, God promised and God with us: Give us peace as we need peace; give us courage to live in times without peace. Awaken us to the hope of your reign, but restrain us from vain hopes in the dominions around us. Free us to claim our own welling-up joy, and sustain us when joy seems far. Lead us to service in your world; strengthen our feeble attempts to serve. Spirit of holiness and good tidings, we come through Advent again, and again we learn the meaning of incarnation. Form and receive our words of praise, prayer, and prophecy, for we magnify your name and rejoice in your salvation in the Christmas moment and the journey of our years and lives. Amen.

(MCT)

OR

God of the simple and the common, when we look upon the beautiful image of the Christ child we are struck by contrast: our schemes are not visible, our thoughts are not clear, and our motives are often mixed. We have mistaken skepticism for wisdom, excuses for discretion, and indulgence for wealth. By the remembrance of your nativity, may we see once more the native goodness of each human life! In the company of the child, may we shed every encumbrance and attain the freshness, the intimacy, and the joy of life. Is it not your desire that we now bear the image of Christ and live as your children? So be it!

(APH)

## FIRST SUNDAY IN CHRISTMASTIDE (INTERCESSION)

Gracious God, we pray this day for all who have come with us to Bethlehem. We pray for those who are poor and cold and hungry like the shepherds, that they may hear good news. We pray for those who are wandering and searching like the magi, that they may find the place to leave their gifts and their burdens. We pray for those who are busy, hurried, preoccupied like the innkeeper, that they may know the peace that comes from a genuine act of hospitality. We pray for those like Herod who have power, that they may use it with good will. We pray for ourselves—we who each need comfort and peace, even joy, in this starlit season and all the days of our lives. Amen. (MCT)

## SECOND SUNDAY IN CHRISTMASTIDE (YEAR C, LUKE 2:40)

O Christmas God—the tinsel falls, the year turns, and the carols fade. The blessing of Bethlehem that touched all the gray in our lives with star silver is past. We read that the holy child grew and became strong and God's favor was with him. In this string of nameless days we long for just such steady becoming—for renewal amid the routine, for courage in current events, for the assurance of God's presence beyond our holidays and into the wintering times of our lives. Amen. (MCT)

# LITANIES

## CHRISTMAS EVE (PS. 29, ADAPTED)

LEADER: Ascribe to God glory and strength!

PEOPLE: Ascribe to God the glory due God's name.
Worship God in the beauty of holiness.

LEADER: The voice of God is upon the waters;
the God of glory thunders;
God is upon the mighty waters!

PEOPLE: The voice of God is a powerful voice.
The voice of God is a voice of splendor.

LEADER: The voice of God breaks the cedar trees;
God breaks the cedars of Lebanon.

PEOPLE: God makes Lebanon skip like a calf
and Mount Hermon like a wild young ox.

LEADER: The voice of God sharpens lightening shafts,
the voice of God shakes the wilderness,
God shakes the wilderness of Kadesh.

PEOPLE: The voice of God makes the oak trees shudder and strips the forest bare,

LEADER: And in the temple of God everything cries:

PEOPLE: Glory!

LEADER: God sits enthroned above the flood;
God sits enthroned as ruler forevermore.

ALL: God shall give strength to God's people.
God shall give the blessing of peace.

*Silent Prayer*

*Collect*

ALL: Now, God of all, a new ruler sits over your creation, the one of your own choosing. Your word of peace shakes the trees and rattles the walls of the earth. Tonight with the angels we cry out, "Glory," for you have done a new thing through our Christ; in Christ's name. Amen.                    (JWR)

## CHRISTMAS DAY

LEADER: Emmanuel, we affirm that you are God-with-us this Christmas morning and all the days of the year.

PEOPLE: Emmanuel, we confess that we need both the tender words of the comforter and the shouted challenge of the herald.

LEADER: Emmanuel, we believe that you are the shepherd of our lives;

PEOPLE:    We come this morning to be nurtured for strength;

LEADER:    We come this morning to be gathered from the scatteredness and fragmentation of our hurried days;

PEOPLE:    We come this morning to be held and carried through the places of pain, sorrow, and fear;

UNISON:    We come this morning to be gently led into new paths of service as we become, by your strength, your shepherds for one another.

LEADER:    And so hear us, Emmanuel, as we pray together your prayer.

*Here follows the prayer of our Savior.*                                        (MCT)

OR

LEADER:    O Christ, light of the world, come to our lives and reveal meaning and truth.

PEOPLE:    O Christ, hope of the despairing, come to our lives and teach us simple joy.

LEADER:    Jesus Christ, bread of the soul, come to us and nourish us to true and eternal life.

PEOPLE:    Jesus Christ, shepherd of the flock, come and lead us to the springs of living water.

LEADER:    Living Christ, just and gentle judge, come and reveal us to ourselves.

PEOPLE:    Living Christ, healer of the wounded, come make us whole. Show us the way to new life.

ALL:       Jesus Christ our life, we celebrate your birth today. May our celebration be more than mere remembrance; may our worship be an opening of ourselves to you, in Spirit and in truth. Be born in us today, renew our spirits, and strengthen us to be your people in the world, through the indwelling power of your Holy Spirit. Amen.                                        (RCD)

# PASTORAL PRAYER FOR THE CHRISTMAS SEASON
## (alludes to Isa. 11:6; Amos 5:24; Ps. 103:8; Luke 2)

O God, whose love blesses and unites us in this place and time, we come before you with hearts gladdened by this holy season, its lights, its colors, and, most especially, its message of peace and good will to all.

In the birth of Jesus, you have given our weary and struggling world reason to rejoice. In the cry of an infant, you have given hope to all who cry. By the light of a star, you have helped us find our way again.

We thank you, good and generous God, that in Jesus the Christ, you have made yourself known and have beckoned us to join you in the continual creation of a world where wolf and lamb shall dwell together and justice will roll down like waters.

Create in us, O God, hearts devoted to shaping that world and bless especially those for whom such a world seems only a distant dream—the poor, the imprisoned, the ill, the lonely, the despised. Open our hearts, Spirit of Life, to the news of angels and the wonder of shepherds that these days may renew us for the days to come.

Grant us, for the sake of Christ's ministry, hearts that may discern how to make meaningful the gospel which we cherish. Grant, to your glory, that those whose lives we touch may hear in our words and see in our lives that truly you are merciful and gracious and abounding in steadfast love! These things we ask, trusting in your care for us today and always. Amen.

(ABD)

# COMMISSION FOR CHRISTMAS

## (Luke 1:38)

Mary spoke the words of faith and became the human vessel through which God entered history. Let her words be our own: "Let it be to me according to your word."

(JTF)

# Resources for Epiphany

## INTRODUCTION

In order to encourage theological depth in the celebration of Epiphany, we have based the resources at the beginning of the season on readings and meanings that differ from traditional celebrations of the Western churches.

We encourage churches to celebrate Epiphany on January 6 even when it falls on a weekday. The order for an Epiphany festival comes from a congregation in which Epiphany is celebrated each January 6 as a high point in that church's life.

In this section we depart from Western tradition by assigning greater importance to the incarnation of the Word and the baptism of Christ than to the magi as central themes of Epiphany. In the West, when Epiphany has been celebrated, the text and theme of the magi have been central. However, Epiphany originated as the Eastern celebration of the incarnation. In areas of the East where the Gospel of John was central in Christian celebrations, chapters 1 and 2 of the Gospel of John provided the themes for Epiphany and the weeks following: the incarnation of the Word, the baptism of Jesus, the calling of disciples, and the wedding at Cana. (Refer to A. Allan McArthur, *The Evolution of the Christian Year* [London: SCM Press, 1953], 31–76, for a fuller history of the season and exploration of its themes.)

The incarnation of the Word and the baptism of Jesus are, in our opinion, central to the gospel of Jesus Christ and worthy of a major liturgical feast such as Epiphany. The story of the coming of the magi is also important, pointing to the universal import of the coming of Christ. However, it appears only in Matthew's Gospel (unlike the baptism of Jesus, which appears in all four Gospels), and some scholars have questioned its historicity. (Refer to Raymond Brown, *The Birth of the Messiah* [Garden City, N.Y.: Doubleday & Co., 1977], 165–201.)

Therefore, it seems important to me that Matt. 2:1–12 (about the magi) not, as often happens, displace the readings about Jesus' baptism, especially when there is no weekday celebration of Epiphany. (For further theological reflection on these issues, refer to *A Handbook for the Lectionary,* ed. Horace Allen [Philadelphia: Geneva Press, 1980], 31–34; or Bryan Spinks, "Revising the Advent-Christmas-Epiphany Cycle," in *Studia Liturgica* 17 [1987]: 166–75.)

As an alternative to making the story of the magi the main focus of Epiphany celebrations, we suggest using Matt. 2:1–12 on the first Sunday of Christmastide, Year A, and Matt. 2:13–15, 19–23 on the second Sunday of Christmastide, Year A. Realizing that some may choose to follow this suggestion, while others will prefer to continue the Western focus on the coming of the magi, we have put the resources for Matt. 2 in a separate section, immediately following "An Epiphany Festival." Other resources for Sundays after Epiphany immediately follow the resources for Matt. 2.      (RCD)

# AN EPIPHANY FESTIVAL

Epiphany always falls on January 6, one of the earliest fixed dates of Christian worship. In early centuries one of the three major festivals of the Christian calendar (along with Easter and Pentecost), Eastern churches still keep it in its glory. Epiphany does not usually fall on a Sunday. Therefore our congregation (First Church in Cambridge, Massachusetts) gathers on the festival day, after school or work, with a potluck dinner.

After dinner, we have a candlelight procession through a darkened church building until we reach a side chapel. There we have a vesper service entirely by candlelight with readings, prayers, and a combined children's/adult sermon illustrating one of the evangelical texts about Jesus' baptism.

From the vesper service we proceed to the chancel area of our main sanctuary, where we gather around a baptismal font, turn on all the lights, baptize (or remind ourselves of our common baptism), receive new members, sing hymns, and generally rejoice in the life and ministry we share with Christ. We usually close with an older person reading the *Nunc Dimittus* (Luke 2:29–32) and by having everyone extend the right hand of Christian love or share a kiss of peace.

This sequence and its liturgical expressions are infinitely variable—by, for example, using evening hymns if there is not an Epiphany hymn in the book. Epiphany festival has become one of the major events in our annual church life, a special opportunity to baptize or remind ourselves of our discipleship as we recall the baptism of Jesus and the beginning of his ministry. What follows is the order we used one year:

CANDLELIGHT PROCESSION

OPENING SENTENCES: Isa. 42:1–9

COLLECT FOR EPIPHANY

NEW TESTAMENT: 2 Pet. 1:16–19

SOLO: "O Splendor of God's Glory Bright"

GOSPEL: Luke 3:15–22

A DOXOLOGY FOR EPIPHANY
*Refer to the metrical service music, pages 233–40.*

SERMON

INVITATION

BAPTISMAL PROCESSION

HYMN: "Of Eternal Love Begotten"

BAPTISM

ANTHEM

RECEPTION OF NEW MEMBERS

BLESSING: *Nunc Dimittis* (Luke 2:29–32)

EVENING HYMN: "Now, on Land and Sea Descending"

RIGHT HAND OF CHRISTIAN LOVE

*The entire congregation is invited to greet the new members.* (APH)

# RESOURCES FOR MATTHEW 2 GOSPEL READINGS

## CALLS TO WORSHIP

LEADER: The magi came from many places, following a star.

PEOPLE: We come to worship, and the star sheds light on our lives.

LEADER: The magi brought gifts to offer the Child.

PEOPLE: We too bring gifts—ourselves, our hopes, our dreams.

LEADER: Shepherds and magi—the meek and the mighty—all were welcome in Bethlehem.

PEOPLE: We too come to Bethlehem and then return to our homes rejoicing. (MCT)

OR

We come bearing gifts.
Starstruck, we advance toward the light
and the cradle—where newborn dreams sleep
awaiting the awakening,
and we worship
while Dream beams brighten the dawn. (JWH)

OR

LEADER: Although the beckoning star heeded by wise travelers long ago no longer leads the way,

PEOPLE: The manger-born Christ is still to be found and followed.

LEADER: We are not brought to our knees in surprise as were those journeyers of old,

PEOPLE: Yet our desire to worship can be as deep as theirs.

LEADER: And though we do not bear gifts of gold, frankincense, and myrrh,

PEOPLE: We offer ourselves and what we have.

LEADER: The story continues. The good news abounds. There is a living Christ to discover and worship and serve.

PEOPLE: Let us rejoice and be glad! (GER)

## INVOCATION (ISA. 60)

Radiant God, all nations are drawn to your light; all people proclaim your praise. You befriend the forsaken and the hated; you are the help of the oppressed; for you have come to us in Jesus Christ. We rejoice in your great love for the world, and rise to praise you, together with people of all nations. Glory be to you, O God! Amen. (RCD)

## PRAYER OF CONFESSION

God of perfect light, lead us as we proceed through life. Forgive us when, like Herod, selfish ambition makes us willing to hurt others. Forgive us when, unlike the magi, we refuse to follow the light you give us. Shine in our lives through the light of your Christ, in whose name we pray. Amen. (alludes to "We Three Kings of Orient Are")          (RCD)

## PRAYER FOR ILLUMINATION

Guiding God, bless us on the road we have chosen to seek your star. Light-shedding God, light up our minds with your truth that lets us ignore the bad-news-Herods and keep on going toward that certain glow in the sky of our lives. Beckoning God, help us to bring gifts worthy of the Christ. Then, we too shall be known by you as wise women and men. We pray in Christ's name. Amen.          (GER)

## OFFERING PRAYER

Loving and receptive God, who acted in the Bethlehem birth and who sustains the whole human family, we come to you seeking to be wise men and women. May our gifts be a sign, as were the gifts for those travelers of old, that wisdom is marked by an offering of self and substance to the Christ in whose name we pray. Amen.          (GER)

## BENEDICTIONS AND COMMISSIONS

LEADER:  Go forth in the light of God's star. Go forth committed to a journey of faith and courage. Go forth to give the precious gift of your life to Christ.

ALL:  We will go forth and let the star guide us.
We will share with others the journey of life.
We will praise God, for the gift we have received is beyond measure—Jesus the Christ.          (MCT)

OR

May the image of Christ, the hunted Child, move people of faith to oppose the paranoia of dictators today. May the image of Christ, the refugee in Egypt, move people of faith to provide sanctuary for the homeless. May we resolve never again to tolerate cruelty or neglect, but to live in tenderness toward all people, through Jesus Christ, the compassionate. Amen.          (JTF)

# CALLS TO WORSHIP

## FIRST SUNDAY AFTER EPIPHANY (JOHN 1:1–9, ADAPTED)

LEADER: In the beginning was the Word.

PEOPLE: The Word was with God,

LEADER: And the Word was God.

PEOPLE: The Word was with God in the beginning.

LEADER: All things came through the Word,

PEOPLE: And not one thing had its being except through the Word.

LEADER: All that came to life had life in the Word,

PEOPLE: And that life was the light of all people,

LEADER: A light that shines in the deepest night,

PEOPLE: A light that could not be overcome.

LEADER: Someone came, sent by God.

PEOPLE: His name was John.

LEADER: He came as a witness,

PEOPLE: A witness to speak for the light,
so that everyone might believe through him.

LEADER: He was not the light,
only a witness to speak for the light.

ALL: The Word was the true light
that enlightens all people.
The Word has come into the world.
Thanks be to God!

(JWR)

OR

## (Year B, Isa. 61:3)

READER 1: We enter this place of worship in search of light to guide our way.

READER 2: We seek to exchange the ashes of mourning for the garland of joy.

READER 1: We come because we have seen the light afar off and desire to come closer.

READER 2: We want to join with others in walking in the light so we may enjoy true human communion.

READER 1: We worship that our light may shine and draw others to God's light.

READER 2: In Christ, the light has come into the world, the bright expression of God among us.
Let us worship God!

(DBB)

## SECOND SUNDAY AFTER EPIPHANY (PS. 36:6, 7b, 8, 9 NIV, ADAPTED)

LEADER:    Your love, O God, reaches to the heavens,
             your faithfulness to the skies.

PEOPLE:    Your righteousness is like the mighty mountains,
             your justice like the great deep.

LEADER:    Earth's children, high and low, take refuge in the shadow of your wings.

PEOPLE:    We feast on the abundance of your house;
             you give us drink from your river of delights.

ALL:    For with you is the fountain of life;
             in your light we see light.
             Glory be to you, O God, our life and our light!      (RCD)

## THIRD SUNDAY AFTER EPIPHANY (PS. 118:24, ADAPTED)

God has made this day.
Let us rejoice and be glad in it.
Let us worship the living God!
To God, Fountain of Life, Living Word, and Spirit of Holiness, be praise in all the
earth.      (RCD)

## FOURTH SUNDAY AFTER EPIPHANY (YEAR A, MATT. 5:1–12)

LEADER:    Come, all who are poor in spirit;
             come, all who mourn;
             come, all who are meek;
             come, all who hunger and thirst after righteousness.

PEOPLE:    Come, all who would be merciful;
             come, all who would be pure in heart;
             come, all who would be peacemakers.

LEADER:    Let us come together—the weak, the simple, the powerless, the foolish.

PEOPLE:    Let us confess that the source of our life is Christ Jesus. Let us worship the
             God of every blessing.      (MCT)

## FIFTH SUNDAY AFTER EPIPHANY (YEAR A, MATT. 5:13–16)

LEADER:    We have been called the salt of the earth.

PEOPLE:    Let us remain hidden and distinctive.

LEADER:    We have been called the light of the world.

PEOPLE:    Let us shine brightly in the midst of pain or confusion.

LEADER:    We have been called a city set on a hill.

PEOPLE:    Let us, like Jerusalem, lift our gates, lift our hearts, lift our voices in the
             worship of God, the Sovereign of hosts and the Savior of the humble.    (MCT)

OR

LEADER: To disciples, then and now, Jesus has said, "You are the light of the world.
. . . Let your light so shine before all, that they may see your good works
and glorify your Parent who is in heaven."

PEOPLE: We have come together to be community, to receive light, and to be light. To
this end we dedicate ourselves.

LEADER: We have come together to be windows through which, instructed and
illuminated by God, we might see the world more clearly.

PEOPLE: We have come to be windows through which the world might know the light
and love of God. To this end we will praise and magnify God.          (JRC)


## SIXTH SUNDAY AFTER EPIPHANY (YEAR C, JER. 17:7–8; 1 COR. 15:12–20)

LEADER: Let us praise God, who gives living water,
through whom the faithful flourish.

PEOPLE: Like trees planted by the water, God,
are those who trust in you.

LEADER: Like trees with deep roots
are those who place their faith in you.

PEOPLE: Like green trees in winter
are those who receive their life from you.

ALL: We praise you, God, for life that has no end,
through Jesus our risen Christ!                                       (RCD)


## SEVENTH SUNDAY AFTER EPIPHANY (YEAR B, ISA. 43:21, 19d; 2 COR. 1:20, 22)

LEADER: We are a people created to sing praise to God!

PEOPLE: We praise the God who gives rivers in the desert.

LEADER: We worship the God who has said, "Yes!" to humanity in Jesus Christ.

PEOPLE: We give thanks to the God who gives the Spirit in our hearts.

ALL: Glory be to God, Creator, Christ, and Spirit, giver of all good gifts.   (RCD)


## EIGHTH SUNDAY AFTER EPIPHANY

LEADER: We come seeking the holy love of God, that we may become whole and
loving.

PEOPLE: As Jesus Christ has shared the life of earth, through Christ we may share the
life of God, in growing holiness, justice, and love.

LEADER: In awe, faith, and thanksgiving, let us rejoice in God's presence and share
God's life!

ALL: Let us worship God.                                               (RCD)

## TRANSFIGURATION (YEAR B, 2 COR. 4:3–6)

LEADER: The glory of God transfigures the everyday!

PEOPLE: The light of God transfigures familiar faces!

LEADER: At the heights of our worship,
may God's presence shine through the commonplace.

PEOPLE: At the depths of our pain and struggle,
may God's presence give us courage and peace.

ALL: May God's light, shining in the face
of Christ, illumine all our days! Amen.      (RCD)

## ST. VALENTINE'S DAY

We are in midwinter—Christmas is behind us and the crocus is ahead. It is cold; the days are short; and we find it dreary to look at dirty snow. Some of us are despondent and lonely. But today is St. Valentine's Day—a day to celebrate love. In the secular world it is celebrated by lace hearts and candy and flowers. As we gather to worship let us know the presence of love in our midst—God's love for us and the love that God enables us to share with one another. Amen.      (MCT)

# INVOCATIONS

## FIRST SUNDAY AFTER EPIPHANY

Holy God, Eternal Spirit, we thank you for baptizing us into one body in Jesus the Christ. Wash over us with your Spirit, that, like Jesus, we may serve you in serving humanity. Baptize us with the fire of your truth, through Jesus Christ. Amen.     (RCD)

## SECOND SUNDAY AFTER EPIPHANY

With different gifts, with a variety of talents, with an array of interests, we come to worship you, our creating God. We are here to unite our spirits, to be made one in Jesus Christ, to be merged in hope as your children. Bless our differences, that the unique gifts and perceptions of each may strengthen our oneness. Drawn into your Spirit, we give you the thanks of our hearts, in the name of the living Christ.     (LLK)

## THIRD SUNDAY AFTER EPIPHANY

We thank you, O God, for calling us into your church to be your people. We have gathered, God of grace and wisdom, because we have heard your call. You have reached out to us in Jesus Christ, you have touched us with your Spirit; and we have turned toward you, seeking to love as we have been loved. We call upon your holy name: empower us to worship and serve you, walking gently on this earth, through the grace of Jesus Christ. Amen.     (RCD)

## FOURTH SUNDAY AFTER EPIPHANY (YEAR A)

We have come before you, God,
like those who gathered around Jesus
on a faraway hill, long ago,
to find new meaning for our lives.
We want our lives to sound in harmony
with your song of love.
We want to live with integrity and wisdom,
with a spirit of truth.
Do not disappoint us, God,
but allow us to know your presence
and hear your voice.
Come among us, holy God,
for we pray in the name of Jesus. Amen.     (RCD)

## FIFTH SUNDAY AFTER EPIPHANY (YEAR C, ISA. 6)

Holy God, we come before you with awe,
for you are great in love and power.
Some of us come with reluctance, and some with joy,
some with sadness, and others full of fear,
yet we know you receive us as we are.
Touch us, God, with your healing fire.
Speak to us through your word.
Send us back into the world renewed
and eager to do your will.
For we pray in the name of Jesus Christ. Amen.                    (RCD)

## SIXTH SUNDAY AFTER EPIPHANY

O God, it is good to be here
in your presence, among your people.
Make us radiant with the light of your Christ.
Help us to worship with reverence,
and serve you with joy in the world.
May our words, our songs, and our thoughts,
be pleasing to you, O God.
For we pray in the name of Jesus our Sovereign.
Amen.                    (RCD)

## SEVENTH SUNDAY AFTER EPIPHANY
## (YEAR A, 1 COR. 3:10–23; MATT. 5:27–37)

Steadfast Lover of humanity, we come to you as those who search for ways to love more
wisely, more genuinely, more steadily. We seek to base our lives on the love of Christ,
that from day to day we may be passionate and patient, faithful and forgiving, in loving
one another and this world of many peoples. Through your Spirit, build your church
into a living temple, a sign of your presence on earth; through Jesus Christ, our
foundation. Amen.                    (RCD)

## EIGHTH SUNDAY AFTER EPIPHANY

Living God, come, be known among us.
Help us to perceive your presence,
as near as breath, yet hidden.
Help us to seek you as you are seeking us.
Speak your word of power.

Make us true disciples of Christ.
Transform us through your fiery Spirit.
All glory be to you, O God, in Christ and the church forever! Amen. (RCD)

## TRANSFIGURATION

Mighty God, stay with us always,
as we worship and
as we share
the risk and challenge of living our faith.
By your powerful Spirit, turn our fear
to courage and our confusion to confidence.
Your glory shines in the face of Christ.
Shine in our hearts and lives.
May your name be praised, glorious God!
Amen. (RCD)

# PRAYERS OF CONFESSION

### FIRST SUNDAY AFTER EPIPHANY (YEAR A, ISA. 42:1–9)

Tender, holy God, you have come in Christ to bring forth justice. Yet we confess we have been unjust to others, though seeking justice for ourselves. Your Chosen One nurtures the bruised reed and protects the dim light. Yet we say, "Only the strong survive," and reject the weakness in ourselves and others. Your Servant does not become discouraged but tirelessly seeks justice on earth. We quickly grow tired and quit trying. Our hope is in you, gracious God. Forgive us and lead us by your hand, that we may show ourselves to be the people who bear Christ's name. Amen.　　　　(RCD)

### SECOND SUNDAY AFTER EPIPHANY

Infinite God of all peoples and all places, you created the earth, with its mountains and valleys, oceans and plains, with no boundaries. Yet we have parceled out your good earth, and built great armaments to protect our separate parcels.
Forgive us, and breathe your Spirit of unity into all peoples, that the world may live in harmony, and war shall be no more; through Jesus, the power of peace.　　　　(RCD)

### THIRD SUNDAY AFTER EPIPHANY

We admit, O God, that we are attracted to false gods who lure us from you. The "god of easy answers" whispers that we need not accept the cost of discipleship, but only its joy. The "god of busy schedules" tempts us to delay doing your will until tomorrow. The "god of cozy friendships" calls us to love those who love us, rather than laboring to build Christian community among diverse personalities. Forgive us that we are drawn toward false gods. Hold us close in your love, that we may never forsake you, but always serve you faithfully; through the grace of Jesus Christ. Amen.　　　　(RCD)

### FOURTH SUNDAY AFTER EPIPHANY (YEAR A, MATT. 5:1–12; LUKE 11:10a)

*Responsive Prayer of Confession*

LEADER: Blessed are the poor in spirit, for theirs is the realm of heaven.
PEOPLE: Forgive us our spiritual arrogance.
LEADER: Blessed are those who mourn, for they shall be comforted.
PEOPLE: Forgive us our false independence.
LEADER: Blessed are the meek, for they shall inherit the earth.
PEOPLE: Forgive us our misplaced aggression.
LEADER: Blessed are those who hunger and thirst, for they shall be satisfied.
PEOPLE: Forgive us our gluttony.
LEADER: Blessed are the pure in heart, for they shall see God.

PEOPLE: Forgive us our half-hearted commitment.
LEADER: Blessed are the peacemakers, for they shall be called the children of God.
PEOPLE: Forgive us for waging war.
LEADER: Blessed are those who are persecuted for righteousness' sake, for theirs is the realm of heaven.
PEOPLE: Forgive us for not taking a stand.

*Assurance of Pardon*

Rejoice and be glad!
Blessed are those who seek the face of God.
Everyone who asks, receives, and the one who seeks, finds.
Blessed are those who ask for forgiveness, for they shall be forgiven.
Blessed are those who repent, for they shall be freed to live fully in the present.   (MEW)

## FIFTH SUNDAY AFTER EPIPHANY

You are our light, O God. In your presence our lives are illumined, our way becomes clearer. Our own light comes from you: Like small candles lit from the Christ candle on Christmas Eve, we are able to shine with love and hope because you love us and give us reason to hope. Yet we confess to you, O God, that we often hide our light under a bushel. Not trusting our perceptions, we do not share our truth with others. Not trusting our abilities, we do not risk sharing our gifts in community. Not trusting our skills in relationships, we do not reach out in friendship, we do not raise issues which should be raised, we do not break the silence of anger to give or seek forgiveness. Help us to trust in you where we cannot trust ourselves. Radiate through us with your holy love and wisdom, healing the hurts of the past, giving us courage for the future. Warm our coldness; relax our tight muscles; give us clarity and peace. We pray in the name of Jesus Christ, who came to reveal your light to the world. Amen.   (RCD)

## SIXTH SUNDAY AFTER EPIPHANY (YEAR B, KINGS 5:1–14)

Healing River, Source of Life, forgive our lack of faith in you. Heal our diseases and wash away our sin. Free us from our demons and from every desire that enslaves us. Help us always to come to those shores where the rivers of your love can make us clean and whole; through Jesus Christ we pray. Amen.   (RCD)

## SEVENTH SUNDAY AFTER EPIPHANY

*Call to Confession*

God's love has been shown to us in Jesus Christ, yet we sometimes live as if that made no difference to us. Let us confess to God.

*Prayer of Confession*

Compassionate God, we confess the times when we have closed ourselves to your love. We cling to our fear, our guilt, our self-hatred, rather than to let ourselves be warmed and healed by your love. We close our hearts, refusing to be channels of your love to others. We are frozen like winter ice and snow. Forgive us, and give us courage to trust you and to let your love flow through us to others; through Jesus Christ we pray. Amen.

*Assurance of Pardon*

This is the good news in Jesus Christ: God loves us more than we love ourselves. God forgives us, encourages us, and frees us to love others. Thanks be to God.          (RCD)

## EIGHTH SUNDAY AFTER EPIPHANY (YEAR A, MATT. 5:38–48)

God of pure, unbounded love, we are a people who long to be loving, and a people who often fail. Forgive us when our actions hurt ourselves and others. Forgive us when we do not choose our words with care, lest they hurt our family, friends, or neighbors. Help us to go the second mile in loving and giving of ourselves; make us strong and wise in our loving. Teach us what it means to love our enemies. Hear now as we pray to you for healing in our relationships: with you, with our loved ones, with friends and associates, with our world neighbors, and with ourselves. Through Jesus Christ we pray. Amen.                                                                          (RCD)

## TRANSFIGURATION

God of mercy and of hope, we confess that we come with mixed thoughts and uncertain dreams. We could not meet our daily needs without the labor of others; yet we take them for granted. We are offended by slight offenses or oversights against us and hardly consider our neglect of your Word, our patience with evil, and our slowness to act for others. We could not sense the beauty or meaning of life without your Spirit, yet we have not noticed signs of the eternal in the ordinary moments of our lives. We have not allowed our habits and perceptions to be transfigured by the glory of your grace and presence. Grant us a taste of your love so we may acquire an appetite for justice and a capacity for fulfillment. Sharpen our hunger and thirst for you, O Christ! Amen.    (APH)

# UNISON PRAYERS

## FIRST SUNDAY AFTER EPIPHANY

God of light that shines through all creation, your word has called us back into your light. May you shine through our lives, we pray, making us your children and helping us bear witness to the light that dwells among us; through Christ, our Way, our Truth, and our Light. Amen.

(JWR)

## SECOND SUNDAY AFTER EPIPHANY

Fountain of life, we thank you that you have come among us in Jesus Christ. Recalling Jesus' first sign at the wedding of Cana, we pray that at Jesus' word our lives may be changed. May the waters of baptism lead us to the cup of joy, through the Spirit of Christ among us. Amen.

(RCD)

## THIRD SUNDAY AFTER EPIPHANY

Source of Light, Giver of Life, satisfy our searching spirits in the One who is the image of your glory; the unfailing light, the everliving Christ. Grant that each day our lives may abound with this life in obedience to your Word. May our spirits shine as a bright star guiding the world toward your presence. Amen.

(MGMG)

## FOURTH SUNDAY AFTER EPIPHANY

We thank you, O God, for calling us into your church to be your people in the world. We are ready, God, to hear your word; speak to us, God, and give us courage to do your will. With all our doubts and fears and shortcomings, we have decided to follow Jesus in our time and place. Guide us by your loving Spirit. We pray in Jesus' name. Amen.

(RCD)

## FIFTH SUNDAY AFTER EPIPHANY (YEAR C, ISA. 6)

Before you, Holy One, we are people of unclean lips and hearts. Touch us with the fire of your love, that we might praise you worthily. Speak your call to us, and give us courage to respond, "We will!" Show us your way, that we may walk in paths of goodness and truth, through the grace of Jesus Christ and the power of the Holy Spirit. Amen.

(RCD)

## SIXTH SUNDAY AFTER EPIPHANY (YEAR C, LUKE 6:17–26)

Hope of the poor, friend of the persecuted, advocate of the suffering, O God, we praise you, for you have been our help. Turn our tears to laughter and give us what we need to live. Then keep us faithful, that we may never be satisfied until all have what they need. May all people receive your blessing, through Jesus Christ who died, and rose again, and in whom we find life. Amen.                                    (RCD)

## SEVENTH SUNDAY AFTER EPIPHANY (YEAR B, ISA. 43:18–25; MARK 2:1–12)

Creative God, from whom new possibility springs, we call your name; for we are the people you have sealed in your name. Make a way for us where there has been no way. Quench the drought of our spirits with living water, that we may sing your praise. Free us to welcome your newness of life; through Jesus Christ we pray. Amen.          (RCD)

## EIGHTH SUNDAY AFTER EPIPHANY

Amazing God, whose glory outshines the sun, open our lives to the inspiration of your Holy Spirit, that we may more fully reflect the glory of your love. We know that you can do this, O you with no limits. Our love is "like a morning cloud, like the dew that goes early away." Your love is as solid as the great mountains, as wet as the rain, as hot as flames, and as constant as the air we breathe. Our prayers are sometimes clear and sometimes foggy. Reach into our hearts and minds and touch us tenderly, we pray. Amen.                                                                        (MEW)

## TRANSFIGURATION

God of Abraham and Sarah,
God of our mothers and fathers,
we thank you that you make yourself known to us.
For Moses, the burning bush was a sign of your presence. Peter, James, and John saw you in Jesus when he was transfigured and shone as bright as the sun. Your people at Pentecost knew your Spirit had come near, descending in tongues of flame. We yearn, mysterious God, for clear signs of your presence, for fiery epiphanies and not faint glimmers. We would like to live by certain knowledge and not by faith. Yet we know that the faithful have gone out trusting in you, not knowing where you were leading, and that we too must live in faith. Teach us, God, to trust the still, small voice as well as fire and thunder. Take our hands and stay beside us, that we may follow your will as far as we understand it. Heal our sorrows; calm our fears; set us on sure paths. Help us to be your people indeed, through the presence, the word, and the example of Jesus Christ. Amen.                                                                       (RCD)

# ADDITIONAL RESOURCES

## AFFIRMATION OF FAITH (BAPTISM OF JESUS)

LEADER:  The earth has been sanctified, O Word, by your holy birth.
The heavens with the stars declared your glory.
Now the waters are blessed by your baptism in the flesh,
and humanity has been restored once more to nobility.
Christ is baptized.
Coming up from the waters,
he carries the universe.

               (from the Orthodox liturgy, trans. Kenneth Leech)

PEOPLE:  God is joined with humanity.
As Jesus is baptized,
we too are baptized into renewed life.
We discover the dignity of being human;
we are empowered to forsake the thrall of death.
God has sanctified creation:
The waters are blessed,
as are earth and sky and all creatures.
While humans threaten to destroy this world,
our Creator works to restore all creation.
We join with this God who has joined with us:
in upholding human dignity and working to renew our world,
in challenging the rule of death and claiming the dominion of life.    (MLP)

## RENEWAL OF BAPTISM

LEADER:  By his baptism Jesus witnessed that we turn from sin and turn to God. By our baptism we have accepted God's grace and joined God's people. Let us now profess the faith of the community into which we were baptized. Do you renounce evil and all its empty promises?

PEOPLE:  I do.

LEADER:  Do you believe in God, Creator, Redeemer and Sustainer?

PEOPLE:  [Recite a confession or statement of faith.]

LEADER:  Let us pray: God of eternal mercy, we thank you that through Christ Jesus we have been led through the waters of death and come home to you. Through the power of your Spirit renew in us, we pray, this newness of life, that we might serve you in trust and zeal; in Christ Jesus. Amen.    (JWR)

## OFFERING INTRODUCTION AND PRAYER (YEAR A, DEUT. 30:15–20)

We are poor, unless God blesses us.
We are rich, when we offer up what we have to God.
Let us receive our morning offering.

*Prayer*

O God of blessing and of curse,
of life and of death,
grant that we might have ears to hear the word of life in Christ with all its stark
demand. Enable us to hear good news when Christ asks us to give up our attachment to
all earthly values, and give us courage to do so. May these gifts be used in this spirit
that we may attain to your blessing. Amen.                    (RCD)

# LITANIES

## ON THE OCCASION OF MARTIN LUTHER KING, JR.'S BIRTHDAY

READER 1: Miriam hid a baby in the bullrushes, disobeying pharaoh's edict to kill the male children of the Hebrew slaves. The child grew to adulthood. Called by God, he liberated his people from Pharaoh's bondage—and Miriam sang a freedom song!

READER 2: Jonah, called by God to preach repentance to his enemies in Nineveh, resisted. He fled from Nineveh in a storm-tossed ship. Rescued from the depths of the sea, he returned to the enemy city, preached, and witnessed the Ninevites' salvation when they turned to God.

READER 1: Mary, the mother of Jesus, accepted her call from God with rejoicing, saying, "God has filled the hungry with good food and sent the rich away empty."

READER 2: Paul, the apostle, journeyed over the known world founding Christian communities. Called by God, he preached reconciliation to Jew and Gentile, creating controversy among his colleagues as he pursued God's purpose of peace among estranged people.

READER 1: The women with the banners and petitions were called suffragettes. They wanted peace among men and women and peace based on justice between races. Called by God, they struggled seventy years to win the right to vote in the United States so that their granddaughters could take up the work they had begun.

READER 2: Black and white marched together in Alabama, Mississippi, Chicago, and Washington, D.C., called by God to turn the nation around. Martin Luther King was our drum major keeping rhythm as we walked toward a new day when liberty and justice would be shared in peace by all.

READER 1: The march continues, as we raise our voices with women, hispanics, gays, lesbians, children, and poor people from the developing countries in every corner of God's world, crying out for a just peace.

READER 2: Christ, our peace: we hear your call; we experience your ministry through the lives of peacemakers and justice seekers. Guide us as we follow the path of shalom. We thank you for the cloud of witnesses who have known your presence in their struggles every step of the way to peace. Your promise is sure that peace is possible when we follow in the way you lead. Amen.

(CLC)

## SECOND SUNDAY AFTER EPIPHANY—GOD'S CALL
### (1 SAM. 3:4; MARK 1:17–18; JOHN 4:7, 19, 28; ISA. 6:8;
### EXOD. 3:11, 13; 4:13; LUKE 1:34, 38; JER. 1:5, 6; JOHN 20:15, 18)

LEADER: A child once dreamed that God called him by name—"Samuel." Fisherfolk from the Galilean Sea once met a young man who told them to lay aside their nets and follow. A woman, drawing water from a well, once spoke with a prophet whose words sent her back to town in a rush.

PEOPLE: I heard the voice of God saying, "Whom shall I send? Who will go for us?" Then I said, "Here am I! Send me."

LEADER: Moses stood before a burning bush, protesting God's call upon him: "Who am I to go to pharaoh to free the children of Israel? . . . What will I say when they ask who sent me? . . . O God, I beg of you, send someone else!"

PEOPLE: I heard the voice of God saying, "Whom shall I send? Who will go for us?" Then I said, "Here am I! Send me."

LEADER: Mary stood before God's messenger, amazed at the news she was hearing: "But how is it possible for this to take place? . . . Yet, I am God's servant. So, let it be done as you have said."

PEOPLE: I heard the voice of God saying: "Whom shall I send? Who will go for us?" Then I said, "Here am I! Send me."

LEADER: Jeremiah stood in despair before God who had appointed him a prophet while he was still within his mother's womb: "Sovereign God! I don't know how to speak to the nations; I am too young!"

PEOPLE: I heard the voice of God saying, "Whom shall I send? Who will go for us?" Then I said, "Here am I! Send me."

LEADER: Mary Magdalene stood in joyous tears before the risen Christ, framing the message she would bring to her grieving companions: "I have seen the Lord!"

PEOPLE: I heard the voice of God saying, "Whom shall I send? Who will go for us?" Then I said, "Here am I! Send me."                                    (CLC)

# EUCHARISTIC PRAYER FOR EPIPHANY

*Alludes to UCC Statement of Faith and to Phil. 2:5–11*

In response to God's infinite love and boundless grace
we rejoice to give thanks at all times and in all places,
to the one who created order out of chaos,
who penetrated the night of sin with the light of the world,
and whose light cannot be overcome by human resistance.
We thank you, God, living Spirit,
for sending a star to guide the wise to Christ.
But even more we praise you for signs and witnesses
in every generation that lead us to your Christ.
We thank you that Christ identified with sinners,
preached good news to the poor,
proclaimed release to those shackled by ignorance, prejudice, and injustice,
and brought life and immortality to light by living the gospel-life.
We bless you for the gifts you have lavishly given us, though undeserving:
for new definitions of power and wisdom,
for disarming the principalities and powers,
for removing the estrangement of sin,
for inviting all to faithful discipleship,
for promising courage in the struggle for justice and peace,
for your presence in trial and rejoicing,
for the sacrament of your extravagance,
and for inviting us to dwell in your presence forever.
Mighty God, we worship and praise you.
With magi and shepherds, apostles and martyrs,
we sing your glory.
At the name of Jesus let every knee bow,
every tongue confess,
and every heart join in the song of the heavenly host,
singing. . . . [Followed by the *sanctus.*]

(JTF)

# BENEDICTION

## (Includes Isa. 60:1, adapted)

Arise, shine, for your light has come,
and the glory of God has risen upon you.
God has loved us from before all time.
In our here and now
let us receive and reveal God's love,
through the grace of Jesus Christ,
and the power of the Holy Spirit. Amen.

(RCD)

# Resources for Lent

## CALLS TO WORSHIP

### ASH WEDNESDAY (YEAR A, JOEL 2:12–18)

LEADER: Blow the trumpet in Zion; sanctify a fast; call a solemn assembly; gather the people.

PEOPLE: Let us gather and sanctify all of this congregation—young and old, male and female, joyful and sorrow-filled.

LEADER: This is a day of true repentance, a time to return to God with all our hearts.

PEOPLE: We return to God in true repentance for all those things which we have done that we should not have done and those things we have left undone which we should have done. We rend our hearts and not our garments.

LEADER: We seek God's amazing forgiveness.

PEOPLE: We affirm that God is gracious and merciful, slow to anger and abounding in steadfast love.                                                                    (MCT)


### FIRST SUNDAY IN LENT

LEADER: Welcome, travelers, to the journey of faith.

PEOPLE: The faith journey is the best route through the land called life.

LEADER: Then come and continue the quest, acting out your faith by living life to the fullest.

PEOPLE: We will let our spirits soar like eagles;

LEADER: taking a deep breath we will stretch ourselves to the limit like fully inflated balloons, colorful, hopeful, ready to sail and to soar,

PEOPLE: and to drink in the world's color, absorbing its light and texture, inhaling its fragrance, dancing to its music.

LEADER: This is the way we worship God.                                              (JWH)

## SECOND SUNDAY IN LENT

We gather this day to worship our God, whose words and ways challenge us.

God invites us to lose our selfishness to find ourselves.

God calls us to be fools in the world to show forth the wisdom of Christ.

God urges us to empty ourselves to discover life's fullness.

God bids us to be obedient to a divine will so we might know true freedom.

We come to worship our Creator, seeking to have our faith challenged into growth.

We root our faith in worship seeking to find nourishment for our spirits in this growing season of Lent.                                                                          (GER)

## THIRD SUNDAY IN LENT (YEAR C, EXOD. 3:1–8, 13–15)

LEADER:   Moses saw a burning bush and he took off his shoes, for he expected to be on holy ground.

PEOPLE:   We have come to worship with our shoes on and our minds distracted. How shall we find holiness?

LEADER:   As in Moses' time so also now, God always hears the cries of people and comes to be with them.

PEOPLE:   Our prayers are full of cries. How shall we know that God answers?

LEADER:   "I AM," God told Moses, and then God asked him for commitment.

PEOPLE:   In this time of worship may we recognize God's name and respond to God's call.                                                                               (MCT)

## FOURTH SUNDAY IN LENT (YEAR C, LUKE 15:1–3, 11–32)

It is the young man whom we know as the prodigal son who said in desperation, "I will arise and go to my father and I will say to him, 'Father, I have sinned against heaven and before you; I am no longer worthy to be called your child, treat me as one of your servants.'" In this time of Lent we recognize our own unworthiness and inadequacy.

Even as we return home to God, we hear the unexpected words of forgiveness, "Rejoice, my child—you were dead and are alive again; you were lost and now are found." Let us rejoice that we are at home in God's house.                                             (MCT)

## FIFTH SUNDAY IN LENT (YEAR A, EZEK. 37:11–14)

LEADER:   Sometimes we say that we are a people of dry bones; we are a people without hope.

PEOPLE:   God says that we shall be raised from our living graves and we shall be filled with Spirit.

LEADER:   Sometimes we say that we are cut off from one another, and our sources of joy are dried up.

PEOPLE: God says that we shall be at home with one another and we shall live with celebration.

LEADER: Sometimes we come to worship aimless and fearful.

PEOPLE: Then God reveals wondrous works of love and we come to know God.

(MCT)

## EVENING LENTEN SERVICE

This is the season of Lent and we remember Jesus' journey to Jerusalem. We follow him. We follow with our minds the stories of scripture; we follow with our hearts the passion of Christ and the passions of our brothers and sisters; we follow with hands and feet through recommitment to justice and reconciliation; we follow with the wings of the spirit in prayer and meditation. May our minds be open; may our hands be strong; may our hearts be gentle; may our spirits sing. May this evening worship so transform us that in the week to come we will, indeed, share with others our Jerusalem journeys and follow Jesus in the way of life. Amen.                              (MCT)

## PASSION OR PALM SUNDAY (YEAR C, LUKE 19:28–40; PHIL. 3:10)

LEADER: Cry out, people of faith!
Rejoice and praise God!

PEOPLE: If we did not sing praise,
the very stones would cry out!

LEADER: Cry out, people of faith,
for your Savior draws near to Jerusalem.

PEOPLE: Hosanna! God saves!
Blessed is the One who comes in God's name!

LEADER: Blessed is Jesus Christ,
who did not turn back for fear of the cross.
Let us praise the God who loves us,
sharing Christ's sufferings,
and facing with courage our path of faith.

ALL: Hosanna! God saves!
Blessed is the One who comes in God's name!              (RCD)

## MAUNDY THURSDAY

LEADER: This is a day to remember.

PEOPLE: We remember the Passover Jesus shared with his disciples.

LEADER: We remember his new covenant of broken bread and cup.

PEOPLE: We remember his night alone in the garden in prayer.

LEADER: We remember his arrest, his trial, his suffering, the denial of his friend.

PEOPLE: We remember this day and thank God for Jesus' presence with us then and with us now.                                                                (MCT)

## GOOD FRIDAY

A cradle and a cross
And between these—a life
Bethlehem and Jerusalem
A birth and a death
One "of sorrows"
Who often wept
One of joy who also kept
Sensitivity and compassion
Alive and real
Today let us feel
The surge of that life
The beauty of that love
The power of that cross.                                                           (TEJ)

# INVOCATIONS

## ASH WEDNESDAY

Gentle God, we thank you for your Lenten walk through Galilee and our lives. We thank you for healing grace and teaching challenge; we thank you for the miracle that our little gifts are turned into many loaves. We thank you for the parables that tease us, the supper of Passover and Passion that makes us whole, the cross and tomb and heaven that call us. Gentle God, we thank you that what is written in the gospels and in our hearts is the story of Jesus of Nazareth. Amen.                                         (MCT)

## FIRST SUNDAY IN LENT (YEAR B, GEN. 9:8–15; MARK 1:12–15)

We come before you, O God, in the shadow of the cross, grateful for your great love for us. As you came to us in Jesus to win our love and obedience, reveal yourself among us still. Give us courage to follow Jesus over rocky hills where we carry our crosses and green valleys where you restore our souls. For we pray in the name of the shepherd whose life was laid down for the sheep. Amen.                                         (RCD)

## SECOND SUNDAY IN LENT

O God, there are many things that stand between us and the life you intend us to lead. Like frozen ground stifling back a bulb's expression of life, these things subdue spirits struggling to bloom.

A lack of courage chills the ground of our being and prevents our challenging the cold grip of injustice.

A snow-covering of indifference keeps problems out of sight and makes us believe there is no life below the surface.

A sense of self-importance allows the dormancy of faith and permits us to be content without growing into the world. As we worship, God, thaw us out. Through all the chill of self-importance, indifference, lack of courage, we feel the life-giving warmth of your love. Help us to bloom as persons nourished by that love. In the name of Jesus Christ. Amen.                                         (GER)

## THIRD SUNDAY IN LENT (YEAR C, EXOD. 3:1–15)

Most holy God, we do not take off our shoes for worship, nor do we set you apart in a holy of holies visited only by priests. Still, we come to you with awe and wonder, aware of the mystery of life, reverent before your holy love and power. Sharpen our awareness of the sacred; startle us with the joy of discipleship; and strengthen us to accept the cost of following Jesus Christ. In Christ's name we pray. Amen.                                         (RCD)

## FOURTH SUNDAY IN LENT

Holy God, we come before you thankful that you love us as we are. We are creatures of your hand; we are a community formed by your Spirit. You are the potter; we are the clay. With your sure and loving hands, shape us, through the grace of Jesus Christ. Amen.                                                                                          (RCD)

## FIFTH SUNDAY IN LENT (YEAR A, EZEK. 37; JOHN 11)

Mother of mercy, we come to you dry and lifeless, seeking your breath of life. Lead us to the place where our hopes lie buried and call us out from the tombs of despair. Call forth our faith that, with Martha, we may know you to be the resurrection and the life, in this world and the world to come. Amen.                                        (RCD)

## PALM SUNDAY

As crowds of people welcomed Jesus when he rode into Jerusalem, acclaiming him as their ruler, so we welcome you, God, Creator, Christ, and Spirit. Above all human powers and dominions, you lay rightful claim to our praise, our love, and our obedience. Therefore we have come to worship you and to hear your word. We love you, God, and we pray that we, with all people, might do your will on earth:
*The Prayer of our Savior follows.*                                                        (RCD)

## MAUNDY THURSDAY

Spirit of Christ, be with us now. Guide us in the hour of trouble; awaken us when we sleep. Help us to face the cross upon which you died for our sakes; help us to face the crosses we must carry. For we are your disciples—we will follow you even in fear and fainting, if you will consecrate us in truth, both spirit and flesh. Lead us through life and into death. We know that nothing can separate us from the love of God in you. Amen.                                                                                                (MCT)

## GOOD FRIDAY (YEAR A, ISA. 53)

Gracious God, on this day we gather to remember with love and tears the suffering and death of Jesus of Nazareth. We believe that this despised and rejected man of sorrows has borne our griefs and has been wounded for our transgressions. We come to this worship in deep repentance for our individual sins and in recommitment of our lives to end suffering, pain, and death in all times and all places. Amen.                    (MCT)

# PRAYERS OF CONFESSION

## ASH WEDNESDAY

Eternal and most merciful God, we are children of dust and unworthy of the favors and goodness you shower upon us. We have not loved as you have loved us, nor have we lived as we ought, and our years are soon gone. God, have mercy upon us. Lift us above every past regret and present failure; reveal to us our true selves; and give us grace to accept your mercy and courage to live by your promise. Lamb of God, you take away the sin of the world; grant us your peace. We have no other hope save in you. Amen.

(APH)

## FIRST SUNDAY IN LENT

Merciful God, what a gentle and healing balm it is to come to you with our secret thoughts, our sad discouragements, and our noblest dreams, and find you here to listen, to forgive, and to renew us! We confess our reluctance to understand your will and our hesitancy to act upon it. We are quick to blame others and slow to accept responsibility for ourselves. We wish for signs of your power even while we take for granted the beauty and love with which you have surrounded us. We desire some guarantee of your favor and, at the same time, shudder to think about the suffering of the cross and what it portends for us and for our world. Submerge us in your Spirit and grant us faith to perceive good arising from evil and to sense your immediate presence within the solitude of endless space. Amen.

(APH)

## SECOND SUNDAY IN LENT

God of compassion, you know how we rebel against you. You know how we doubt and fear and hold back, when you call us to freedom and to partnership in Jesus Christ.

God, forgive us. Free us by the power of your cross, that we may serve you without fear. Grant us your peace, through Jesus Christ who was faithful to the end. Amen.

(RCD)

## THIRD SUNDAY IN LENT

Eternal God, from the beginning of time you have called your children into communion with you. Yet we confess that like all the rest, we have turned to our own way and refused your love and grace. Restore us to the joy of knowing you, and of recognizing your reign among us, through Jesus Christ, bringer of your good news. Amen.     (RCD)

## FOURTH SUNDAY IN LENT (2 COR. 5:16–21)

Reconciling God, compassionate Christ, we realize that we have often resembled enemy agents more than ministers of reconciliation. With angry words and vindictive actions we have harmed our brothers and sisters. We have dehumanized those we do not wish to understand. We distance ourselves from those who disappoint us or remind us of our own human frailty. Forgive us, O God; lift us to a higher, holier purpose. Help us to draw as close to each other as you drew to us in Christ. Help us to regard persons no longer from a human point of view but from the vantage point of the cross where all hostility was conquered, all forgiveness assured. Amen.                                    (JTF)

## FIFTH SUNDAY IN LENT

Eternal and Almighty God, you have long sought us and we have fled. You have offered us an easy yoke, and we have tied ourselves down with cares and burdens. You have forgiven us, and we have complained against our sisters and brothers. Give us a conversion that turns us around to face the light; teach us a repentance that lives in works of love; lead us into the narrow path; guide us through the valley of the shadow of death. Call us to follow Jesus Christ and in his way to live and suffer, die and rise again. Amen.                                    (MCT)

## PALM SUNDAY

O God, we are like the people of Jerusalem so long ago.
We are hungry for a hero.
We crave some glimpse of greatness.
We are starving for the spectacular.
We are gathered here like those who watched
the Passion-Parade in Jerusalem,
craning our necks to catch a glimpse of our Messiah.
As we wait here for the Savior to come
let us not be disappointed when the special one appears
even though we are certain to be surprised;
and give us courage to follow
where the one on the donkey might lead us.
Amen.                                    (JWH)

OR

*Call to Confession*

Let us confess before God our tendency,
like the Jerusalem crowds,

to profess our faith in moments of enthusiasm
and deny our faith in moments of stress.

### *Prayer of Confession*

O God, we sing and praise you, happy of heart and strong of spirit, when we are among others who praise you too. But in times of stress, we seek scapegoats to be targets for our anger. We betray those we love and who have loved us and we turn against you, too busy to seek you, too selfish to obey you. Your compassion is without bounds, O God, for you forgive us again and again. You restore us to a right spirit and bring us together to worship you again. God of steadfast love, teach us how to be steadfast; through Jesus Christ we pray. Amen.

(RCD)

## MAUNDY THURSDAY

Ever gracious God, we gather this evening hour as friends gathered with Jesus in an upper room long ago. We come bearing the marks of a bitter and broken world. We come from anonymous places, with dry and thirsty spirits. Remind us in the breaking of the bread of our need and of your sufficiency. Refresh us and make us whole with the cup of forgiveness. Draw us nearer to each other in mutual service and closer to you in the covenant of faithfulness and thanksgiving. As the night advances, deepen in us a sense of your steadfast love for us in Jesus Christ, our friend and redeemer. Amen.

(APH)

## GOOD FRIDAY

### *Call to Confession*

What part of ourselves is found in the shadow of the mob that streamed to Calvary? What part of ourselves creates nails in other forms that wound our brothers and sisters—and our God? Complicity, apathy, guilt oppress us and stifle our joy; let us bring our sins to God in genuine repentance and discover what God will do for us!

(JTF)

### *Prayer of Confession*

Ever-living and ever-loving God, how frayed our lives have become, a collection of loose ends, tarnished glories, and hazy dreams! We have not kept our eyes upon your saving cross nor listened with undivided attention to your voice. We have not sought your presence among the destitute nor accepted ourselves as persons for whom you died. Stretch our boundaries, stir our hearts, and inflame our souls to behold you in every fragment of life, to feel you in every moment of time, and to serve you in every occasion with obedience and joy. Amen.

(APH)

# UNISON PRAYERS

## ASH WEDNESDAY

Creating God,
still Center of the world you have made,
we come to you in this season of turning and returning.
We do not know how to seek you with our whole hearts,
but we know you are our source and our destiny.
In the midst of life,
we return to you, we turn toward you.
We thank you that you receive even the broken heart,
the troubled conscience, the conflicted spirit.
Seeking you in secret,
may we turn around to honor you among humanity;
through Jesus Christ, our path homeward to you.
Amen. (RCD)

## FIRST SUNDAY IN LENT (YEAR A, GEN. 2:7–9; 3:1–7)

Holy God, breathe your Spirit of life into us. We are creatures of earth, and we are your
children, created in your image. We are frightened sometimes in this world full of risk
and confusion. Sometimes things happen too fast, and we find it hard to make good
decisions. We need your help.

God, as you created life at the beginning of time, create and shape us anew. We want
to be clay once more, shaped by your hand, touching earth, contemplating heaven,
loving, working, and playing on this good earth. We want to be a part of the circle of
love you began in Jesus, reaching to embrace the whole world—a circle where the sick
are healed, the dying are comforted, the oppressed achieve new dignity, and all live in
peace. Through your Spirit, let it be! (RCD)

## SECOND SUNDAY IN LENT (YEAR A, GEN. 12; ROM. 4)

On this journey of life, O God, be our companion, be our guide. Show us where to go.
Wherever we are, in the journey from birth to death, grant us your peace. We thank you
for each other, our companions in the journey of faith. We pray for those with whom
we travel on this planet as it makes its rounds of the sun. Bring us together to a new
world of peace, through Jesus Christ, who lived and died that all might be one. Amen.
(RCD)

## THIRD SUNDAY IN LENT

O God, who art the Alpha and Omega, the beginning and the end; may we sojourn in the wilderness with you; may we touch and immerse ourselves in the truly spiritual; may we discover newness of life; may we transcend common worries and know the liberating love of the Christ. Amen.

(JHH)

## FOURTH SUNDAY IN LENT

Gracious and compassionate God, your redemption has come into our hearts like a fiery pillar to lead us to the promised land. We pray that your covenant, full of grace in Christ, might stand forever among us, framed in the faithfulness that only you provide; through Christ's name. Amen.

(JWR)

## FIFTH SUNDAY IN LENT (YEAR A, EZEK. 37:11–14)

Gracious and merciful Redeemer, you are the source of our healing and resurrection. We are lifeless, we are hopeless, we are dried up and cut off from one another like the dead bones of a desert valley. But you cause us to be knit together; you cover us with the flesh of strength; you breathe into us the Spirit of life and hope and prophecy; you raise us out of the graves of our meaninglessness so that we can speak of you who have also died and are also risen again. Amen.

(MCT)

## PALM SUNDAY (LUKE 19:28–40)

God of Joy and Arrival,
  enter our lives as Christ entered Jerusalem.
May we celebrate your coming.
May we cry out with the stones so the world might hear your glad arrival.
Yet do not leave us in the events to come.
This joyous crowd which greets you will turn and flee.
From a crowd of hosannas, we turn into a silent, denying crowd at the Cross.
Do not leave us in the events to come!
Even though we may leave you, do not leave us, O Christ!
Then forgive us, so we can return to you changed.
In Christ's name, we pray. Amen.

(JCW)

Or

O God, your name be praised, for in Jesus Christ you come to visit and redeem your people. Help us to understand Christ's rule, strongest among the oppressed, among the victims, among the hurt and broken ones. Help us to understand Christ's triumph revealed when love speaks the healing and freeing word. Help us to understand glory revealed on a cross.

Then may we sing with children and beings of light: Hosanna! Hosanna! Blessed is the one who comes in God's name to visit and redeem God's people! (RCD)

## MAUNDY THURSDAY (REV. 4:8)

Everlasting God, who was and is and is to come, we are grateful that you have invited us here as guests to a banquet, as witnesses to your holy love. Inspire our singing, our praying, our words of devotion, so that your Spirit may come alive in us once again. Let our worship this evening bring the stories and passions of Scripture to new life for us. In Jesus' name we pray. Amen. (JFDM)

## GOOD FRIDAY (YEAR C, MATT. 27:31–50)

Jesus, crucified and living Savior, we are huddled together in doubt and fear like the disciples of long ago. We do not want to be separated; we do not want to be forsaken; we do not want to say "good-byes"; we do not want to follow you with a cross. But, even as we know you bid us follow you into brokenness and death, we also know that you have gone before—you have faced danger and conquered doubt. As we remember the Good Friday events of long ago, we are brought closer to each other and feel your presence with us, and we know that we can go with you, because your promise abides with us. This promise we remember as we pray together in your words:
*The Prayer of Our Savior follows.* (MCT)

# ADDITIONAL RESOURCES FOR LENT

## ASH WEDNESDAY WORSHIP SERVICE FOR SIX READERS

PRELUDE

### THE CALL TO DISCIPLESHIP

READER 1: After John's arrest, Jesus came unto Galilee, proclaiming the gospel of God, saying, "The time has come at last—God's reign has arrived. You must change your hearts and minds and believe the good news" (Mark 1:14–15 PHILLIPS).

READER 2: We must change our hearts and minds.

OPENING HYMN

READER 3: While he was walking by the lake of Galilee Jesus saw two brothers, Simon Peter and Andrew, casting their large net into the water. They were fishermen, so Jesus said to them, "Follow me and I will teach you to be fishers of humanity." At once they left their nets and followed (Matt. 4:18–20 PHILLIPS).

READER 4: Jesus calls—and we follow. At least we try to follow!

READER 3: Trouble is, he's always out ahead of us, moving faster than we do.

READER 4: Lent is a time for deciding to follow Jesus, a time for re-turning to his path.

READER 3: Tonight, we can lay down some of the heavy load we carry.

READER 4: Tonight, we can fall again under the spell of Jesus' love.

### THE BURDEN OF IDOLATRY

READER 5: When the people saw that Moses was so long in coming down from the mountain, they confronted Aaron and said to him, "Come, make us gods to go ahead of us." Aaron answered them, "Take your gold and bring it to me." He took it out of their hands, cast the metal in a mold, and made it into the image of a bull calf (Exod. 32:1–4 NEB abridged).

READER 6: From time before time, this has been our way. We sense the Living Spirit, but can hardly let it work its way before we try to capture and control it, enflesh and entomb it.

READER 5: We want things predictable and safe. But too much safety kills! Jesus knew this: "We must be born from water and spirit. Flesh can give birth only to flesh; it is spirit that gives birth to spirit. . . . The wind blows where it wills; you hear the sound of it, but you do not know where it comes from, or where it is going. So with everyone who is born from spirit" (John 3:5–6, 8 NEB).

READER 6:  And from the Sermon on the Mount: I bid you put away anxious thoughts about food and drink to keep you alive and clothes to cover your body. Surely life is more than food, the body more than clothes. Set your mind on God's reign and God's justice before everything else, and all the rest will come to you as well (Matt. 6:25, 31–33 NEB).

READER 5:  We are idol makers, all of us. We think, first I must have a fine, secure home, and then I will seek out God's ways.

READER 6:  First, I must advance in my job.

READER 5:  First, I must marry someone attractive.

READER 6:  First, I must be healthy.

READER 5:  First, I must get an education.

READER 6:  First, I must raise my children.

READER 5:  First, first, first! But maybe we have it backward. Maybe there is no home, job, marriage, health, education, or parenthood without God.

READER 6:  "Set your mind on God's reign and God's justice before everything else. . . ." What are the idols that you and I put before commitment to God? What are the things that we want to happen before we follow Jesus?

HYMN

### THE BURDEN OF VIOLENCE

READER 2:  "You have learned that they were told, 'Eye for eye, tooth for tooth,' but what I tell you is this: Do not set yourself against anyone who wrongs you. If someone slaps you on the right cheek, turn your left. If someone wants to sue you for your shirt, give your coat as well. If someone in authority makes you go one mile, go two. Give when you are asked to give; and do not turn your back on one who would borrow. You have learned that they were told, 'Love your neighbor, hate your enemy.' But what I tell you is this: Love your enemies and pray for your persecutors. There must be no limit to your goodness, as God's goodness knows no bounds" (Matt. 5:38–44, 48 NEB).

Another burden we carry is violence. We are acutely aware of differences. We remember wrongs done us from long ago. We believe that only weapons will keep us safe from potential enemies.

READER 4:  Jesus knew the violence of our hearts. He knew our liking for grudges, the temptation of bitterness. Jesus counseled a different way: Peter came up and asked how often we should forgive. Jesus said to him, "I do not say to you seven times, but seventy times seven" (Matt. 18:21–22).

READER 2:  Jesus also knew that violence begets violence, that we must resist the temptation to outdo our enemies, that fighting will not lead to peace. Judas, one of the twelve, appeared with a great crowd armed with swords and staves . . . [they] came up, seized hold of Jesus, and held him. Suddenly one of Jesus' disciples drew his sword, slashed at the High Priest's servant and cut off his ear. At this Jesus said to him, "Put your sword back into its proper place. All those who take the sword die by the sword" (Matt. 26:47, 50b–52 PHILLIPS).

READER 4: Fear and anger are such natural human responses.

READER 2: But they lead so easily to hatred and violence.

READER 4: It is not the fear and anger that are wrong,

READER 2: But the way we choose to respond to them.

READER 4: What are the ways we allow fear and anger to encumber us with hatred and violence—either the hatred we carry within or the violence we choose to act out on the outside?

HYMN

## THE BURDEN OF SELFISHNESS

READER 1: It was at this time that the disciples came to Jesus with the question, "Who is greatest in God's realm?" Jesus called a little child to his side. "Believe me," he said, "unless you change your whole outlook and become like little children you will never know God. Whoever can be as humble as this little child is greatest in the kingdom of heaven" (Matt. 18:1–4 PHILLIPS).

READER 5: Like the disciples, we, too, are interested in greatness. Wealth, fame, power—at some level we're all attracted to these. Like James and John, we wouldn't mind being chosen to sit at the left and right hands of God.

READER 1: Jesus, too, was concerned with power. But it was the power to love rather than control, the power to give rather than receive, the power to serve rather than be served.

READER 5: It was before the Passover festival. Jesus knew that his hour had come and he must leave this world and go to God. He had always loved his own who were in the world, and now he was to show the full extent of his love. During supper, Jesus, well aware that God had entrusted everything to him and that he had come from God and was going back to God, rose from table, laid aside his garments, and, taking a towel, tied it round him. Then he poured water into a basin and began to wash their feet and to wipe them with the towel (John 13:3–5 NEB).

READER 1: Jesus had everything: power, responsibility, authority, strength,

READER 5: but he used it to serve—to wash his disciples' feet, to die on a cross.

READER 1: We also have been given power, responsibility, authority, and strength. But how are we using them?

READER 5: Let us ask ourselves how we are weighed down by not using our power with love and our responsibility with wisdom.

HYMN

## FORGIVENESS AND NEW LIFE

READER 3:   We have examined the burdens of idolatry, violence, and misuse of power as they weigh down our lives and keep us from following Jesus.

READER 6:   These are a heavy load, indeed! Yet the good news of our faith is that Jesus seeks out people like us.

READER 3:   Said Jesus: "It is not the healthy who need the doctor, but those who are ill. I have not come to invite the 'righteous' but the 'sinners'—to change their ways" (Luke 5:31–32 PHILLIPS).

READER 6:   Come and celebrate with me . . . for I have found that sheep of mine which was lost. I tell you that . . . in heaven there is more joy over one sinner whose heart is changed than over ninety-nine righteous people who have no need of repentance (Luke 15:5b, 6).

READER 3:   "Salvation has come to this house today! . . . [for] it was the lost that the Son of Man came to seek—and to save" (Luke 19:9–10 PHILLIPS).

READER 6:   Come, you who have won my God's blessing! Take your inheritance—the realm reserved for you since the foundation of the world! . . . [for] I assure you that whatever you did for the very humblest ones, you did for me (Matt. 25:34, 40 PHILLIPS).

READER 3:   In light of the promises of Jesus, let us renounce the burdens of idolatry, violence, and selfishness that weigh us down. Let us allow the cleansing fire of the Holy Spirit to purify our hearts. And let us pray for the love of Jesus to dawn on our hearts and draw us closer to the life he offers.

## THE ASHES OF FORGIVENESS

PASTOR:   Ashes are a symbol of purification. As a fire burns, it can separate what is valuable from what is valueless, just as an assayer's fire can separate a base metal from one that is precious. In this same way, these ashes are pure. They are a symbol of the new space that is now present within us for a new life. Let us claim the new life Jesus offers us by praying to our God:

ALL:   God of love and mercy, we come to you in prayer, seeking to change our hearts and minds. We confess the baggage of idols, bitterness, and self-concern that we so often drag along with us, struggling under its weight all the while we attempt to follow Christ. Cleanse us from our attachment to these old things. Burn away their power in us and purify our hearts. In place of old ways fill us with the new fire of your Holy Spirit. Open up new opportunities for us to follow Jesus in loving you and our neighbors. In Jesus' name we ask these things. Amen.

PASTOR:   Friends, receive the good news of our faith, for in the name of Jesus, I announce our sins are forgiven. The old has died. Behold, the new has come!

## THE SIGN OF THE CROSS

PASTOR:   Those who wish, now come forward and receive the mark of these ashes as a sign of your forgiveness and new life.

*Participants come up the center aisle to the front of the chancel. One by one, the clergyperson marks a cross on their foreheads using his or her thumb. As the cross is made, she or he says to each person, "The old has died. The new has come."*

BENEDICTION

POSTLUDE

(DJS)

## AN AFFIRMATION OF FORGIVENESS

Forgiveness is the spring flower which blossoms in confidence outside the human ovens of Dachau.

Forgiveness is the laughter in a field hospital of a child whose leg has been blown off by a hidden land mine.

Forgiveness is the opening of a new school built upon a mass grave in Kampuchea.

Forgiveness is a mother's lighted candle of remembrance for a teenage son found dead in Nicaragua.

Forgiveness is a Red Cross medic searching for life amidst the rubble in Beirut.

Forgiveness is the rejuvenation of scarred earth after the searing heat of a lightning fire.

Forgiveness is the love of a God who knows our sins, yet forgives us and offers us the chance to begin again. Amen. [May be used in conjunction with the Lenten lectionary reading of Luke 15:11–32.]

(HWW)

## LITANY FOR PALM SUNDAY (YEAR A, PHIL. 2:5–11)

ALL:       Surprising God, you come to our lives in ways we do not expect.
LEADER:   We ask for success;
PEOPLE:   you teach us acceptance.
LEADER:   We ask to be loved;
PEOPLE:   you ask *us* to love.
LEADER:   We ask for ease;
PEOPLE:   you challenge us.
LEADER:   We ask for a triumphant Messiah,
PEOPLE:   you come as one obedient to death.
LEADER:   We glorify the winner,

PEOPLE:    you glorify the loser
                who died on a criminal's cross.
ALL:         Walk among us, surprising God of peace.
                Sanctify our joys and our successes;
                turn our hearts to you.
                At the name of Jesus, we bow before you.
                May your name be glorified in your church,
                now and always. Amen.                                                                (RCD)


## COMMISSIONS FOR LENT

Go forth, in Christ's name, to transform existence, to bring consolation to the desperate, hope to the hungry and homeless, reconciliation to a community and world divided. And in Christ's name, find a cause you can live for, a self you can live with, and a Redeemer for whom you can die.                                                                (JTF)

*Palm Sunday*

Go into the world in peace.
Jesus Christ is victorious over all the powers of this earth.
You are free to live and die with courage,
trusting in God your strength,
and the Holy Spirit your comfort. Amen.                                                (RCD)


## OFFERING SENTENCE AND PRAYER FOR PALM SUNDAY

*Sentence*

To be a Christian in this day and age is to offer up our lives and deaths to God. These gifts are a sign of the offering of our whole selves.

*Prayer*

God of all true power and glory, we thank you that Jesus Christ came to Jerusalem not with a sword to challenge the power of this world, but with love, recognizing your authority in human life. Enable your church to choose your ways, winning the victory over sin and death. Establish your righteous realm on earth. Use our gifts and our lives to your glory, through Jesus, who comes in your name. Amen.                                (RCD)

# *Resources for Eastertide*

## CALLS TO WORSHIP

### EASTER SUNDAY

LEADER:   Easter begins in despair.
                Our life, our love, our hope forever dead,
                crushed by boulder, bottled up in a cave.

READER:   Who will roll away the stone?

LEADER:   Easter takes us by surprise, early in the morning.
                The obstacles we expect to face are removed.
                Where once death and despair laid
                locked in time
                now the bright light of hope sprouts wings
                to fly from emptiness.
                It is, at first, too good to be true.

READER:   Where have you laid him?

LEADER:   When faced with a miracle,
                our first reflex is to run.

READER:   Be not afraid.
                Ye seek Jesus of Nazareth who was crucified.
                He is risen; he is not here:
                see the place where they laid him.
                But go your way.
                Tell his disciples and Peter
                that he goes before you into Galilee.
                There you shall see him.

LEADER:   Suddenly the realization dawns. It may rise as quietly as the sun creeping over the horizon, or it may explode like fireworks, painting the world with dazzle. We recognize the One who was dead as he comes to life in us.

READER:   Christ is risen, risen indeed!

READERS:    Alleluia!

LEADER:     And all who encounter the Risen One
whether gently roused by the sunrise
or surprised by the sudden burst of joy
will join the Resurrection Procession
one by one, slipping into step,
some of us singing,
some of us silently soaking it in,
and all of us feeling like dancing.

READERS:    Alleluia! Christ is risen, risen indeed!                    (JWH)


## SECOND SUNDAY IN EASTERTIDE

We are now in the season called Eastertide. Perhaps it is a fitting time to consider that our resurrection faith has tidal qualities.

It breaks upon us as waters upon the shore, molding and shaping. Sometimes it smooths our rough and jagged edges and at other times it pulls at us to expose new sharpness. It uncovers what has previously been hidden.

Faith brings surprises, laying them before us as though they were dropped by an outgoing tide. Its offerings connect us with people in far-off places; its gifts include living things such as hope and charity.

Faith tells us of God's power and grace, both ever in motion as the seas, both ever present whether we are at high or low points in our lives.

Faith constantly beckons. It seems to stretch toward us as the waters of a new-broken wave reach out to the walker on the shore.

In gathering together during this season, we open ourselves to a God who changes us, surprises us, informs us, draws us. May our worship be Eastertidal, our community filled with Spirit.                    (GER)


OR


LEADER:    Christ our Savior is risen from the dead! Alleluia!

PEOPLE:    Break forth into joy! Sing together! God comforts those whose hearts are broken in sorrow.

LEADER:    We who once suffered in death, we who once cried in despair—

PEOPLE:    Now we know victory over death!
Now we know joy over despair!

ALL:       For God has raised Christ from the grave!
The tomb is empty and death has been defeated for all the earth!     (JCW)

## THIRD SUNDAY IN EASTERTIDE (PS. 30:4, 5b, 11, 12, ADAPTED)

LEADER:  Sing praises to God, you faithful,
           give thanks to God's holy name!
PEOPLE:  Weeping may linger for a night,
           but joy comes in the morning.
LEADER:  You turn our weeping to dancing, God;
           you remove the garments of mourning
           and clothe us in gladness.
ALL:      May we praise you and not be silent!
           We will give thanks to you, O God,
           forever!                                                                    (RCD)


## FOURTH SUNDAY IN EASTERTIDE (REV. 5:12; 7:9–12, PARAPHRASED)

LEADER:  Jesus Christ, the Passover Lamb who was slain, lives!
PEOPLE:  Worthy is the Lamb to receive power and wisdom and glory and blessing!
LEADER:  Myriads of the faithful, freed and called to be a nation of priests of God, sing
           praise:
ALL:      Blessing and honor, glory and power be unto God, for ever and ever.
           Amen!                                                                        (RCD)


## FIFTH SUNDAY IN EASTERTIDE (PS. 117:14, PARAPHRASED)

LEADER:  God has made this day.
PEOPLE:  Let us rejoice and be glad.
LEADER:  The God who raised Jesus Christ from the dead raises us to new life daily.
PEOPLE:  Thanks be to God.
ALL:      Glory be to God our Creator,
           to Jesus our risen Christ,
           and to the Spirit our Comfort. Amen.                                     (RCD)


## SIXTH SUNDAY IN EASTERTIDE

God holds out to us the promise of new life. Life as unpredictable, as unrehearsed, as
explosive as life at the very beginning. God calls us to respond to this gift with
creativity, with joy, and with courage. In worship, we can begin to accept this gift of
new life. Let us worship God.                                                        (MGMG)

## SEVENTH SUNDAY IN EASTERTIDE

LEADER:   Praise God, who has raised Jesus Christ to reign in power!

PEOPLE:   Praise God, who sends the Spirit to empower the church.

LEADER:   Praise God with trumpet sound; praise God with flute and harp!

PEOPLE:   Praise God with timbrel and dance; praise God with strings and pipes!

ALL:   Let everything that breathes praise God!       (RCD)

# INVOCATIONS

## EASTER

Gracious Redeemer, we come to you in the morning of the resurrection. We expect to find you among the tombs and grave clothes of our world, but you are alive. Sin cannot hold you; death cannot bind you; and, just as we have been weeping and mourning that you have been taken from us, you meet us in the garden of the new life and send us running to share the good news of the gospel to the very ends of the earth. You are risen, indeed. We have seen you and so we believe that joy comes from grief. Because we are not left alone, we can join hands with one another and pray your prayer. *The Prayer of Our Savior follows.* (MCT)

Or

Giver of new life, we come this morning with our alleluias, our banners and flowers and trumpets and song. We come to worship in beauty and in truth because we have faith that Jesus Christ is raised from the dead, because we have hope that the resurrection will enter into each of our lives and transform them, and because, through Christ's spirit, we have come to love one another. Accept our worship, gracious God. Be present with us as daystar, miracle, and mystery, and as the tender hands of grace. Amen. (MCT)

## SECOND SUNDAY IN EASTERTIDE

God of Resurrection,
we cry out to you as empty people in a fractured world.
We live in a world of Good Fridays:
where the innocent suffer and die,
where midday darkness smothers the light,
where hopes and dreams dissolve,
where evil seems to triumph.
God of Resurrection,
we long to discover your presence,
we long to feel the rhythm of your power,
we stumble toward the tombs in our lives
and long to find them empty.

Bring Easter to our hearts, to our eyes and ears, to our lives, this morning.
In the name of Christ,
whose life and love could not be stamped out,
whose resurrection hope is the hope
which plants love and laughter in our lives

and lures them to sprout and bloom and blossom
like spring flowers in the morning sun, we say,
Amen.                                                                                (JWH)

### THIRD SUNDAY IN EASTERTIDE (YEAR A, LUKE 24:13–35)

We come before you, O God, in Easter joy, seeking to be a people of the resurrection.
Be known among us; grant us the assurance of your presence, your love, and your
renewing power. Through your Word and Spirit, reveal to us your purpose in our lives.
We pray in the name of Jesus Christ. Amen.                                        (RCD)

### FOURTH SUNDAY IN EASTERTIDE

Risen Lord, live in us that we may live in you. We gather to thank you that in your
resurrection we are renewed and transformed. Like the butterfly, we unfold and fly free,
free from the cocoon, free from all the graveclothes that have bound us—our prejudices,
our fears, our angers, our self-centeredness, our loneliness. We thank you that in your
resurrection all those who have died who are dear to us now live with you. In you they
have victory over suffering, peace never known on earth, and the joy of your presence
always. We thank you that in your resurrection we ourselves may hope for the end of
pain, grief, tears, weakness, and for everlasting life in the beauty of your spirit. Alleluia,
we pray in Christ's name, Amen.                                                  (MCT)

### FIFTH SUNDAY IN EASTERTIDE

God, you are the source of our life.
Gather us now together, we pray.
Form us into a holy community of your own people,
molding us by the breath of your Holy Spirit,
and revealing in this corporate body
the face of your anointed Christ. Amen.                                          (CLC)

### SIXTH SUNDAY IN EASTERTIDE

New every morning is your mercy, O God; your faithfulness is as boundless as the
heavens. We gather to worship you, thankful for all your gifts. We thank you that Jesus,
in dying and rising for us, has overcome the power of sin and death. Help us to accept
the freedom Christ offers us, through your presence among us. In the name of Jesus
Christ we pray. Amen.                                                            (RCD)

## SEVENTH SUNDAY IN EASTERTIDE

Resurrected Savior, Savior of new life and new hope, we come to you in humble prayer and joyous song, for Easter has changed our lives. We are no longer frightened people—because you live, we have courage to face life and to face death. We are no longer lonely people—because you live, we can accept ourselves and reach out to each other. We are no longer scattered people—because you live, we may come together to worship and to witness in our weakness and our strength to the presence of your reign among us and the promise of your reign to come. Amen.                                    (MCT)

## ASCENSION DAY

Great and loving God, we who come to worship are also persons who sometimes feel that you have abandoned us or left us to fend for ourselves. Although we rely upon your ever-presence, we suspect your absence. Encourage us, O God, when we doubt your promise to be with us always.

In our worship, grant us the gifts of discernment and hope. Enable us to recognize your workings in the commonplace and the everyday. Open us to faith and help us to perceive not only what is, but also what, by your grace, might be.

We offer this prayer in the name of Jesus Christ. Amen.                          (GER)

# PRAYERS OF CONFESSION

## EASTER

God, we come before you as those who have been baptized into the death of Jesus Christ, and who seek to be raised to new life in Christ. Yet we confess our fear of death. We fear death as life's ending, and its threat hidden in poverty, danger, or sickness. We fear death as letting go of old ways, old relationships, old self-understandings. We confess our fear of life. Sometimes we want to build shells to protect ourselves from people who come too close, from change that comes too fast, from possibilities that seem too bewildering.

God, help us trust our lives into your keeping, accept the embrace of your loving arms, and receive your forgiveness and your promise of life eternal in Jesus Christ. Raise us to walk in newness of life—whether in the faltering steps of infants or the sure steps of mature Christians; through Jesus Christ, who has promised to be with us always. Amen. (RCD)

## SECOND SUNDAY IN EASTERTIDE

God of all worlds and all time, we gather voicing thanks for this season of resurrection. May our worship be as an Easter tide.

Wash over us and seep into us to refresh and to cleanse. Dissolve the prejudices that cling to us like barnacles, the jealousies that lodge in crevices of memory. Move toward us with power and might when we are rock-rigid in our views and when we are unforgiving as granite. Let us hear the thunderous sound of good news as it breaks upon our hardness of heart. And bid us, God, to dare to journey upon the sea of the Spirit. May the waves of an Easter tide buoy us up and beckon us to the adventure of resurrection living. Amen. (GER)

Or

Gracious God, we confess before you our slowness to embrace the new life you offer.

You offer springtime to our souls, but we prefer the winter of coldness and indifference.

We continue in despair and self-doubt, rather than rejoicing in knowing you love us.

We forget that we have been baptized into the death and resurrection of Christ. Afraid to die, we cannot receive new life.

Rejoicing that you forgive us, with our coldness, self-hate, forgetfulness, or fear, we pray to you with the confidence of your children.

*The Prayer of Our Savior follows.* (RCD)

## THIRD SUNDAY IN EASTERTIDE (YEAR A, LUKE 24:13–35)

God, we confess that there are many hours when we are not mindful of your presence. We give up the comfort and avoid the challenge that come from your Word and Spirit. Forgive us and restore the joy of knowing you. May Christ be known among us in the breaking of bread. Amen.                                                    (RCD)

## FOURTH SUNDAY IN EASTERTIDE (YEAR A, ACTS 2:42–47)

Revolutionary God, in raising Jesus Christ you loosed great energy, creating a new people who shared common life, witness, prayer, and belongings. Yet we confess that we are afraid to risk selves and goods in creating your new world. We are even afraid to pray honestly with one another. God, forgive us. Blow through us with the Spirit of your Christ. Give us new energy to build community, peace, and justice on earth. Amen.                                                                          (RCD)

Or

God of life and death, we confess that sometimes we are not alive to the possibilities you offer. In the midst of pain, unfairness, and fear, we find little reason for hope. We feel despair or blame others, but we do not turn to you for help. Forgive us and show us how to share the new life you offer, through Jesus Christ. Amen.          (RCD)

## FIFTH SUNDAY IN EASTERTIDE (YEAR B, JOHN 15:1–8)

Gracious God, Dresser of Vines, we confess that we have been more willing to consume the fruits of others than to bear fruit ourselves. We have refused to give of ourselves when the harvest is uncertain. We have not been fruitful because we depended too much on ourselves and not enough on you. Help us, God, to be channels for your grace, branches who feed on your life-giving Spirit, bearers of your word of love and joy, in Jesus Christ. Amen.                                                          (JTF)

## SIXTH SUNDAY IN EASTERTIDE (PS. 121)

Keeper of heaven and earth,
guardian of our coming and going forth,
of our times of tender reflection
and our moments of turmoil.
Our life is fragile.
We violate each other in personal relationships, as nations, as inept keepers of life's beauty.
Sharpen our sensitivities. Stir in us preference for listening over speaking, for tenderness over aggression, for solidarity and community over alienation.

Deepen for us the meaning of the resurrection, that we not only speak words of transformation but embody those words in our life.

Healer, Renewer, Sustainer, Source of Hope and Joy, we offer thanks and praise, Alleluia, Alleluia, Amen.                                    (EEB)

## SEVENTH SUNDAY IN EASTERTIDE

*Call to Confession*

God's love is steadfast, and God's faithfulness endures from age to age. Our love falters, and our faithfulness waxes and wanes from day to day. Let us confess our sin and our need for God.

*Prayer of Confession*

Gracious God, you encourage us with your love, bringing new life out of death. We confess that we need your life-giving power in our lives and our relationships. We have hurt others and been hurt by them. We are often angry or afraid. We are not sure when to assert our needs and when to care for others' needs. We continue to live in ways which do not lead to peace and justice. Forgive us, O God. Pour your Spirit of wisdom and healing upon us, that by our lives and our loving, we may glorify you, through Jesus Christ the Risen One. Amen.                          (RCD)

# WORDS OF ASSURANCE

### CHRIST IS THE WAY (JOHN 14:6)

For all who have come believing in Christ as the Way, there is rest from your fruitless labors, forgiveness of your sins, and the guarantee of eternal life. Let us then continue our journey of faith and obedience, through the grace of Jesus Christ. Amen.　　(JTF)

### VINE AND BRANCHES (JOHN 15:11)

If you are serious about the confession you have made, God will bless your efforts and you will feel more "at home" than you have before. Your past is forgotten, your future will be fruitful and Christ's words will become your personal benediction: "These things I have spoken to you, that my joy may be in you, and that your joy may be full."

(JTF)

# UNISON PRAYERS

## EASTER (ACTS 10:34–43; JOHN 20:22)

Powerful and loving God, you have raised Jesus Christ from the dead. God, raise us too. May fresh life burst among us like buds awakening to the spring. May shells of distrust and self-hatred which keep us from loving be broken away so that new life can emerge. May new community spring up where fear has kept us from the stranger. Keep us patient in making peace and building justice. Teach us to trust the slow process from seed to stem, from stem to flower, from flower to fruit. Breathe on us with your Spirit, through the risen Christ. Amen.

(RCD)

OR

Alleluia! God, may all praise your name, for you have brought life out of death, and hope out of despair. You have raised Jesus Christ from the dead to be the first fruit of resurrection and the pledge of your victory of love over evil.

Wise God, you know our doubts, our fears, and our failures, which we bring to the tomb on Easter morning. Through your Spirit, nurture the small growth of hope, courage, and faith within us, that we may forever live to praise and serve you, in the name of Christ Jesus, in whom we pray. Amen.

(RCD)

## SECOND SUNDAY IN EASTERTIDE (JOHN 20:19–31)

God of the Risen Christ, you love us so much as to raise Christ from the tomb. In you we find only life and grace. You grant us peace in Christ. You give us forgiveness of sin. You welcome us back—without revenge—when we have been faithless. Bring us your peace and lead us to forgive others. Carry us through our times of disbelief.

May we believe that Jesus is the Christ! In that belief may we have life in Christ's name! In the name of the Risen One, we pray. Amen.

(JCW)

## THIRD SUNDAY IN EASTERTIDE

God of grace, you have come to us in Jesus Christ so we might have a new life—here on earth with each other. You seek that we surrender to your grace and completely change our lives—so we might know new strength in you, so we might love beyond frustrations, so we might help and serve others as a witness to your power and grace.

Be in all our days, for we pray in the name of the Risen Christ. Amen.

(JCW)

## FOURTH SUNDAY IN EASTERTIDE

We thank you, God, for raising Jesus Christ to new life, to live among us forever. We thank you for the new life you offer us, that hope, not fear, and love, not coldness, may rule our lives. May we know the risen Christ among us today, through the power of your Spirit. Amen.

(RCD)

## FIFTH SUNDAY IN EASTERTIDE

God, we thank you for your love and your grace so abundant, so overflowing, that you receive us in spite of our fear and our timid lives of faith. As you encouraged the first Christians to witness in the face of all risks, encourage us to follow your call rather than to cower before the powerful. Grant us peace in midst of the challenge; and fill us with your Holy Spirit, through the risen Christ. Amen.

(RCD)

## SIXTH SUNDAY IN EASTERTIDE (YEAR C, JOHN 14:23–29)

Gracious God, comfort of the grieving, peace of the troubled, we turn to you. Bring to our minds awareness of what it means to live in Christ's presence. Give us heart to love and to risk as your friends. Send your Spirit to guide us in everything, through the word and promise of Jesus the Christ. Amen.

(RCD)

## FESTIVAL PRAYER FOR THE DAY OF ASCENSION

Glorious God of wonder and might, you have spoken your eternal word in Jesus whom you have given to teach, to suffer, to love, and to rise with new life; may those who suffer raise their sights toward the ascended Christ and renew their hope in the eventual triumph of righteousness and peace. Beyond the pain and assaults of cruel and heartless authorities, we plead for your justice and your salvation, which you would so willingly lavish upon the weakest and the lowliest. Stir us to action and faith by our confidence that good will overcome evil and that the gentle breath of your Spirit will blow away every cloud of doubt and despair.

Come, lamb of sacrifice and judge of nations: crush every tyranny, expose every defeat, dispel every falsehood, wash away every vain desire, and rule with truth and mercy. Ascend in our hearts and in the affairs of nations until the earth itself becomes the place of your habitation and the garden of your delight!

Glory to you, O Christ: you are our friend, our savior, our only hope and sovereign. Yours is the victory beyond every tragic defeat, through time and past death! Glory be to you forever! Amen.

(APH)

## SEVENTH SUNDAY IN EASTERTIDE (ACTS 17:28)

Spirit of Life,
in whom we live and move and have our being,
we worship you.
We thank you for your presence among us
and in your whole creation.
Fill us with your power,
that by truthful words, just actions, and shared life
we may witness to the resurrection of Jesus Christ,
in whose name we pray. Amen.                                    (RCD)

# ADDITIONAL RESOURCES FOR EASTERTIDE

## LITANY (JOHN 15:1–8)

LEADER:   Planted in love by God and nourished by the life-giving vine that is Christ,
PEOPLE:   Our lives in this world can be fruitful.
LEADER:   Fruitfulness is the sign that we are being fed by Christ and not some other. The vine will bear for its planter.
PEOPLE:   But will the branch that we represent be pruned or burned?
LEADER:   It is not our responsibility to be the Source of life.
PEOPLE:   It is our responsibility to be the channel,
ALL:   The willing vehicle of God's bounty for all peoples!

(JTF)

## PRAYER OF CONSECRATION FOR EASTER COMMUNION (FOLLOWS THE *BENEDICTUS*)

Blessed indeed, our God, is that One who comes in your name. Blessed is Christ who came in the power of your name and the nature of your love. Blessed is Jesus of Nazareth who in life, in death, and in undying life brought life to us and led us to you. Blessed indeed is the courage by which he died and the choice by which he lived.

Remembering his life, his teachings, and especially now his costly choice of the way of the cross, the way of true love, we offer to you these your gifts of bread and wine, praying that you will hallow both them and us by the presence of your Spirit; that the bread we break may be the bread of his broken life, and the cup we bless and share the cup of his sacrifice.

And so we pray with confidence for the coming of your reign . . .
*The Prayer of Our Savior follows.*

(DLB)

## A POEM FOR COMMUNION SUNDAY

ON THE WAY TO EASTER

Face what must be faced.
Life moves with great complexity.
Stark simplicity marks death.
Avoidance of life and fear of death
would keep us alive but lifeless.
Join Jesus in death
by partaking of the cup.
Break bread and share fish.
This supper is common fare for those

whose goal is communion at the cross.
>This way through death
>>makes life endurable.
>Emerge now with all fullness.
Burst sanctuaries with lilies.
>Raise the day with singing.
>>God's word is light.
>The baptism of little ones
>>makes death acceptable
>>through a dark night.
>>On the way to Easter expect death and resurrection.
>Meet and greet each one
as a creation of God's love
>and open to JOY!

(DLJ)

## OFFERING (YEAR C, JOHN 21:15–19)

*Sentence*

Since our cups run over with the gifts of grace, let us respond with our love and ourselves and with our gifts.

*Prayer*

O God, we thank you that Christ has entrusted us with the task of feeding your people. Make us faithful and courageous in our ministry of love and may we use these gifts to your glory. Amen.

(RCD)

## CLOSING PRAYER FOR EASTER SUNRISE SERVICE

Loving Creator, Forgiving God, Source of all goodness, we offer these closing words of prayerful thanks for the wondrous gift of Christ's resurrection. Hear our prayer.

We have much to celebrate this Easter day. In the chill morning air we can appreciate the warming Spirit that you have placed within each one of us alone and all of us together. We can rejoice that beyond our tendency toward disbelief is a capacity to be captured by faith. We can gladly confess our surprise that a cross of execution has become our symbol of liberation, that an empty grave has served as the womb of new life.

O God, we awake this Easter morning to express gratitude in word and song. We offer our thanks that when you could have abandoned us you chose instead to affirm a steadfast presence. And we offer our thanks that the amazing graciousness of what you will for your children far exceeds our expectations, our imaginings, even our hopes.

In days to come, may we live for Christ. Show your power through us as you did through the crucified one. Draw forth our faithfulness from places of entombment; bring it to the light of day; set it free.

    We pray in the name of the resurrected and risen Christ. Amen.         (GER)

## BENEDICTION FOR EASTER

Because the tomb is empty your life can be full, so go into every place and every day as people brimming with the love of God.

    Be graceful in spirit, hopeful in word, faithful in deed.

    Live for the risen Christ as Christ lives in you.

    Alleluia and Amen!         (GER)

## BENEDICTION FOR A BAPTISM SUNDAY IN EASTERTIDE

Go forth as those baptized into Christ's death
to embrace newness of life,
through the love of God which seeks us
from our parents' arms,
the grace of Christ which renews us,
and the communion of the Holy Spirit which binds us. Amen.     (RCD)

## A PASTORAL PRAYER FOR EASTERTIDE

We thank you, Redeeming God,
for the glorious message
that you bring new hope out of despair,
resurrection out of defeat,
and new life out of death.
You call dry bones to dance.
You give living water so that new life blossoms.
You urge flowers to push their way through winter-hardened soil.
We bring before you the dead and dried-out places in our lives,
that through your touch we may discover newness of life.
Forgotten dreams, lapsed intentions,
hardened resentments,
griefs to which we cling
like children who cling to a worn but cherished toy or blanket:
these we hand over to you,
knowing that you will return them,
mended, washed, renewed, transformed.
We bring before you

the places in our lives and in our world
where despair reigns unchallenged.
With grief we bring our concerns for the Middle East and other parts of the world
where the cycle of violence goes on and on.
Point us toward actions, however small,
which lead to a more hopeful future
for ourselves and for our world.
Gracious God,
we thank you that you walk beside us as we journey through life.
Because you are with us,
we accept each new day, with its joys and sorrows,
as a gift.
Because you are with us,
we gain courage to meet the challenge of the day,
choosing life and not death as we move through time.
As you raised Jesus from the dead,
raise us to new life day by day.
For we pray in Jesus' name. Amen.                                    (RCD)

# Resources for Pentecost Sunday
## and the Sundays after
### Pentecost

## CALLS TO WORSHIP

### PENTECOST SUNDAY

LEADER: Do not give easy or unthinking response to this day's call to worship. For today we ask God's Spirit to fill us, that we may prophesy, and dream dreams, and see visions. The call to worship today is a summons to be touched by holy fire.

PEOPLE: Even now the flames may dance above our heads,

LEADER: Igniting our opinions on peacemaking so that they blaze into commitment.

PEOPLE: Even now the flames may be burning into our hearts,

LEADER: Animating us, leaving us no peace as individuals until God's justice and peace fill the earth as the waters fill the seas.

PEOPLE: Prophets, visionaries, dreamers! Let us all worship with courage and with hope.

(MSG)

*Originally published by UCC Stewardship Council for use for Peace Pentecost*

### FIRST SUNDAY AFTER PENTECOST

LEADER: Let us worship the eternal God,
the Source of Love and Life,
who creates us.

PEOPLE: Let us worship Jesus Christ,
the Risen One, who lives among us.

LEADER: Let us worship the Spirit,
the Holy Fire, who renews us.

ALL: To the one true God be praise
in all times and places,
through the grace of Jesus Christ!

(RCD)

## SECOND SUNDAY AFTER PENTECOST (YEAR B, MARK 2:23—3:6)

LEADER:   You were not made for the sabbath, but the sabbath was made for you.

PEOPLE:   We choose to gather on this sabbath to worship, to pray, and to share with one another.

LEADER:   Jesus asked, "Is it lawful on the sabbath to do good or to harm, to save life or to kill?"

PEOPLE:   We choose compassion and justice and healing. In this sabbath time together we choose life.                                                                                                        (MCT)

## THIRD SUNDAY AFTER PENTECOST

LEADER:   The Holy Spirit has given us life and pours on us the power to become new people!

PEOPLE:   The winds of the spirit have given us breath and the fire of the spirit has enkindled in us a love for God and each other.

LEADER:   Come here in faithfulness and be ready for the surprises that God's Spirit brings.

PEOPLE:   We open our lives to the presence of God and trust God's promise to us that we can live new lives of freedom and grace. May God help us to be true people of spirit, letting holy surprises fill our days!                                                (SEG)

## FOURTH SUNDAY AFTER PENTECOST (GEN. 1:1, 2; JOHN 1:1)

LEADER:   In the beginning God created the heavens and the earth.

PEOPLE:   Behold our God is a Creator.

LEADER:   In the beginning was the Word, and the Word was with God, and the Word was God.

PEOPLE:   Behold our God is a Redeemer.

LEADER:   The earth was without form and void, and darkness was upon the face of the deep; and the Spirit of God was moving over the face of the waters.

PEOPLE:   Behold our God is a Holy Spirit.

UNISON:   Let us worship the God who is one in three, three in one, who heals our brokenness and gathers up all our meanings.                                                        (MCT)

## FIFTH SUNDAY AFTER PENTECOST

LEADER:   Come, let us worship Almighty God.

PEOPLE:   Let us lift up our songs, our prayers, our praises.

LEADER:   Come, let us honor Christ Jesus.

PEOPLE:   Let us love Christ with our hearts, our minds, our spirits.

LEADER:   Come, let us be filled with the Spirit of the Living God.

PEOPLE:   Breathe in us, Breath of God. Alleluia.                                                                  (MCT)

## SIXTH SUNDAY AFTER PENTECOST (YEAR C, LUKE 9:51–62)

LEADER: We have been called here to face into God's gracious way of living. We are to leave the past behind us and walk into these new days of our ministry.

PEOPLE: Sometimes we'd rather remember how things used to be. Sometimes we are afraid to be disciples.

LEADER: But this is a new day, and Christ is sharing freedom with us. It is a day to put aside all fear, to leave doubting behind, and to take courage in God's loving call.

PEOPLE: We will look to the new day, and we will set ourselves on the Jerusalem road. We will strive for faithfulness, even at the cost of popularity, and we will be disciples of Christ, renewing and healing the world around us. (SEG)

## SEVENTH SUNDAY AFTER PENTECOST

LEADER: Praise be to God who reigns above the heavens.

PEOPLE: Praise be to God who dwells within our hearts.

LEADER: Let the majesty of creation worship in reverence.

PEOPLE: Let each man, woman and child pray in faith.

ALL: Praise be to God. (MCT)

## EIGHTH SUNDAY AFTER PENTECOST

LEADER: We come to this worship lonely or empty or frightened.

PEOPLE: We come to this worship sick or grieving or discouraged.

LEADER: We come from households spiky with anger. We come from unfinished projects, ruined plans, and multiple irritations.

PEOPLE: We come from broken diets, hidden drinking, unanswered mail, and a week without bedtime prayers.

LEADER: We come from nuclear paralysis and the refusal to read the newspaper for fear of learning how we might help someone.

PEOPLE: From inadequacy we seek God's wholeness; from delinquency we seek God's forgiveness; from self-imposed impotence we hope to be freed for love and service by the gospel's power. (MCT)

## NINTH SUNDAY AFTER PENTECOST

LEADER: We have been called to walk the faithful road and to choose the way of God's justice.

PEOPLE: We are here because we believe strongly that our God is good, and that we live in that goodness. We are here to proclaim our faith and to seek direction along this faith journey.

LEADER: Come together, then, to be God's people. Follow Christ and listen for the good things that God has done. Rise up in praise and thanksgiving!

PEOPLE: We will share with others the goodness that we have found in God. May our lives be an expression of that goodness. (SEG)

## TENTH SUNDAY AFTER PENTECOST (YEAR A, ROM. 8:26)

LEADER: The Spirit of God calls to us,

PEOPLE: With sighs too deep for words.

LEADER: The Spirit of God calls to us,

PEOPLE: Claiming us,

LEADER: Summoning us to become more than we now are.

PEOPLE: Calling us by name: God's children. (MSG)

## ELEVENTH SUNDAY AFTER PENTECOST

LEADER: Let us rejoice, for morning has dawned. A new day has been born, and we are newly alive to enjoy it.

PEOPLE: We know the beauty of God's creation and the wonder of the human family. We remember those whose love has shaped our lives and those whose struggle for justice has been unsleeping even in nighttimes of loneliness.

LEADER: We gather in our church to worship God, to share prayers and gifts, to pledge ourselves to God's work in the world.

PEOPLE: May God bless us, so that what we do in this time together may be honest, sacred, and filled with hope. (MCT)

## TWELFTH SUNDAY AFTER PENTECOST (YEAR C, HEB. 11)

LEADER: In faith, Abraham and Sarah set out for a new land.

PEOPLE: In faith, we seek to follow God in our lives.

LEADER: In faith, the church seeks to discern the future to which God calls us in our age.

PEOPLE: In faith, we gather now to worship, seeking new life in Christ.

ALL: God of present, past, and future, guide us now to your new age of promise. (RCD)

## THIRTEENTH SUNDAY AFTER PENTECOST

LEADER: We come, like Abraham, Sarah, and John, people with vision.

PEOPLE: We come, like Job, Thomas, and the Samaritan woman, people with questions.

LEADER: We come, like Moses, Jeremiah, and Mary, people with self-doubts.

PEOPLE:  We come, like Joshua, Deborah, and Stephen, people with courage.

LEADER:  We come, like David, Mary Magdalene, and Paul, people with sadness and sin in our memories.

PEOPLE:  We come, like Rebekah and Samuel, like Hosea and Esther, like Nathaniel and Martha, like John Mark and Priscilla, people with a part to play in the story of faith.

(MCT)

## FOURTEENTH SUNDAY AFTER PENTECOST (YEAR B, JOHN 6)

Come to Christ, the living bread, who satisfies those who hunger and thirst for what is right.

Come to Christ, who gives living water, that you may never thirst again.

Come to Christ, that being filled yourself, you may minister to the hunger and thirst of others.

Come to God, in worship and praise, through Jesus Christ, who gives us life.    (RCD)

## FIFTEENTH SUNDAY AFTER PENTECOST

LEADER:  What does this worship service need?

PEOPLE:  Quiet where faith can grow, song that blossoms hope, scripture that remembers love, honest words to untangle a small length of knotty existence, gifts offering service of the heart.

LEADER:  Who shall come to this worship service?

PEOPLE:  All who have prayer in the center of their lives and all who are lonely for the touch of God.

(MCT)

## SIXTEENTH SUNDAY AFTER PENTECOST

LEADER:  May the peace of God rest upon your busy lives so that you may be quieted into prayer.

PEOPLE:  May the love of God flow through your worship words that they may be alive with opportunities for service.

LEADER:  May the grace of God seek out your every need and may the restless gospel set your hearts afire.

PEOPLE:  Amen and Amen.

(MCT)

## SEVENTEENTH SUNDAY AFTER PENTECOST

LEADER:  In autumn beauty blue sky and golden land is clothed. Apple-gathering children and nut-gathering squirrels alike prepare for winter.

PEOPLE:  In our tradition, harvest is a time of rejoicing in God's natural bounty and the ingathering of our lives.

LEADER:   We praise God for all we have received. Seasons turn but God's love is changeless.

PEOPLE:   We praise God for all we have received. Maple leaves dancing, crisp breezes blowing, the good news stories of Jesus' sojourn in Galilee, and the restless winds of the Spirit rushing through our lives—all these assure us of God's faithful presence.                    (MCT)

## EIGHTEENTH SUNDAY AFTER PENTECOST (YEAR B, JAMES 3:17–18)

LEADER:   God's wisdom is pure, peaceable, gentle, open to reason, full of mercy and good fruits, without uncertainty or insincerity.

PEOPLE:   Our wisdom is none of these things. We compete for knowledge, and our learning fosters belligerence. Our understanding is insufficient and our compassion limited. We long for certainty and sacrifice too much for its sake. We strive only for conditional sincerity.

LEADER:   The harvest of righteousness is sown in peace by those who make peace.

PEOPLE:   We cannot know with God's wisdom, nor always walk in God's righteousness, but we can come together to share our thoughts, to read Scripture, to sing, to pray, and to make peace.

LEADER:   Let us worship together.                    (MCT)

## NINETEENTH SUNDAY AFTER PENTECOST

LEADER:   God be praised for turning seasons—blustery winter with its snow-face, the fragile wings of spring, and hot, heavy, growing, grazing summer.

PEOPLE:   Now two-faced autumn begins with burnished days and drizzling days.

LEADER:   Autumn—September crimson, October orange and cat-black, November gray.

PEOPLE:   Autumn—golden leaves, ripe red Cortlands, school bells, football cheers, pumpkin pie, cider, mince, the smell of cold and smoke, the touch of homecoming.

LEADER:   Autumn—when between the boughs of leaf-lost trees squirrels race winter. We gather in the harvest of our lives, the plenty, the good, and rake up the scatterings—dried hopes and fallen dreams.

PEOPLE:   And we offer all the end-year bounty and gleanings before Almighty God.                    (MCT)

## TWENTIETH SUNDAY AFTER PENTECOST (ISA. 25:6–9)

LEADER:   We wait for God that God might save us.

PEOPLE:   Let us be glad and rejoice in God's salvation.

LEADER:   God will swallow up death forever and will wipe away the tears from all faces.

PEOPLE:  Let us be glad and share in God's salvation.

LEADER:  God will take away all reproach and will make a feast for the peoples of the earth.

PEOPLE:  Let us act with compassion so that we may dry tears. Let us walk with justice so that we may silence reproach. Let us make festival with all people so that God's feast may be well-prepared. (MCT)

## TWENTYFIRST SUNDAY AFTER PENTECOST (YEAR A, PHIL. 4:7–8)

LEADER:  Paul the Apostle commends to us whatever is true and honorable and just.

PEOPLE:  Let us hear these words that we may be challenged.

LEADER:  Paul also offers us whatever is pure and lovely and gracious.

PEOPLE:  Let us seek these ways that we may be blessed.

LEADER:  We are to set before ourselves whatever is excellent and worthy of praise.

PEOPLE:  Let us think upon these deeds in our time of worship together.

UNISON:  And the peace of God which passes all understanding will keep our hearts and minds in Christ Jesus. (MCT)

## TWENTYSECOND SUNDAY AFTER PENTECOST

LEADER:  God has given us this beautiful earth and all that grows and runs upon it.

PEOPLE:  Thanks be to God.

LEADER:  God has given us breath to live and spirit to sing.

PEOPLE:  Thanks be to God.

LEADER:  God has gathered us into a community of care and worship.

PEOPLE:  Let us worship God with love, thanksgiving, and praise. (MCT)

## TWENTYTHIRD SUNDAY AFTER PENTECOST (YEAR B, JER. 31:7–9)

LEADER:  God has called people from the farthest places of the earth.

PEOPLE:  From east and west, from north and south, the people of God are gathered.

LEADER:  God has called the blind and the lame, pregnant women, and those with nursing infants.

PEOPLE:  From all ways of life and every experience the people of God are gathered.

LEADER:  Those who are weeping will be consoled, those who are thirsty will be led by brooks of water, those who stumble shall find a straight path.

PEOPLE:  We hear God's call through prophet words, and we come as this congregation to be the gathered people of God. (MCT)

## TWENTYFOURTH SUNDAY AFTER PENTECOST (JOHN 10:10)

Jesus said, "I came so that you may have life, and have it more abundantly." Yet even in the season of harvest we are hungry. We gather today to be fed. May God's presence fill us and refresh us anew. Let us worship God with such great expectations.     (MEW)

## TWENTYFIFTH SUNDAY AFTER PENTECOST

LEADER:   This is sabbath—we seek deep within our restful selves for re-creation.

PEOPLE:   This is Sunday—we celebrate the bright resurrection and its good news.

LEADER:   This is the day which God has made.

PEOPLE:   Let us rejoice and be glad in it.     (MCT)

## TWENTYSIXTH SUNDAY AFTER PENTECOST
## (PSS. 96:4; 81:9; 100:4)

LEADER:   God is great, and greatly to be praised!

PEOPLE:   We thank you, God, for families and friends. We thank you for the warmth of kitchens, quilts, and good neighbors.

LEADER:   God, how great is your name throughout the earth!

PEOPLE:   We thank you, God, for newborn kittens and faithful dogs, for pine trees and sunlight and crisp, clear air.

LEADER:   Blessed be God, the rock of our salvation!

PEOPLE:   We thank you, God, for the sound of laughter and the touch of love, for brand new mornings and for dreams held close.

LEADER:   Let us come into God's presence with thanksgiving; let us make a joyful noise with songs of praise. Come! Let us worship God.     (JJS)

## TWENTYSEVENTH SUNDAY AFTER PENTECOST (YEAR B, REV. 1:8)

LEADER:   Our God is Alpha and Omega.

PEOPLE:   We are a people of many beginnings and endings.

LEADER:   Sovereign God who is and was and is to come is the Almighty.

PEOPLE:   Within God's time we each find our little times—our memories, our concerns for today, our hopes for the future.

LEADER:   This is the hour we set aside to worship God in deep reverence through great praise.

PEOPLE:   With our human hearts and sinews, with our reason and our spirit, we rejoice in God's presence with us here and find ourselves within God's presence.

(MCT)

## ALL SAINTS' DAY OR REFORMATION SUNDAY (ISA. 6:8)

LEADER:   There are many who have walked the path toward God before us, showing us
the way with their lives.

PEOPLE:   We come to give thanks for them.

LEADER:   As they were called, so are we called to live as Jesus did, answering the call
of God, saying, "Here I am! Send me."

PEOPLE:   We come to ask for guidance and courage.

LEADER:   We are, each of us, like those who have gone before us, a strange mixture of
saint and sinner. God accepts us that way and fills us with the Spirit, who
empowers us to act.

PEOPLE:   We come to worship the Holy God.                                    (JJS)


## THANKSGIVING

LEADER:   Let us gather together in thanksgiving to God.

PEOPLE:   For God has made us and this earth which gives us nurture.

LEADER:   Let us gather together in gratitude to one another.

PEOPLE:   For we are the bearers of God's blessing and love for the earth and its
people.

ALL:   Let us praise God; let us join hands; let us reach out in care and courage so
that the goodness of life may be for all God's children. Amen.          (MCT)

OR


LEADER:   Today we offer thanksgiving for those other things.

PEOPLE:   For troubles that shape and sharpen our patience, for doubts that let faith
moments shine, and for confusions that keep our lives from being rigid.

LEADER:   For sufferings that help us share another's grief, for fears that mark real
terror in the world, and for pains that open our eyes to joy.

PEOPLE:   For sorrows that join our hands to hope and for loneliness that leads us to
the heart of God.

LEADER:   For all these gifts by which we have become more human, we give thanks.

PEOPLE:   Let our thanks reach out and embrace the daily small ingratitudes of our
lives.                                                                   (MCT)

# INVOCATIONS

## PENTECOST SUNDAY

Send forth your Spirit, O God, and renew the face of the earth. Dwell among us, even though your presence will startle and unsettle us. Grant us your peace, we pray, as justice and love pour down upon the yearning earth. Amen.

(MSG, drawing on an ancient prayer)

## FIRST SUNDAY AFTER PENTECOST

O God, there is a dark and lonesome gulf in worship, a cavern of the awesome into which we rarely go. We prefer catchy tunes, bright vestments, and holiday prayers. We would rather exchange fellowship than touch holiness. Enable us in this precious time to venture into the depths of worship which can never be found totally in individual spirituality but which open slowly before the shared pain, struggle, and love of the communion of the saints. Amen. (MCT)

## SECOND SUNDAY AFTER PENTECOST

O holy God, we know the beauty of this June day and we are grateful. We experience the warm stirring of summer and the fullness of bountiful earth, and we are grateful. We share the love of family and friends and the family and friendship that is our church, and we are grateful.

Through the grace of Christ Jesus, we know the opportunity to bring new selves to this new day that we might worship with our community in joy and thanksgiving and be filled with the good news we would offer everyone. For all these things we are deeply grateful. Amen. (MCT)

## THIRD SUNDAY AFTER PENTECOST (YEAR C, LUKE 7:11–17; ISA. 43:1–7)

God of wondrous love,
  you have touched us
    and never left us in despair.
  You have held us
    in our grief and chaos.
  You have never deserted us.

  You paid us a visit
    and your visit has never ended.
  You clung to us
    when we were given up for dead.

In life and in death—
   you raise us anew!
This we know!
This we experience!
This is your word of assurance!

God of wondrous love,
   touch us again in this time.
Stay with us—
   as we continue healing
   our memories and lives.

In Christ's name, we pray. Amen.

(JCW)

## FOURTH SUNDAY AFTER PENTECOST

Gracious God, we give you thanks for June with its roses and its rains, for all that is green and alive and growing, for weddings and their anniversaries, for school children counting the days till summer vacation, and for reunion times of remembering childhood days. All these rejoice our hearts, and so we give you thanks. We also thank you for those assurances of our faith that are beyond the changing of the seasons—for the promise of forgiveness and healing, for the resurrection and our trust in eternal life, for the scriptures of Israel's history and the gospel story of God's love made flesh for us in Christ Jesus. For all that blesses us, as a congregation and as individuals, we give you thanks and praise, O gracious God. Amen.

(MCT)

## FIFTH SUNDAY AFTER PENTECOST
## (YEAR C, I KINGS 19:9–14; ALLUDES TO 2 KINGS 2:6–14)

Gracious God who has the power to create the whirlwind and the wisdom to speak to us in the still, small voice, we ask that you bring your love to us today. We are in need of the strength of your spirit. We live in the hope of your call. We depend on you; there is no other who gives us such hope and life. Be with us, care for us, comfort and confront us with your love and grace. Through the power of the Spirit we pray. Amen.

(SEG)

## SIXTH SUNDAY AFTER PENTECOST

God of the sojourners, we ask your presence with us on our journey through life. Help us to be faithful to your ways of love and grace. Keep us from helpless despair. Give us the power to make your love known, even in this world that seems so bent on war and hate. With your courage in our hearts, we will walk the Jerusalem road together. Amen.

(SEG)

## SEVENTH SUNDAY AFTER PENTECOST (YEAR A, MATT. 11:28)

Gracious God, we thank you that we can rest in you, secure amid the conflict and confusion of life. We thank you that you provide for our needs and that you have trusted us to one another's care. Help us to receive with humility and to give with joy. Help us to share what we have without fear of tomorrow. May we be peacemakers and justice makers, that one day humanity may choose bread over weapons and fairness over greed. Amen.                                                                        (RCD)

## EIGHTH SUNDAY AFTER PENTECOST

Merciful God, Just God, Faithful God, God of blessing and God of our most difficult times, we come to you for a moment of quiet in our self-made busyness. We come to you for energy in our weariness. We come to you for challenge when we are willing to settle for our own small plans and dreams. We long for the peace of your presence, even as we are afraid of the urgency of your call. Enter, Spirit of God, into each of our lives and enliven us; enter, Spirit of God, into our community and enable us to love and serve you and all your children. Amen.                                              (MCT)

## NINTH SUNDAY AFTER PENTECOST

O God, our joy and our comfort, we gather in your name to give thanks for all the gifts of this day. Our spirits abound with your gift of joy. Of all the many things we have received from your hand, the flame of joy is the most precious. We have also come to this hour of prayer bearing in our hearts the sorrows of our world. Comfort us with your presence that we may be strengthened to continue to proclaim your goodness and deliverance in all the earth; through Jesus Christ our Savior. Amen.             (MGMG)

## TENTH SUNDAY AFTER PENTECOST (YEAR A, ROM. 8:23, 26, 27)

Spirit of holiness and life, be within our community as we worship this morning. Search within each of us for the sighs too deep for words and make them articulate so that we may share our hopes and fears and bring out of our silence life-changing prayers for ourselves and, in intercession, for all precious, groaning creation. Amen.             (MCT)

## ELEVENTH SUNDAY AFTER PENTECOST

Gracious and holy God, we come to you because you have first come to us. We know you because you have revealed yourself. Give us in this morning hour of worship a new sense of your Spirit breathing through us. Lift our hearts with the wings of song, heal our souls with the balm of prayer, enliven our minds with the words of scripture and interpretation, and newly enable us to dedicate our strength, our substance, and our service to your work in the world. We pray in the name of Jesus Christ. Amen.     (MCT)

## TWELFTH SUNDAY AFTER PENTECOST

Holy God,
we thank you that you receive us
not according to our failing goodness,
but according to your overflowing grace.
You receive us as we are.
You show us what we can be.
You have come to us in Jesus Christ
to share our common lot and reconcile us to yourself.
Sweep over us with your Spirit,
change us by your love,
that we may sing with joy before you,
and live to your glory in the world.          (RCD, quoting the UCC Statement of Faith)


## THIRTEENTH SUNDAY AFTER PENTECOST (ISA. 40:31)

Creator, Redeemer, and Spirit of all holiness, be in our midst with your baptism of
power and your communion of love. We wait upon you in stillness and patience because
you turn strength into weakness and weakness into strength. In the moments of victory
and joy you do lift us up on wings of flight. In the days of routine and duty you enable
us to run a sure course without weariness or collapse. In the hours of pain and fear, in
the times of trial, in the nights of grief and death, you help us walk, hand-held and
step-steadied, so that we do not faint. You are our God and we are your people. Amen.

(MCT)


## FOURTEENTH SUNDAY AFTER PENTECOST

Spirit of the Living God, be with our kaleidoscopic church. We are many-colored and
multi-shaped, with fragments that focus and focus again always in different patterns as
we turn to the light of your presence. Help us to love the patterns and the turning, and
to trust in the beauty of a wholeness we may rarely see. Amen.          (MCT)


## FIFTEENTH SUNDAY AFTER PENTECOST

*This is especially appropriate for use after Labor Day.*
Gracious God, we ask your blessing presence among us. We gather today after we have
been scattered to many places, and we begin a new church year full of excitement, even
if wistful for summer relaxation. Bless this church family—bless singers and pray-ers and
workers and teachers and servers of so many kinds that all worship and ministry might
be to your greater glory and that our gifts of the spirit might build up the body of
Christ. Amen.

(MCT)

### SIXTEENTH SUNDAY AFTER PENTECOST (YEAR A, MATT. 18:15–20)

We worship you, O God, and thank you that you receive us when we turn to you. We turn to you now, trusting the promise of Jesus Christ to be with us whenever two or three gather in his name. Come to us, and fill us with your Spirit of unity and truth, that we may serve you in the world; for we pray in Jesus' name. Amen.          (RCD)

### SEVENTEENTH SUNDAY AFTER PENTECOST

Our Sovereign God, Light of lights, Word of words, Life of all living, Peace of perfect peace. We praise you and thank you for the faith we have, for the hope we can always rekindle, for the love we experience in creation, redemption, and the spirit which dwells in the vortex of the universe and the breath of every child. Bless and consecrate the worship we share this day that in it we may affirm the grace and wonder of our relationship with you. Amen.          (MCT)

### EIGHTEENTH SUNDAY AFTER PENTECOST

Almighty God, you have created a tabernacle for the sun, the moon, and all the lights of heaven and are present to all things in all times and yet never can be contained. We know that you are not limited by the houses of worship which we build with our hands, but rather that your love always shelters our worshipfulness. Bless and consecrate our gathering in this place and the love we share in this time. May your touch of peace be upon our restless hearts, and may we always in greater reverence find you in our midst, even when we find you in the least likely of our sisters and brothers. Amen.          (MCT)

### NINETEENTH SUNDAY AFTER PENTECOST

For earth we give you thanks, O God. For rest we give you thanks. For work we give you thanks. For blue heaven we give you thanks. For meaning that is simple and sacred, for bonding of family and friendship and church, for the possibility to hope and live into the future, we give you thanks. For the light of day and the darkness gentle in the night, for the turning seasons of the year and the celebrations by which we mark our time, we give you thanks. For the gospel story, for the salvation of souls, for the promise of life eternal, we give you thanks and praise, God of holiness and splendor, even as we gather together in the name of the One who makes all love incarnate, Christ Jesus. Amen.          (MCT)

### TWENTIETH SUNDAY AFTER PENTECOST

Holy Spirit of God, who gathers the church into one body, gather us once again in your presence and strengthen the bonds of affection that hold your people together. Bless us with grace to cooperate with one another in love and service that we may be the signs of your uniting love to our fractured world. Teach us to show compassion for those in need, to face challenges with imagination, and to counter disappointments with prayerful trust. So may your church bring forth your will and your reign. Amen.     (MGMG)

## TWENTYFIRST SUNDAY AFTER PENTECOST

God of life and all living, we give you thanks on this November Sunday for the chilly, windy beauty of these late autumn days—for the leaf-lost trees and wet streets, for geese and birds vanishing south, for squirrels finishing their acorn gathering, for early dark and for the sober brown and gray of earth and sky and pond which remind us of pilgrim garb. We thank you for the warmth we find in family, friends, and church that sustains us now and in the winter months of our lives. We thank you for the harvest of good words we find in the Good News, the ingathering through forgiveness of all who confess their sins and the reconciliation of so many people. We thank you for Jesus Christ who is our model, strength, redeemer, and friend, and in whose name we gather together to worship today. Amen.     (MCT)

## TWENTYSECOND SUNDAY AFTER PENTECOST

Gracious Redeemer, we come to you in our times of indecision. We do not know where to turn; we do not know how to stand; we do not know what to choose. Set our feet now upon your paths, incline our hearts to your call, give us new opportunity to decide for your ways. Be with us, faithful God, in this hour of commitment and in all our hours. Amen.     (MCT)

## TWENTYTHIRD SUNDAY AFTER PENTECOST

Our gracious God, like a loving parent you nurture and encourage and challenge us to grow in grace. Grant that by sensing your Spirit's presence in our midst, we may be enabled to mature in our commitment to you. Forgive our failures and show us once again our possibilities. Prepare us to be servants of your will and agents of your love in all the world. Amen.     (MGMG)

## TWENTYFOURTH SUNDAY AFTER PENTECOST

Eternal God, we gather as your people to worship you. By your Spirit break the bonds that hold our minds captive to the petty concerns of our lives that we may know the freedom of new possibilities. Quiet the din of our distracted spirits that we may hear your gentle voice calling us. Transform our very lives that we may go forth from this hour with deeper commitment to doing your will, with a firm assurance of your presence. Amen.     (MGMG)

## TWENTYFIFTH SUNDAY AFTER PENTECOST

Dear God, we thank you that you never forsake us, that you never stop loving us. Trusting in your unfailing love, we have gathered to worship and praise you. Through your Holy Spirit, touch us, renew us, comfort us, challenge us; for we pray in the name of Jesus Christ. Amen.                                                                        (RCD)

## TWENTYSIXTH SUNDAY AFTER PENTECOST (FOR A COMMUNION SUNDAY)

We gather before you, God, thankful that you receive us when we come to you. Skillfully, through your Spirit's fire, find the places where we hurt and shine on them with healing light. Find the places where we run from you and gather us home. Then mold us, shape us, make us one as the grains on many hillsides become one loaf, one bread, one body in Jesus Christ. Amen.         (RCD, drawing on a prayer in the Didache)

## TWENTYSEVENTH SUNDAY AFTER PENTECOST (PS. 8)

O God, supreme power of the universe, we thank you that you care about us. When we think of your vast creation, we are amazed that you are mindful of us. Yet we dare to ask you to come and be known among us. Rule among us. We are your people. Fill us with your Spirit of life, through the grace of Jesus Christ. Amen.                        (RCD)

## WORLDWIDE COMMUNION SUNDAY

Spirit of the living God, though we are many, we have come together with one purpose—to worship you with scripture and song, with silence and sacrament. We witness that we are members of one another and wait for your word spoken clearly in our midst. May your presence be among us in this hour: touch us with tenderness, brush us with ecstasy, strengthen us into commitment, through Jesus Christ our Savior. Amen.
                                                                                            (MCT)

# PRAYERS OF CONFESSION

## PENTECOST SUNDAY

Almighty and ever gracious God, we confess that we have failed to open our hearts to the power of your Spirit. We continue the divisions of Babel, speaking in tongues that confound rather than clarify, hurt rather than heal, separate rather than unite. Though we are not deserving, we pray for the gift of fellowship that confirms your presence among us. Restore our fractured lives that we, with one voice, may ever give you thanks and praise. Amen.

(LKH)

## FIRST SUNDAY AFTER PENTECOST

O Holy God, we acknowledge to you, to ourselves, and to one another that we are not what you have called us to be. We have not stood by our faith, shared our hope, or reached out with love. We have done unkind and shameful deeds, and we have left undone deeds which could have made a difference in the lives of those around us. We have failed to speak and act for peace and justice in our world. Have mercy upon our repentance, forgive our sin, and change our lives, for we pray in the name of Jesus Christ our Savior. Amen.

(MCT)

## SECOND SUNDAY AFTER PENTECOST (YEAR C, LUKE 7:1–10)

O Thou, whose very name is Love, we mean to do well, but our intentions are soon discarded. We try to be faithful, but we are diverted by so many things. We do not wish to harm anyone, but, for lack of consideration, we sometimes hurt those we love the most. We sympathize for those who suffer more often than we act with them. We refuse to accept the help of others because we are unwilling to admit our needs. We, too, can say with the man who came to you, "Lord Jesus, I am not worthy that you should enter my house; only say the word and I shall be healed!"

(APH)

## THIRD SUNDAY AFTER PENTECOST (YEAR C)

*Call to Confession*

God has always been there for us, loving us and calling us to be all that we can be. Let us tell God all about ourselves, not leaving anything out.

*Prayer of Confession*

Everloving, everliving God, you have given us life itself and have asked us to be life-giving people in your name. But we, in turn, have cared more about ourselves and the comfort that we have than about your people in every place. There are people in our very presence who are left out of our thoughts and prayers, because our minds and hearts are too crowded with all the things that will make us feel self-satisfied. The world aches for peace, while we proclaim power to be more important. People on our streets go hungry because we make sure that we are full before even thinking about them. God, give us the purpose that you gave to people of Jesus' time: to be faithful disciples in your care. Through Christ we pray. Amen.                                                    (SEG)

### FOURTH SUNDAY AFTER PENTECOST (YEAR B, 2 COR. 5:17)

God of new life, we often say that anyone who is in Christ is a new creation. Yet when we consider our lives, we confess our failure to live in Christ. You promised to be present with us always, yet our fear for the future shows we do not trust in you. You love us with a great, eternal, and costly love, yet our self-hatred shows that we have not opened ourselves to your love. You promise that where your Spirit is, there is freedom, yet the injustice within your church shows that we have not let you set us free. God, guide us on the slow journey of growth. Free us from our fears, our prejudice, and our self-hatred, that we may live in Christ in the freedom of your Spirit. Amen.          (RCD)

### FIFTH SUNDAY AFTER PENTECOST

Christ Jesus, we have lived as if we did not need you, pretending that life is what we make it. In those exceptional moments of openness when we received the gift of faith, we have assumed it was given for ourselves alone. Awaken us by your Spirit to fuller dimensions of faith. Lead us to find in our neighbors the opportunities for love, in the social order the possibilities for justice, and in the affairs of nations the potential for peace. Reform our attitudes and behavior until in every circumstance we may, by your grace, be the instruments of your saving Word. Amen.                                        (APH)

### SIXTH SUNDAY AFTER PENTECOST

Most holy and most merciful God, in your presence we must face the sinfulness of our nature and the errors of our ways, intended and accidental. You alone know how often we have failed by wandering from your paths, wasting your gifts, and underestimating your love. Have mercy upon us, O God, for we have broken your requirements for justice and overlooked opportunities for kindness. Humble us with your truth and raise us by your grace that we may more nearly be the people of Christ and the witnesses of your Spirit. Amen.                                                                          (APH)

### SEVENTH SUNDAY AFTER PENTECOST (YEAR C, LUKE 10:4)

God, if we carry excess baggage on life's journey, teach us to travel more simply. If our possessions own us, free us to trust you and share with others. If our need for control keeps us anxious and demanding, help us to relax. If we carry loads of guilt, may we hand them over to you, trusting you to forgive us. God, make us simple: simple in trust, simple in life, simple in commitment to you. Prepare us for your mission. Allow us to join your labor to heal the hurting, feed the hungry, and bring good news to the poor. We pray in the name of Jesus Christ, in whose name we are baptized and sent on mission. Amen.                                                              (RCD)

## EIGHTH SUNDAY AFTER PENTECOST (YEAR C, LUKE 10:25–37)

O Holy God, we come in confession for our lack of love. We have neither loved ourselves nor our neighbors. We have passed by suffering and misfortune because of fear or busyness or preoccupation. We have held prejudices against people as deep as those against the Samaritans. Heal our pains, amend our faults, and guide us in ways of danger and compassion, for we pray in the name of Jesus, our most beloved neighbor, who cared for us even to the cross. Amen.                                          (MCT)

## NINTH SUNDAY AFTER PENTECOST (YEAR C, LUKE 10:38–42)

*Call to Confession*

Even when we have been too busy to notice, God has been constantly loving us and encouraging us to grow in the light of God's love. We can trust God with our deepest confession.

*Prayer of Confession*

Mighty, Gentle God, you have shown us your love and called us to be your servants. But we have made ourselves too busy and worried to notice. Like Martha, we have been anxious about much we cannot control, and we have forgotten you. We have been worried about what other people think of us, and we have missed the point of your care. We resent the Marys who act freely, trusting in your grace. We are angered by people whose service draws attention away from us. Forgive us, God, that we have worried over the wrong things. Free us, body and soul, for your service of love and grace. Amen.
                                                                          (SEG)

## TENTH SUNDAY AFTER PENTECOST

O God of love, God of power, we have heard your promises of abundant life and have been afraid to believe them. We have worshiped you with our lips but have reserved parts of ourselves for our own purposes and plans. We are bound by our need for absolute certainty and so we often miss your living presence in the surprises of life. Renew us by turning our trust to you again. Amen.                              (LKH)

## ELEVENTH SUNDAY AFTER PENTECOST

Gracious God, we open our hearts and confess our sins—against you, against our neighbor, against even ourselves. For the wrongs of our minds, our hearts, our hands, our spirits—forgive us. For our silence and lack of compassion—forgive us. For our self-love and our self-hatred—forgive us. For our anger and our fear—forgive us. For the waste of your gifts—forgive us. For our part, known and unknown, in the suffering of all of your children—forgive us. For our failures in justice and peace—forgive us. For all the times we do not walk the way of love—forgive us in the name of Jesus Christ who goes before us, so that we can know love. Amen. (MCT)

## TWELFTH SUNDAY AFTER PENTECOST (YEAR C, HEB. 11)

God of Abraham and Sarah, God of Jesus Christ, God of our mothers and fathers, you are a God who acts in history. Yet we confess that we are too busy with our own lives to perceive you at work in our time. We fall into fear and despair about our troubled world, as if you had no care for us. Forgive our lack of faith and help us to join you as you labor to bring new life on earth; in the name of Jesus Christ we pray. Amen.

(RCD)

## THIRTEENTH SUNDAY AFTER PENTECOST

God our Creator, we come to you a rebellious people. We have denied your intentions for us; we have sought our own ways rather than the way of Christ. We have refused to learn the lessons of the past, and still we remain bound up with past offenses. We dream of what cannot be and yet do not devote ourselves to laying a foundation for genuine hope. Forgive what we have been, amend what we are, and direct what we shall be in order to rise with Christ and serve you with trust and joy. Amen. (APH)

## FOURTEENTH SUNDAY AFTER PENTECOST

Merciful God, whose care never ceases, we come to you as we are. We are tired from trying to do more than we can manage. We are anxious about problems which go unresolved. We are worried about events beyond our control. We do not easily let go. For mistakes we cannot redeem, for tasks left undone, for uncertain goals, we need your forgiveness and ask for your understanding. For recovery of strength and enthusiasm, we pray for your Spirit. For fullness of life, generous hearts, and contented souls, we pray to be followers of Christ Jesus. In your mercy, restore us and lead us. Amen. (APH)

## FIFTEENTH SUNDAY AFTER PENTECOST

Christ Jesus, our teacher and our friend, we have not listened for your word amid the clamor of words all around us. We are more pleased to repeat familiar tunes than to listen for new melodies and strange harmonies. We try harder to defend what we think we know than to reach for that which is beyond our grasp. Slow to trust, afraid of the unknown, we are cautious to hear and do your will. We pray for ears to hear the cries of our neighbors and for hearts which resonate with your Spirit. Silence us and instruct us until we learn afresh to sing the songs of faith, hope, and love. Amen.     (APH)

## SIXTEENTH SUNDAY AFTER PENTECOST

God who loves us, you have always given us what we need. You have taken care of us even when we could not care for ourselves. You have given us life and breath. Why is it that we still doubt you? Why do we still go on our own way, rebelling against you? Why do we persist in doing everything our own way? God, we have hurt ourselves and others by being so fiercely independent. Give us courage enough to place our trust in you. Through the constant presence of the Spirit, we pray. Amen.     (SEG)

## SEVENTEENTH SUNDAY AFTER PENTECOST

Gracious God, we confess that our hearts are closed tight against your love and mercy. We hold on to unlove for ourselves, resentment against those for whom we care, anger at our helplessness, and complicity in the structures of society. We have protected ourselves emotionally, socially, and spiritually; and our selfishness has nourished the pain of the world rather than its hope. Open, loosen, and unbind us, God. Enable our frozen hearts to love, our clenched hands to help, and our stifled spirits to breathe and pray, in the name of Christ Jesus. Amen.     (MCT)

## EIGHTEENTH SUNDAY AFTER PENTECOST

O God, you search after us when we have gone far from you, yet we confess that we have become consumed with our own affairs. We seldom pause to listen for the wind in the trees or hear the happy voices of children. Sometimes we feel that the burdens of the world fall entirely on our shoulders, and we have been slow to put our trust in you or to cooperate with others. When we take ourselves too seriously, remind us that we are only human! Make us patient with our mistakes, even as we are willing to forgive others. And remind us that we are also precious, not because we are good but because you have accepted us and called us to be your very own. Amen.     (APH)

## NINETEENTH SUNDAY AFTER PENTECOST

Gracious God, we humbly confess our faults. For anger, impatience and quickness to misunderstand—forgive us. For thoughtlessness, indifferences, and self-centering—forgive us. For unkindness and the lack of kindness—forgive us. For not speaking out against injustice and suffering—forgive us. For all the times we have not followed Jesus in the way of love—forgive, heal, and transform us anew into your servant people. In the name of Christ Jesus we pray. Amen.                                            (MCT)

## TWENTIETH SUNDAY AFTER PENTECOST

Gracious God, we confess to you that we have not been your servant people. We have not been as loving, caring, sharing as we should. We have been weak in the cause of justice, slow to opportunities for kindness, quick to anger and hurting words. We have each put ourselves in the center of our world. We have turned away from our neighbor's need. We have not thanked you, nor been your ministers, nor prayed as we should. Accept the burden of our sinful selves, heal our pain, and set us free. In the name of Christ Jesus we pray. Amen.                                            (MCT)

## TWENTYFIRST SUNDAY AFTER PENTECOST (YEAR A, MATT. 22:1–14)

We thank you, God, for inviting us to live in covenant with you and one another, and for remaining faithful to your promise. Yet, like people of all ages, we find it difficult to be faithful to you. We despise those who remind us of your call. We grieve you by our rebellion against your word and our slowness to be your partners. We are not worthy, God, but, we pray, do not give up on us. May we share with you at your table of joy and welcome all your friends as our friends; through Jesus Christ, your word of love, we pray. Amen.                                            (RCD)

## TWENTYSECOND SUNDAY AFTER PENTECOST

Gracious God, we come before you to confess our sins. When we have acted out of fear, when we have acted out of anger, when we have acted out of selfishness, we have sinned. When our thoughts have been small-minded, when our thoughts have been unruly, when our thoughts have been bitter, we have sinned. When our words have been unfeeling, when our words have been thoughtless, when our words have been admirable but empty, we have sinned. When we have wasted your gifts and possibilities, when we have not lived out of love, we have sinned. But you are the source of love and life, and we ask your forgiveness and your re-forming of our very selves, for the sake of Jesus Christ, our Risen Savior. Amen.                                            (MCT)

## TWENTYTHIRD SUNDAY AFTER PENTECOST

Majestic and merciful God, we come to you a wayward people. We have forgotten your intentions for us; we have rejected the way of Christ; we have disregarded the power of your Spirit; and we have worshiped ourselves and the things we have made. Forgive us, restore us in the knowledge of whose we are, and make us alive to serve you with faith, hope, and love; through Jesus Christ we pray. Amen.                              (APH)

## TWENTYFOURTH SUNDAY AFTER PENTECOST (YEAR B, DEUT. 6:4; MARK 12:29–30)

Gracious God, we confess that we have not loved you with all our heart, our soul, our strength, our mind. We have not loved our neighbors with a deep and abiding compassion. And we have not loved ourselves and cared for our own truest needs. Transform our shallowness, enliven our deadness, heal our wounded, broken places, and so fill us with your spirit that we can be forgiven, even as we forgive ourselves and others. For we pray in the name of Jesus Christ who brings us love that has no end. Amen.                                                                     (MCT)

## TWENTYFIFTH SUNDAY AFTER PENTECOST

Glorious God of power and majesty, you bow down to hear our every sigh; deliver us from arrogance and empty vanities. Prevent us from trying to raise ourselves by lowering the position of others. Cast down our pride that we may grow in humility. Take away the barriers of self-defense; grant us the firm security that comes from trust in you and is built with neighborly cooperation and mutual respect. Lead us in the lowly steps of Jesus until we attain the end of a pure joy and eternal victory, through Christ, our servant and sovereign. Amen.                                             (APH)

## TWENTYSIXTH SUNDAY AFTER PENTECOST

### Call to Confession
God has told us that the heavenly realm is near. God calls to each of us to listen and act. Let us place ourselves before God and open our minds and our hearts to God's loving forgiveness.

### Prayer of Confession
God, who has promised eternal life to all, we come before you as humble people. You give us many opportunities to serve, but we turn away. Sometimes we think of ourselves before we think of others. We take paths that lead away from you not toward you. We need you, God! Be with us on our journey. Help us to grow closer to you and to reach out to those in need. Through God the Creator, Redeemer, and Sustainer, we pray. Amen.                                                                      (MM)

## TWENTYSEVENTH SUNDAY AFTER PENTECOST (YEAR A, MATT. 25:31–46)

*The first paragraph may be spoken by one person, or a number of readers may, in turn, speak each sentence.*

We admit to you, God, that we were not thinking of you. We saw a homeless person, and we laughed. We applauded when a prison door was locked. We heard of people dying of thirst, and we changed the channel. We did not protest when the poor were killed in our name. We bought good clothes, filled our refrigerators, but we forgot about you. We enjoyed our friends and ignored a newcomer. Then we came to church and said we love you best of all.

Forgive us, God, and stay near us always, that we may never forget you when people are hungry or homeless or sick or afraid. May we never again separate our love for you from our love for the world and its people. We live in hope that you will come and rule on earth.

Through Jesus, our Sovereign, we pray. Amen.                                   (RCD)

## CHILDREN'S SUNDAY

God, we are sorry for all the times that we have seen you and turned away. For the times that a child was hungry and we told jokes about it, we are sorry. For the time a child cried in church and we made the child feel unwelcome, we are sorry. For the time a child was abused and we pretended the abuse never happened, we are sorry. For the time a child needed us to listen and we didn't have time, we are sorry. For the children who hunger and thirst for righteousness while we turn our heads away from their cry, we are sorry. God, we know that you have given birth to all children and that you love everyone. Help our love and care to grow that strong. Amen.                  (SEG)

Or

Dear God, you made the whole universe and every one of us, but sometimes we forget you. We are sorry when we make mistakes: when we get mad at our brothers, sisters, and pets; when we get mad at our children, parents, and friends. We are sorry when we neglect people we should help and people whom we love. We are sorry when we forget to clean up after ourselves and when we do not take care of the earth. We are sorry when we fight even while we live in fear of wars. We know that you hear us and that you will help us to do our best for others and for you. Amen. (Children of First Church UCC, Cambridge, Massachusetts, with the help of their teachers)

## THANKSGIVING CELEBRATION

*Prayer of Confession*

God of remembrance, do not forget your mercy. Remind us of your desire for us to share the fullness of life with all your children. We forget those who deserve our gratitude. We take our friendships too much for granted. We too often do not remember the right gesture until it is too late. Make us thankful and generous with all that has been given us. Restore us to the joy of your salvation. Inspire us that we may rightly remember the past by building a legacy of hope for those who follow us, that they also may know the goodness of Jesus Christ our Savior. Amen.                    (APH)

*Assurance of Pardon*

There is no chasm that cannot be bridged, no loss that cannot be recovered, no mistake that cannot be forgiven, no life that cannot be redeemed—by the grace of God in Christ Jesus! All you who reject vain desires and put away unwarranted fears and who put your confidence in the mercies of God may assuredly know that you are forgiven and that the ability to begin again is yours. Glory be to the Holy One who can make all things new! Alleluia!                    (APH)

## ASSURANCE OF FORGIVENESS FOR
## THE PENTECOST SEASON

LEADER:   There is no greater joy in the heart of God than the moment when a son or daughter opens to the gift of forgiveness. God's Spirit reaches out to assure us of welcome in Christ.

PEOPLE:   In the name of Jesus Christ we are God's by grace. With great joy we are made alive. Thanks be to God. Amen.                    (DBB)

# UNISON PRAYERS FOR THE PENTECOST SEASON

## PENTECOST SUNDAY (ACTS 2)

Holy Spirit of God,
    pour upon us your gift of guidance.
We live in this day which specializes in confusion.
We live in this time where your Spirit sounds suspect to rational minds.
Confirm in us your courage for faith in this suspicious age.
We are your church! Guide us with your renewing Spirit!
Give us the heart to awaken to your wonders and the faith to welcome your signs of
hope around us.
In Christ's name, we pray. Amen.                                              (JCW)


## TRINITY SUNDAY

Holy Trinity, you are Sacred Three,
    Blessed One,
    Elusive God.
We pray to you:
    Creator, that we may give forth new life.
    Christ, that we may be rooted deeply in this life.
    Spirit, that we may soar beyond possibilities.
May your strange and comforting ways be our ways.
Amen.                                                                        (MEW)


## SECOND SUNDAY AFTER PENTECOST (YEAR B, 2 COR. 4:7)

Our God, sometimes we feel we are made of mere clay and we do not trust ourselves at
all. At other moments we feel that we're precious jewels—your gift to the world—and
we take ourselves too seriously.

Help us, God, to understand ourselves and one another. Remind us that if we are
priceless, it is because we have been named and formed by your love. As we busy
ourselves shaping our lives and our world, remind us that the business of creating and
sustaining is your work.

Yet we know there is much in this world that requires our care. Grant us the strength
to bear that burden and the capacity to trust and to laugh. In all our works, O God,
draw forth your ways of redeeming, where cross and tomb are but doors to new life. We
pray, as we would live, in the name of the One who opens every door for us, Jesus our
Christ. Amen.                                                                (MLP)

## THIRD SUNDAY AFTER PENTECOST

God of all life and grace, we thank you for the seasons of this earth, for the seasons of planting and sowing, for the seasons of harvest and reaping. So also you give us seasons of heart. Grant that in a drought of grace we may find your oasis of prayer. Grant that in a storm of grief we may find your shelter of Easter faith. Grant that in the seasons of our days we may find your rich soil for your seeds of hope. God of all life and grace—stay with us! Be our strength and hope in all times! In Christ's name, we pray. Amen.

(JCW)

## FOURTH SUNDAY AFTER PENTECOST (YEAR C, LUKE 7:36–50)

O God, we thank you that no sin is too great for your forgiveness. Grant us the humility, tears and kisses of the woman with the alabaster flask of ointment, that we may grow closer to you through simple acts of love. As she once anointed you, may you anoint and bless us. Amen.

(MEW)

## FIFTH SUNDAY AFTER PENTECOST (YEAR C, 1 KINGS 19:9–12)

Spirit of God, move among us and free us to love and serve you and all people. Refresh our spirits, that we may not be weary in seeking your ways. Whisper to us in a still small voice; show us what you have for us to do. Guide us to others with whom we may share the labors of peace and justice; through the grace of Jesus Christ. Amen.

(RCD)

## SIXTH SUNDAY AFTER PENTECOST (YEAR C, GAL. 5:1, 13–25)

Freeing God, it is you who calls us to freedom.
It is you who sets us free.
But this is not the freedom to judge others.
This is not the freedom to spoil our lives.
This is not the freedom to live as we see fit.
Your truth will set us free!
We live the freedom of Christ's way!
We lose our worldly life so to live in the freedom of love.
Free us from the captivity of our ways!
In Christ's name, we pray. Amen.

(JCW)

## SEVENTH SUNDAY AFTER PENTECOST (YEAR A, EXOD. 2:1–10)

O God, Strength of the faithful,
Encouragement to all who have defied the powerful to protect human lives, strengthen us now. Through your Spirit of power, may we find courage and resolve to protect

children from abuse and violence. Guide us as we seek to build a world where all children will be loved and nurtured, that they may grow to fulfil your purpose in their lives; through Jesus Christ, who welcomed the little ones. Amen.          (RCD)

## EIGHTH SUNDAY AFTER PENTECOST

God, we call you by so many names: Father, *Abba,* Mother, Loved One, Counselor, Goddess, Friend, Guide, Alpha and Omega. Yet every name reflects your relationship to us, your creation. Each name pushes us beyond imagination to think of you without thinking of ourselves. We cannot think of you without us, and for that we give you praise. As Ruth said to Naomi, let us say to you, O you upon whom we must depend, "Where you go, we will go; where you lodge, we will lodge, your people shall be our people." In your name, intimate and everloving God, we pray, Amen.          (MEW)

## NINTH SUNDAY AFTER PENTECOST (MATT. 13:33)

Bakerwoman God, your presence is the leaven which causes our hopes to rise. With your strong and gentle hands, shape our lives. Warm us with your love. Take our common lives and touch them with your grace, that we may nourish hope among humanity. We pray trusting in your name, through Jesus our Christ. Amen.          (RCD)

## TENTH SUNDAY AFTER PENTECOST (YEAR C, LUKE 11:5–13)

Faithful God, you care for our needs like a loving father or mother.
When we seek you, you make yourself known to us.
When we knock at heaven's door, you open your heart to us.
When we ask, you give us the gift of your Holy Spirit.
From your hand we receive our daily bread.
Receiving your forgiveness, we are enabled to forgive others.
Trusting in your great love, may we daily persist in prayer, and weekly assemble to worship you,
ready always to receive your gifts,
through the Spirit of Jesus Christ. Amen.          (RCD)

## ELEVENTH SUNDAY AFTER PENTECOST (YEAR B, PS. 34:11–22)

You call to us as children, compassionate Maker of all, and you urge us to seek peace and pursue it. Embolden us, we pray, that we might recognize your peace, even amid the confusion of our lives, and be delivered from our pain; through Jesus Christ we pray. Amen.          (MEW)

## TWELFTH SUNDAY AFTER PENTECOST (JOHN 7:53—8:11)

God of compassion and justice, you know best the accomplishments and sins of our lives. Stay our hands from throwing stones of condemnation, so that we might be cleansed from sin. With you, all things are possible, so we pray with faith and hope. Amen.

(MEW)

## THIRTEENTH SUNDAY AFTER PENTECOST (YEAR A, MATT. 15:21–28)

We thank you, gracious God, that you answer all who call upon your name from every nation. Make us bold to ask for your help and to persist beyond all discouragement. May our faith in you transform our troubled lives into testimonies to your love and power; through the grace of Jesus Christ. Amen.

(RCD)

## FOURTEENTH SUNDAY AFTER PENTECOST (YEAR B, PS. 67; 2 SAM. 23:4)

Spirit who dawns upon us like the morning light, be gracious unto us and bless us, we pray. May your touch enliven us as the rain makes the grass grow greenly, so that we might give forth your praise. It is through your blessing that we live, and in your name that we pray. Amen.

(MEW)

## FIFTEENTH SUNDAY AFTER PENTECOST (YEAR B, EPH. 6:10–20)

As we rise in the morning, Beloved One, may we don garments of your truth. May we wear the mantle of your protective blessing, and shoes that will guide us on your path. May our every breath be a prayer, so that we might truly and fully proclaim the mystery of the gospel. It is through you and with you that we design our day. Amen.

(MEW)

## SIXTEENTH SUNDAY AFTER PENTECOST (YEAR B, JAMES 1:17–27)

True Reflector, you are the mirror of our lives, for by facing you we see ourselves more clearly. May the sight of our true faces humble us and encourage us to be doers of your word, not merely hearers of it. It is only through you that our intentions and actions may be united; so we pray in your name. Amen.

(MEW)

## SEVENTEENTH SUNDAY AFTER PENTECOST (YEAR B, MARK 8:27–38)

O God, we often recognize you at one moment, as Peter recognized Jesus as Christ, and then we, too, turn away from you. It is not you who hides from us but we who hide from you. Help us to come to our senses and discover in you the way to true life; through Jesus the Christ, in whose name we pray. Amen.

(MEW)

## EIGHTEENTH SUNDAY AFTER PENTECOST (YEAR B, JAMES 3:13–18)

Spirit of Wisdom, in whose presence is peace, inspire us in this moment, that we may turn our minds from cleverness to kindliness; inhabit our hearts that we may embrace mercy; and inflame our spirits with the love of peace, so that wise in mind and heart and spirit, we may sow the seeds of peace and reap a harvest of justice. Amen. (MGMG)

## NINETEENTH SUNDAY AFTER PENTECOST (YEAR B, JOB 42:1–6)

O God of truth and understanding, generation after generation you have listened patiently while your people questioned your love. We too have doubted your love and judged you without knowing you. Awaken us to your presence that we may know through our own experience that you are faithful in caring for your creation; through the grace of Jesus Christ. Amen. (MGMG)

## TWENTIETH SUNDAY AFTER PENTECOST (YEAR B, MARK 10:2–16)

God of justice, we thank you for Jesus Christ, who calls men, women, and children into new ways of sharing life together. May we receive these new ways with joy, no longer seeking to possess or control any human being. May we commit ourselves to one another in a unity of mutual respect and care. May your life be seen in our relationships. For we pray in the name of Jesus Christ, who cherished all women, children, and men. Amen. (RCD)

OR

### (Year C, 2 Tim. 1:1–14)

God of our parents and our God, whose Spirit blows life from generation to generation, blow among us this day. Transform our trembling hearts with courage enough to bear one another's suffering. Strengthen our will with passion enough to witness to your goodness. And teach us to trust you enough that our children may also know your Spirit in them, until that great day when all generations have finished their charge and are at rest in you. Amen. (MGMG)

## TWENTYFIRST SUNDAY AFTER PENTECOST (YEAR B, PS. 90)

Holy God, Sustainer of life for time out of mind; we recall the many times of sorrow and struggle through which your presence has comforted us. We remember with hope that all our hurried days are held in your embrace, and we are refreshed by the gifts you share with us in the wonders of creation. Comfort, embrace, and refresh us this day, that your will may be done in us and in all the world. Amen. (MGMG)

## TWENTYSECOND SUNDAY AFTER PENTECOST (YEAR C, LUKE 18:1–8)

Blessed God, who calls us to be a blessing to the world, guide us in our search for justice. Save us, we pray, from the fear of powerful people. Inspire us to speak up for those who have been silenced by a loud voice. Grant us such persistence in prayer that we may perceive the reign of Christ, even as we await its coming. Amen.       (MGMG)

## TWENTYTHIRD SUNDAY AFTER PENTECOST (YEAR A, RUTH 2:1–13)

O God, constant and compassionate, you protect all those who trust in you. Each new day you call us to venture from our homes and families and follow you into difficult places among people we may consider strangers. Grant that we, like Ruth, may find your blessing in the wandering in our lives. And shelter us under your wings, that we may find our true home in you. Amen.       (MGMG)

## TWENTYFOURTH SUNDAY AFTER PENTECOST (YEAR B, MARK 12:28–34)

Loving God, you are all mystery, and yet each created moment tells us of your goodness. We are ill at ease in a world we cannot control, but you have given us the secret of love. Grant us so to love our neighbors and ourselves that we may find you whom we seek with heart and mind and soul and strength; through Jesus Christ our Savior, who lives and reigns with you and the Holy Spirit, one God, now and always. Amen.       (MGMG)

## TWENTYFIFTH SUNDAY AFTER PENTECOST (YEAR B, MARK 12:38–44)

Gracious God, who gives and gives and gives to us again, hear our plea for one more gift: a generous spirit, that we may find and use and return to you all that you have given of ordinary and extraordinary, for you are the source and gift of life itself. Amen.       (MGMG)

## TWENTYSIXTH SUNDAY AFTER PENTECOST (PROV. 31:10–13, 19–20, 25–31)

Holy God, blessed and wise, you teach us the wisdom of work and the blessing of generosity. Grant us who are called Christian, teachable spirits that we may remain loyal to you; courage that we may risk a new venture of love; and dignity that we may recognize your image in all people and so bring honor to the name of Christ, in whose name we pray. Amen.       (MGMG)

## TWENTYSEVENTH SUNDAY AFTER PENTECOST (YEAR A, MATT. 25:31–46)

Suffering God, present with all human beings: Help us to know you in the hungry, the
stranger, the ill, and the prisoner, that our souls may be fed with the fruits of justice,
our hearts made glad with healing and hospitality, and our feet set to dancing with the
freedom of your Spirit alive in Jesus Christ. Amen.                         (MGMG)


## THANKSGIVING EVE OR DAY

Infinite God, who fills the universe with your presence and dwells in every human heart:
As music fills this place, so may cadences of compassion and harmonies of hope accent
our lives. With grateful hearts and renewed minds, may we celebrate and realize your
peaceable realm. Amen.                         (TEJ)

# ADDITIONAL RESOURCES FOR PENTECOST

## OFFERING PRAYER/PRAYER OF DEDICATION FOR PENTECOST

O God, on this day of Pentecost we celebrate your Spirit so freely given and so powerfully active within your church. As that Spirit moves in our midst, may it inspire us towards generosity and fire us with an energy to serve you well. We ask this in the name of Christ whose promise of ever-presence the Spirit fulfills. Amen.

(GER)

## PRAYER OF CONFESSION FOR A SUNDAY EMPHASIZING PEACE AND JUSTICE

Spirit of the living God, we confess that we have not accepted the challenge of your peace in the world. We define peace in ways that preserve our own self-interests, forgetting that your peace may call us to great sacrifice. We are content to believe that speaking of peace is sufficient, forgetting that your peace calls us to action and transformation. Merciful God, forgive our lack of imagination and courage, and empower us to strive anew to make our world a place in which your loving peace abounds. In Jesus' name we pray.

(CJC)

## DISMISSAL FOR TRINITY SUNDAY

This is the faith which Christians proclaim:
The power of God which created the world is the
   power of love.
The power in Jesus which rescues the world is the
   power of love.
The power in us which changes the world is the
   power of love.
Therefore, I bid you go in the name of love.

(DLB)

## LITANY FOR PROPHETS

LEADER: Scripture tells us that God declares, "I will pour out my Spirit on all flesh."
PEOPLE: We wonder what this means for us today.
LEADER: "Your sons and your daughters shall prophesy."
PEOPLE: We wonder if there are prophets in this place today.
LEADER: "Your young shall see visions and your old shall dream dreams."
PEOPLE: We suspect those who have visions. It doesn't usually happen to us.
LEADER: "I will pour out my Spirit upon you and you shall all prophesy."
PEOPLE: We want to understand what this means for us. We want to know if we are prophets.

LEADER:     "And it shall be that whoever calls on the name of God shall be saved."
PEOPLE:     Save us, we pray, from denying your Spirit. Save us, we pray, from denying
            our response to your Spirit. Save us from denying your gift of prophecy.

                                                                                    (MEW)


## PRAYER FOR THE FEAST OF THE TRANSFIGURATION REMEMBERING HIROSHIMA AND NAGASAKI (AUGUST 6)

O God, we look with awe upon your creation: the beauty, the intricate connections of
life with life. But we observe with horror the human record of desecration and abuse.
You look with love upon our relationships, while we gaze with terror upon the ways we
have devised to destroy the human family.
Nothing short of transfiguration will bring us to strength, to responsibility, to zeal.
Fill us with your Spirit.
Open us to stirrings of compassion.
Uphold us by your protecting Word
that, like disciples, we might discover that your grace will return us to fidelity, trust,
justice, and radical love. Amen.                                                    (EEB)


## PRAYER FOR SEPTEMBER

O God, this is a month of changes. We can feel it in the cooler air, the drop in
humidity, the gray skies.
    Some of us found our way back to school this month, and we all want to learn. Let
us all grow in wisdom and maturity.
    Some of us are watching our harvest begin, while the gardens of others among us
produce less and less. Let all our hearts produce love and kindness.
    Many of us are leaving vacations behind, but God, you can keep our lives renewed by
filling us with your joy and your rest.
    Creative God, every year the world spins through its seasons and every year brings
new trouble. Steady and soothe your earth that its changes may be good changes and its
struggles end in peace.
    Loving God, who without change remains our steadfast friend, watch over the
changes in our lives. May we stretch and grow but always and ever remain yours, in
Christ. Amen.                                                                       (HAK)


## LITANY FOR AUTUMN

READER 1:   It is the time of the twilight of the seasons. The trees change clothes, then
            shed them. When we look down our streets and at our buildings, we see
            what had been hidden by curtains of green.

READER 2:   O God, we watch your seasons.

READER 1:   We sense the imminent death in nature as clouds increase. With a shudder of anticipation we wonder how severe winter's weather will be. And we wonder at the mysteries of nature as we will soon wonder at the mystery of the one who came and who comes that we might have life.

READER 2:   O God, we wait for your season.

READER 1:   The approaching Advent is the time when we reflect on Christ's meaning that we might act on his challenge. Just as we are never quite sure what a new season holds for us, we are not sure what is held in Christ's next coming into our lives.

READER 2:   We praise you, God.

READER 1:   Will it be nothing more than the gaudiness of commercialized holidays? Will it mean yet another rejection of the Word? Will it be renewed commitment with further death to self as summer dies to fall and fall to winter?

READER 1:   Will it be new creation in Christ or old creatures whitewashed with religious ritual and jargon? Death and rebirth or a lingering death?

READER 2:   O God, help us choose life. Amen.

(AKJ)

## SENTENCES OF CELEBRATION: REFORMATION SUNDAY

LEADER:   Throughout the human story
          the Spirit of God continues to speak,

READER:   in visions and voices,
          in images and ideas,

LEADER:   and in all languages and all times,
          to all people in all places,

READER:   inviting the people of God to discover new revelation.

LEADER:   To Abram it came as a sign in the stars and the sand that he had been chosen by God.

READER:   To Moses it came in the sense that earth was ablaze with God's glory.

LEADER:   To Rahab it came as an unexplainable feeling that her enemies should be befriended.

READER:   To Esther it came as courage to speak, to act, to imagine, to risk.

LEADER:   To Mary it was dramatic, angelic, unbelievable—an overpowering realization that neither her life nor the world—would ever be the same.

READER:   To the disciples and a blind man, and a bleeding woman

LEADER:   and a boy in seizures, and a woman caught in guilt

READER:   and a dying thief

LEADER:   and a Roman soldier

READER:   and to thousands of others

LEADER:   It was the personal touch, the eyewitness experience

of the teacher-healer-storyteller-lover,
the human being they called Jesus of Nazareth.

READER: To three women at the empty tomb
it was a gift in return for their faith,
an ecstasy no one else remained to enjoy,
a story no one else had faith, at first,
to recount or believe.

LEADER: And the words and the life and the power of this Jesus
have tunneled through tomb
and have flown through time and culture
and continue to live for us today.

READER: The Spirit continues to speak

LEADER: in visions and voices,

READER: in images and ideas,

LEADER: in all languages and times

READER: to all people in all places.

LEADER: To people like Irenaeus, Paula, Aquinas, and Theresa,

READER: through prophets and popes and priests and peasants,

LEADER: and through women whose names are forgotten
but whose faith will endure
etched in the hearts of those they have taught and nurtured,
resounding in the songs they have sung and passed on,
incarnate in ideas and questions they shared and inspired.

READER: The Spirit has spoken through people of many faiths
from the Buddha to Gandhi
whose lives and teachings seem to echo those of Christ.

LEADER: To Luther and Calvin and Wesley
and Mary Dyer, Susan B. Anthony and Rosa Parks,
Spirit came as a reformer's fire, blazing in the heart.

READER: And still the Spirit comes to us today

LEADER: in new voices and new visions

READER: and in new understandings of the voices and visions
passed on to us from yesterday.

LEADER: It may burn in our hearts like fire
or whisper in the silence as a still, small voice.
It may sing to us from the stars or sneak up on us from within,
or embrace us in the touch of another child of God.

READER: But we are here today,
because the Spirit speaks to us
and we respond!                            (JWH)

# Alternative
# Lectionary Readings

## WOMEN AND FEMININE IMAGES REDISCOVERED

The Roman Lectionary of 1969 has been adapted, published, and followed by a number of Protestant denominations. (In this article I use the term "the lectionary" to refer to the Roman lectionary and its several ecumenical adaptations.) Increased use of the lectionary has meant that many congregations have used a broader range of biblical texts in worship and preaching than they otherwise would have. The lectionary and resources based upon it have contributed to making scripture more central in the worship of many Christian congregations, and this is good.

However, a revised selection of lectionary texts is needed if the liberation, not the oppression, of women is to be supported. Women of faith must be remembered for their contributions to communities of faith and their sufferings caused by patriarchal injustice. Feminine images of God must be recovered from scripture and placed alongside the masculine imagery which has become predominant in Christian tradition. Passages that enjoin the submission of women and others, while remaining a part of the biblical record, cannot be uncritically proclaimed and should not be among the relatively few passages chosen for lectionaries. Thus, while the use of the lectionary may be beneficial in some ways, critique and revision of present lectionaries are necessary if the humanity of women and men is to be fully honored. (For a discussion of these concerns, refer to Elisabeth Schüssler Fiorenza, *Bread Not Stone* [Boston: Beacon Press, 1984], especially chapter 2, 23–42.)

More than the *selection* of texts is at issue. Feminist *interpretation* of passages is also necessary in order to do justice to women in worship. Such works as *Feminist Interpretation of the Bible* (ed. Letty Russell [Philadelphia: Westminister Press, 1985]) articulate feminist principles for interpretation of scripture and provide interpretations of particular passages. The bibliography of Russell's book lists important and worthwhile books on feminist interpretation of scripture, and includes the names of feminist scripture scholars, many of whom have published additional articles and books since Russell's book was published.

In the pages that follow is a list of passages for use in preaching and worship. The list includes passages which tell the stories of women of faith, as well as passages which suggest feminine imagery for God. Most of those listed are missing from some or all lectionaries based on the Roman lectionary; some of them are appointed for feast days which are not ordinarily celebrated in Protestant churches. The lectionary index used was the one for the *Common Lectionary* proposed by the Consultation on Common Texts for study from 1983–1986 (New York: Church Hymnal Corp., 1983). The *Common Lectionary* is based on the Roman lectionary.

The *Common Lectionary* is continually being revised by the Consultation on Common Texts. Revisions which would include more stories of women of faith and more feminine images of God are now being considered by the consultation to replace some of the texts in the *Common Lectionary.*

For now, the list I present here will enable worship leaders to identify stories of women and images of God that are missing from the lectionary and to substitute them for lectionary readings at appropriate times during the church year. Churches which have been using a three-year lectionary cycle will be able to use an even broader selection of scripture than they do now by substituting these readings some years and using the appointed readings other years. I have suggested specific times during the church year when the passages can be substituted. The list begins with Advent and continues through the church year in order, combining readings from all three cycles by season. I offer comments on the suggested readings which on the whole relate to the interplay of the alternative reading with the other texts for the day or with the season.

This list will also enable worship leaders to identify some of the passages in the lectionary which approve the oppression and submission of women. I suggest that these passages not be used at all. Another course would be to use these passages in worship, but to apply a critical hermeneutic.

Marjorie Procter-Smith has studied the *Common Lectionary* to determine whether and how women are included. She has identified important passages about women which have not been included in the lectionary. Her research and suggestions for change are presented in an article, "Images of Women in the Lectionary" in *Women: Invisible in Theology and the Church* (ed. Elisabeth Schüssler Fiorenza and Mary Collins [Edinburgh: T. & T. Clark, 1985]), which was my main resource for identifying passages relating to women which are not in the lectionary. Phyllis Trible's books, *God and the Rhetoric of Sexuality* (Philadelphia: Fortress Press, 1978) and *Texts of Terror* (Philadelphia: Fortress Press, 1984), were also helpful in determining which passages to suggest.

# ALTERNATIVE READINGS

1. SUBJECT:   Hannah
   SCRIPTURE:   1 Sam. 2:1–10
   WHEN:   Second Sunday in Advent, Year B
   COMMENTS:   In the lectionary, this passage is used only for the Visitation, which is celebrated by Roman Catholics but not by most Protestants. It is placed here rather than with Luke 1:39–55 (the Gospel for the fourth Sunday in Advent, Year C), where it could be used if these two similar texts were the sermon texts, or if one was read and the other sung.

2. SUBJECT:   God intervening in history compared to a woman in labor
   SCRIPTURE:   Isa. 42:14–17
   WHEN:   Third Sunday in Advent, Year C
   COMMENT:   The Gospel (Luke 3:7–18) also speaks of the radical changes brought by God's coming action.

3. SUBJECT:   Hannah
   SCRIPTURE:   1 Sam. 1:3–20
   WHEN:   Second Sunday after Epiphany, Year B
   COMMENT:   Move 1 Sam. 3:1–10 to the third Sunday after Epiphany, Year B, when 1 Sam. 1:3–20 is substituted on the second Sunday.

4. SUBJECT:   Moses implies that God conceived and gave birth to Israel
   SCRIPTURE:   Num. 11:10–25
   WHEN:   Third Sunday after Epiphany, Year C
   COMMENT:   God's providing leaders to "share the Spirit" with Moses complements the epistle reading (1 Cor. 12:12–30) and suggests a model of shared leadership.

5. SUBJECT:   Jephtha's daughter
   SCRIPTURE:   Judg. 11:29–40
   WHEN:   Seventh Sunday after Epiphany, Year A
   COMMENT:   Note the contrast with Matt. 5:33–37 ("Do not swear").

6. SUBJECT:   Male and female created in God's image
   SCRIPTURE:   Gen. 1:26–31
   WHEN:   First Sunday in Lent, Year A
   COMMENT:   This is only in the lectionary during the Easter vigil.

7. SUBJECT:   Jesus as mother hen
   SCRIPTURE:   Luke 13:34–35

WHEN:          Add to Palm Sunday reading, Year C

COMMENT:    The reading listed is Luke 19:28–40. Luke 13:31–35, a related passage, is used in some, but not all, versions of the lectionary on the second Sunday in Lent, Year C.

8.  SUBJECT:     Huldah

    SCRIPTURE:  2 Chron. 34:22–33

    WHEN:          Fourth Sunday in Lent, Year A

    COMMENT:    This passage is appropriately part of the "salvation history cycle," which is the theme of Lenten readings from Hebrew scripture; it has a penitential theme appropriate to Lent.

9.  SUBJECT:     Deborah

    SCRIPTURE:  Judg. 4:4–9

    WHEN:          Fourth Sunday in Lent, Year B

    COMMENT:    The use of this reading here was suggested in *An Inclusive Language Lectionary,* Year B.

10.  SUBJECT:     The anointing of Jesus

     SCRIPTURE:  Mark 14:3–9 (or Matt. 26:6–13)

     WHEN:          Fifth Sunday in Lent, Year C

     COMMENTS:   This passage appears only when the Sunday before Easter is celebrated as Passion Sunday and the longer reading is used. The woman anoints Jesus over the head, a prophetic act pointing to Jesus as Messiah (refer to Elisabeth Schüssler Fiorenza, *In Memory of Her* [New York: Crossroad, 1983], xiii–xiv). The reading appointed for this day (John 12:1–8) does not have the same nuance.

11.  SUBJECT:     Women at the cross

     SCRIPTURE:  Mark 15:1–47

     WHEN:          Good Friday

     COMMENT:    The lectionary uses the passion narrative in John every year as the Gospel for Good Friday. While the passion narrative in John also tells of women at the cross, it would be good to read the Markan passion narrative occasionally.

12.  SUBJECT:     Tabitha

     SCRIPTURE:  Acts 9:36–43

     WHEN:          Anywhere in Eastertide

     COMMENT:    Since Tabitha was raised from the dead in the post-Easter community, her story may be well told in Eastertide.

13.  SUBJECT:     Lydia

     SCRIPTURE:  Acts 16:11–15

WHEN:           Sixth Sunday in Eastertide, Year C

COMMENT:     Another possibility would be to present all of Acts 16:11–40 as a
dramatic reading on the seventh Sunday in Eastertide, Year C.

14.  SUBJECT:      Parable of the leaven
     SCRIPTURE:   Matt. 13:33 or Luke 13:20–21
     WHEN:          Add to the reading for the ninth Sunday after Pentecost, Year A
                    (thus using Matt. 13:24–34, 36–43); or add to the fourteenth Sunday
                    after Pentecost, Year C (thus using Luke 13:20–30).
     COMMENT:     A collect for this reading is provided on page 120.

15.  SUBJECT:      Jesus prevents abuse of woman caught in adultery
     SCRIPTURE:   John 7:53—8:11
     WHEN:          Fourteenth Sunday after Pentecost, Year B
     COMMENTS:    This could replace one of the readings of John 6 in Year B. Refer to
Susan Thistlethwaite's article in the *Feminist Interpretation of the Bible.* A collect for
this reading is provided on page 121.

16.  SUBJECT:      Miriam as leader at the Red Sea
     SCRIPTURE:   Exod. 15:19–21
     WHEN:          Twelfth Sunday after Pentecost, Year A
     COMMENT:     Like the appointed reading about the Red Sea crossing, this
complements the appointed Gospel reading about Jesus walking on water (Matt.
14:22–33).

17.  SUBJECT:      Priscilla
     SCRIPTURE:   Acts 18:1–4, 18–28
     WHEN:          Fourteenth Sunday after Pentecost, Year B
     COMMENTS:    In this way, Eph. 5:21–33, which often is interpreted to enjoin the
subservience of women, is replaced. This passage from Acts could be used with Luke
8:1–3 (also omitted from the lectionary) during Year C, Sundays after Pentecost.

18.  SUBJECT:      Christian social ethics
     SCRIPTURE:   Rom. 13:8–10 (drop 1–7)
     WHEN:          Sixteenth Sunday after Pentecost, Year A
     COMMENT:     Scriptures which urge submission of the powerless to the powerful
are not appropriate selections for the church's public scripture readings (refer to
Procter-Smith, p. 60).

19.  SUBJECT:      Trusting God is compared to being "like a child at its mother's
                    breast"
     SCRIPTURE:   Ps. 131

WHEN:                Eighteenth Sunday after Pentecost, Year B

COMMENTS:   This reading interplays with Mark 9:30–37 and the idea of receiving Christ like a child. The assigned psalm (27:1–6) is used elsewhere.


20.   SUBJECT:        Rock, tower, the shelter of wings as images for God

SCRIPTURE:   Ps. 61:1–5

WHEN:                Twentieth Sunday after Pentecost, Year B and/or Twentythird Sunday after Pentecost, Year A

COMMENTS:   Ps. 128 presents a narrow conception of women as "fruitful vines"; Ps. 61:1–5, with strong and varied images of God, is not in the lectionary.


21.   SUBJECT:        Esther

SCRIPTURE:   Est. 4:8–17

WHEN:                Twentysixth Sunday after Pentecost, Year C

COMMENT:    Bearing witness before rulers is one subject of the Gospel for the day (Luke 21:5–19).

## FOR FURTHER CONSIDERATION

Some other passages concerning women which are not in the lectionary include:

1. Judg. 4:17–22. Jael;

2. Luke 11:27–28. Jesus refuses to define women in terms of their procreative capacities;

3. Prov. 31. Is this a strong or stereotyped picture of a woman? A collect for this reading is provided on page 123;

4. Rom. 16:1–2. Phoebe;

5. Gen. 16. The story of Hagar—a story to mourn, and to tell from Hagar's perspective;

6. Luke 24:1–11, in which the women's testimony to the resurrection is called "an idle tale," is used only in the Easter Vigil, Year C.

Other passages with feminine images of God which are not in the lectionary include:

1. God as a compassionate mother (Jer. 31:15–22; Isa. 66:7–14);

2. *El Shaddai,* sometimes interpreted as "God of the breasts" (Gen. 49:25);

3. God as the one who gave birth to Israel and as a (mother?) eagle (Deut. 32:10–18).

Refer to Phyllis Trible's article, "God, Nature of, in the OT," in the *Interpreter's Dictionary of the Bible, Supplementary Volume* (Nashville: Abingdon Press, 1964, 386–89), and her book *God and the Rhetoric of Sexuality* for examples of feminist exegesis of these and related passages.

The parable of the lost coin is in the lectionary together with the parable of the lost sheep (Luke 15:8–10, seventeenth Sunday after Pentecost, Year C). The story of the prophet Anna (Luke 2:36–38) is also in the lectionary (first Sunday after Christmas, Year B). The challenge worship leaders face in such cases is to call attention to the feminine images or stories about women in spite of the fact that scriptures provide more narrative detail about the male characters.

I hope, first, that these few pages will help worship leaders to reflect on the ways God, women, and men are portrayed in worship services, and, second, that worship planners will avail themselves of the work of feminist biblical scholars. The work of these scholars challenges and enables Christians to worship God in ways that are more just and life-affirming.

(RCD)

# SACRAMENTS AND RITES
# OF THE CHURCH

# *Resources for Baptism*

## A PROLOGUE TO BAPTISM

LEADER: We are a people of the water!

PEOPLE: We worship a God whose love flows through water.

LEADER: Love, like a rain shower,
awakens the sleeping seed within the soul
and lures it to blossom.

PEOPLE: We worship a God whose love flows through water.

LEADER: Love, like a wading pool, inspires the delight of children, jumping, splashing,
spraying each other, shivering with wet joy.

PEOPLE: We worship a God whose love flows through water.

LEADER: Love, like a hot shower after a long day's work, cleanses us, reawakens us.

PEOPLE: We worship a God whose love flows through water.

LEADER: Love, like little drops, drips from fingertips to forehead.
Through baptism, the family of faith makes room for one more. (JWH)

## CALL TO WORSHIP

In worship, we who are called "Christian" gather to express our unity with God and with each other. We are a community which spans the centuries, bound together by a covenant whose signature is baptism. We have inherited this covenant of baptism from those in ages past who bequeathed to us their faith and their faithfulness. In our worship today we renew our commitment to live in this covenant and we draw together a wider community of believers, including those who bore witness at our baptism. As faithful women and men have done for years, let us worship God.          (MGMG)

# PRAYERS FOR BAPTISM

## ACCOMPANYING THE PRESENTATION OF A ROSE

1. Eternal Spirit, send your grace and peace to _____ (name) _____ and to her/his family. As you have ignited the spark of life within her/him, so let us help to kindle that spark into a dancing flame, that _____ (name) _____'s young life may grow in a knowledge and love of Jesus Christ. Guide and protect her/him throughout her/his life. Through this little one, may we learn of your gentleness and love. Amen. (JFDM)

2. Spirit of the living God, once again you have taken the substance of earth in your gentle hands, fashioned it in your likeness, and given it the breath of life. We give you thanks for the life of _____ (name) _____, whom you now entrust to the world's care. Send your blessing and your peace upon this family, that their love for one another and for you may grow. Help us to see your image in this little one, that we may also learn from him/her what life is about. In Jesus' name. Amen. (JFDM)

3. Dear God of gentleness and love, once more you have spoken words of hope in the birth of a child. We delight in this new gift of life. Let your blessing and strength rest upon _____ (name) _____ and _____ (name) _____'s family. May they cherish _____ (name) _____'s life and lead her/him in the ways of faith. In the name of your Chosen One we pray. Amen. (JFDM)

4. Gentle Savior, Giver and Keeper of all life, we offer to you now our thankful praise for the birth and the life of young _____ (name) _____. Let your peaceful assurance rest upon his/her family; gently remind them of your strong presence and sure guidance. Help this church and community to be a good and Christlike influence in his/her life so that he/she may come to know you personally and trust you completely. In Jesus' name we pray. Amen. (JFDM)

5. Gracious God, if one baby is a miracle of love, how much more so is the birth of twins! Hold _____ (name) _____ and _____ (name) _____ in the gentleness of your hands, and their family in the bonds of patient love. May these two little ones grow in the ways of faith and grow to be the best of friends, aware of your tender care and your righteous calling in their lives. In the name of Jesus Christ we pray. Amen. (JFDM)

# Resources for Communion Services

## INVOCATION

God of spirit and flesh,
God of heaven and earth,
God of grape and grain,
we spread our wings in flight toward you.
We stretch our arms in need of you.
We feed ourselves with gifts from you.
We thank you for your love poured out
as we sense your Spirit shining in the sunlight,
sailing on the summer wind,
and singing in the souls of each one gathered here.
Recreate us in your image
as we encounter you today,
that our lives might ignite
a love to light the world,
where despair drips dreary on drowning dreams,
and where heavy hearts shiver in lonely cold.
Let your presence pressing through us
infuse the world with joy
we pray, Amen.

(JWH)

## ASSURANCE OF PARDON

The feast of God is designed to satisfy not our physical appetites but our hunger and thirst for righteousness. The table has long been set and there has always been a place reserved for you. Jesus Christ beckons you, "Come." Beloved, your sins are forgiven. In witness to your new life in Christ and communion with one another, you are asked to gather round the heavenly table. Amen.                    (JTF)

## OFFERING PRAYER FOR A COMMUNION SUNDAY

Loving God, our hunger is never better satisfied than at your table. Our gifts can have no higher value than when they are offered to you. Because you fill our spirits, we hunger to serve. And we pray that these gifts may be as food to nourish the living body of Christ. Amen.

(GER)

# CALLS TO COMMUNION

## (Hos. 11:4; Pss. 131:2; 103:12)

LEADER: Let us give thanks!

PEOPLE: Our God has bent down and fed us!

LEADER: Like a mother, God has held us;

PEOPLE: Our God has calmed and quieted our fear!

LEADER: Like a father God has forgiven us,

PEOPLE: And removed our sins from us!

CELEBRANT: Bless God's holy name!

PEOPLE: And forget not all God's benefits!

ALL: We thank you for the promise of this meal: presence to break the bonds of isolation, power to overcome our powerlessness. We thank you for the promise of this day: new life for tired spirits, victory for the faithful. Help us to reach out to each other in community and be agents of renewal. May your resurrection happen in and through us. Amen.　　　　(JTF)

OR

LEADER: We dare not come to this table trusting in our own goodness or virtue.

PEOPLE: We come knowing we need forgiveness and trusting God to grant it.

LEADER: We come because we are hungry for meaning and need to be fed.

PEOPLE: God, forgive and feed us.

LEADER: We come because Jesus Christ invited us.

PEOPLE: We come as Christ's guests to the heavenly banquet.

LEADER: We come in remembrance, but much more; in recalling the sacrifice of Christ for us we are moved to Christ-like identification with suffering humanity.

PEOPLE: We join here not in passive recollection of ancient signs, but in active reflection of the flesh and blood realities which these signs represent.

ALL: Jesus, stand among us today as host and celebrant!　　　　(JTF)

# AN ORDER FOR COMMUNION

PASTOR:   God in Christ breaks down the walls
that make us strangers to ourselves
and divide us from one another.
We are the body of Christ.
Around this table, we enact our faith.
The body broken is restored to wholeness;
lifeblood poured out brings healing to our world.

SILENCE

PASSING THE PEACE

PASTOR:   At this table we receive God's peace made flesh. What we receive, we now share.

*The people may share God's peace with each other in their own words and gestures.*

## THE EUCHARISTIC PRAYER

PASTOR:   We dream, O God, of community,
but in waking hours we forget such hopes.
Our dreams we call "alien";
our sister and brother we call "stranger."

PEOPLE:   You call us by name.
With arms outstretched as on a cross,
you call us to yourself,
and you name us your own people.

PASTOR:   So with arms outstretched, we now embrace
new friends and forgotten dreams.
The body broken and lifeblood poured
transform our fears, revive our visions.

PEOPLE:   Renew us, O God, with your Spirit,
that we may receive this mystery of our body,
embracing its manifold gifts and needs,
shouting an "Amen!" that resounds through our world.

THE WORDS OF INSTITUTION

*Drawing on one of the scriptural accounts, the pastor recalls Jesus' words and actions at the Last Supper with her or his own words and actions.*

SHARING THE BREAD AND WINE

*The worshipers may sing songs of hope and joy while receiving the loaf and cup.*

Prayer after communion

PASTOR:   All praise is yours, O God. You bring us to this table as sisters and brothers. Lead us now, through each of our moments, to that glorious day when all your children will gather as family. We pray in the name of Jesus Christ,

PEOPLE:   Who is our peace made flesh. Amen!                                    (MLP)

# RESPONSIVE EUCHARISTIC PRAYER

LEADER 1:  O Holy One who created the stars, you have formed us from your womb and have given us life and creativity. You have made us rich in color and speech, and your wisdom has guided us through every age and time.

PEOPLE:  We ask now the presence of your Spirit. We have come from many places and have many ways of expressing our beliefs. Around this table, we are one and we call ourselves your people.

LEADER 2:  We remember those who have gone before us, honoring your earth and your people. We celebrate Ruth and Naomi, who in befriending one another became partners of your promise. We celebrate Sarah, who with great faith, bore the promise of the nations. We give you thanks for Esther and Rebecca, for Miriam and Phoebe, for Leah and Rachel. We thank you for Mary, who risked her life in bearing a child.

PEOPLE:  We thank you that you have surrounded us with so gentle and powerful a host of witnesses. We thank you for models and memories of women in our own lives who have shown us faith and promise.

LEADER 3:  We thank you, God, for the liberation that Christ brought to all people and for giving us new life by dying and rising that life might be more precious to us than death.

PEOPLE:  Thank you for the wholeness that you have given to us in the flesh and blood of Jesus the Christ. Give us courage to live in ways that give life and celebrate living!

ALL:  Through the grace that we have known in Christ and in the lives of those who have gone before us, we pray. Amen.                    (SEG)

## PRAYERS OF THANKSGIVING AFTER COMMUNION

1. For the healing you have given us in the brokenness of bread and the pouring out of cup, we thank you. For the community that you have restored in us through the sharing of life, we thank you. For the courage and strength that you have promised to us, even as we have honored the ones of courage in our own past, we thank you. Send us forth from this place in love, letting justice be worked out with gentleness and power known in the presence of your Spirit. Amen. (SEG)

2. Since, dear God, in this place, at this table, we have touched, we have tasted, and we have heard the signs of your love for us, grant that we may go away from this house filled with our love for you and overflowing with your love for those who are around us and who share our lives. We pray in the name of Jesus Christ our Savior. Amen. (DLB)

# COMMISSIONS

1. For the bread that we have eaten,
   for the cup of blessing we have tasted,
   for the purifying waters of baptism,
   for the life that you have given:
   Creator, Son, and Holy Spirit,
   we will praise you as long as we have breath. Amen.                    (JTF)

2. May we be as living loaves, kneaded and shaped by the hands of God. May we be as wine of the Spirit, poured out that others might know joy. Love be the leaven within. Love be the flavor of thought and word and deed. Peace be among us. Amen.                    (GER)

3. In ways known and unknown our Sovereign God has spoken to each of us this day. We are transformed. In the image of the Christ we shall be peacemakers in our homes, our schools, our jobs, our government, and even the world community. May the spirit of love we feel this day empower us to enhance and enrich the beauty of life lived in faith. Amen.                    (JHH)

# SHORT COMMUNION LITURGY FOR USE AT TABLE
# AT A DENOMINATIONAL GATHERING

## (based on Luke 22:14–20)

LEADER:   Let us worship God.

CLERGY:   "When the hour came, Jesus took his place at the table with the apostles."

LAITY:    We come as apostles following the Savior, in our gathering and in our communion, to rejoice in our Christian faith.

CLERGY:   "Jesus said to them, 'I have wanted so much to eat this passover meal with you before I suffer.' "

LAITY:    We do not know the suffering of other persons or churches, but we come in unity. May this meal be a symbol of the bond we feel for each other in our _____(name denominational body)_____ and world.

CLERGY:   "For I tell you, I will never eat it until it is given its full meaning in the kingdom of God."

LAITY:    We do not know what meal will be our last, but each meal sustains us, reminds us of how dependent we are on God for breath and health and life itself.

CLERGY:   "Then Jesus took a piece of bread."

LAITY:    Let us lift the common bread.

*Each clergyperson takes a roll or bread.*

God of life, we ask you to bless this bread, that it may nourish us and encourage us in following your truth. May it sustain body and soul. Amen.

CLERGY:   "Then Jesus broke the bread . . ."

*Clergy break the rolls or bread.*

LAITY:    This bread reminds us of Christ's body, which was broken on a cross, and our brokenness and sin in Christ's body, the church.

CLERGY:   "Then Jesus gave it to them, saying, 'This is my body, which is given for you. Do this in memory of me.' "

*All share in eating the bread.*

LEADER:   Let us continue.

CLERGY:   "This cup is God's new covenant sealed with the Savior's blood, which is poured out for us all."

*Clergy at each table lift the cup or pass the tray.*

*All drink of the cup.*

LEADER:   Let us pray together.

ALL:      We thank you, God, for refreshing us with this holy feast. Bless now this food and this time together. As you have guided us in the past, so lead us in the days ahead. Adjourn us now, our God, we pray, spiritually renewed, reminded that we are one family, who carry with us your justice and your peace. Amen.

*The meal is now served.*                                                    (RLA)

# A Service of Rededication and Renewal

*This order may be incorporated into a Service of Word and Sacrament following the sermon or it may be used alone.*

INTRODUCTION: Come to the living stone rejected as worthless by humanity but chosen as valuable by God. Come as living stones and let yourselves be used in building the spiritual temple, where you will serve as holy priests.

You are a chosen people, the royal priests, the holy nation, God's own people, chosen to proclaim the wonderful acts of God, who called you from darkness into marvelous light (1 Pet. 2:4, 5, 9 TEV, adapted).

HYMN OF CONSECRATION

SCRIPTURE: Isa. 6:1–8; Eph. 4:11–13; or Matt. 6:36–38

## Litany of Response to God

LEADER:    To be a disciple of Jesus means making a decision to follow Jesus. It means giving up everything—turning away from the temptation to create false gods such as money, comfort, or ambition. Jesus reminds us that possessions do not make our lives secure. Security is not a matter of individual self-sufficiency. The quality of our relationship with God is all important. We are rich in serving God, not that which we own.

PEOPLE:    Jesus said, "Sell all that you have and give it to the poor."

LEADER:    Our love for God finds expression in our relationships with others. We must be prepared to hear God's call and, in obedience, to find joy in meeting the needs of our neighbor. What have you and I done for the hungry, the lonely, the homeless? The quality of our love for others expresses our love for God.

PEOPLE:    Jesus said, "Sell all that you have and give it to the poor."

LEADER:    In the path begun by confessing Jesus as Christ and Savior, we journey from death to life as healed, forgiven children of God. We are called to spend our lives in the service of Christ, who came to serve us all, and who gave his life as a ransom for many.

PEOPLE:   Jesus said, "Follow me."

*Prayer of Commitment*

LEADER:   Let us pray. In a world of violence between persons, clans, and nations; of violence upon the self; where families are fractured through broken relationships, where unemployment causes frustration and suffering, where those who differ from ourselves become scapegoats for our pain and fears, and where hatred and war are common to the news . . . In such a world, God, what do you want us to do?

PEOPLE:   We wait upon you, O God. Guide us.

LEADER:   We remember Abraham, a person to whom you made yourself known. Like him, we are willing to go out, not knowing where you will lead. Yet we trust that you will go before us to guide us.

PEOPLE:   Help us, God, to hear your call above the many conflicting claims of today. Then encourage us, God, to accept your call to go and to do what you want us to do.

LEADER:   We remember Deborah who served as a prophet and a judge over the Israelites.

PEOPLE:   By the power of your Holy Spirit, give us wisdom to respond to your call and, like Deborah, to help others discover how you are calling them.

LEADER:   We remember Paul who sought through his ministry to strengthen the body of Christ so that all its members could work together more effectively.

PEOPLE:   So we of this body seek to witness and work wherever you have placed us, in love for the world.

LEADER:   We remember the woman at the well, who, though unacceptable to some among whom she lived, was called to ministry.

PEOPLE:   God, open our hearts that we may discern in others—and ourselves—the great worth and calling you bestow upon all people, that we may not ignore the world and its needs. Through Jesus Christ we pray. Amen.

*Remembrance and Recognition*

*An opportunity shall be given for persons renewing their faith to share a portion of their faith journey, citing a specific gift they wish to dedicate to God's service. Then each person shall place a special remembrance or symbol of that gift on the altar, silently dedicating it to God's use.*

HYMN OF THE HOLY SPIRIT

*Invitation*

*The leader shall invite those who wish to renew their faith to come forward.*

*Renewal of Baptismal Vows*

*Those renewing their faith shall stand before the leader of the service as they are able.*

LEADER: Do you promise to seek God's direction for your life, to serve God in responsible freedom as a member of this church, in ministry to all people? Will you seek to meet the needs of a broken world and to walk humbly with God all the days of your life?

INDIVIDUALS: I do, asking God's guidance.

LEADER: Do you confess your faith in Jesus Christ as your Savior?

INDIVIDUALS: I confess my faith.

*Persons renewing their faith may kneel as they are able, and the leader, laying her or his hands on the head of each, shall say:*

Dear God, strengthen _____(name)_____ , your servant, that he/she may continue to grow in relationship with you, with others, and in service to the world you have created.

*After all those wishing to renew their faith have done so, the leader shall say to the congregation the following words:*

Do you who witness this act of renewal and rededication promise your love and support to these persons as they live and grow in Christ?

PEOPLE: I do.

*Commission*

*The leader may give the following commission, or another suitable for the occasion, to persons renewing their faith.*

Go forth into the world in peace; be of good courage; hold fast to that which is good; render no one evil for evil; strengthen the fainthearted; support the weak; help the afflicted; honor all people; love and serve God, rejoicing in the power of the Holy Spirit.

*Those renewing their faith shall then take their places in the congregation. The service shall conclude with the sacrament of Holy Communion.*
(HWB)

# Service of Thanksgiving
# for Christian Dying
# into Life

A Christian experiences many little "deaths" and "resurrections" in the journey that begins with baptism and continues throughout life. This rite is designed to give God thanks for such experiences of dying and rising with Christ, experiences of dying into life.

The rite may be used by anyone who has been through an experience of loss, has been resurrected into new life by God's grace, and now wishes to give thanks. Loss experience takes many forms, and includes such things as becoming disabled, surviving sexual assault, becoming widowed or divorced, being released from imprisonment, and losing a home by fire.

The ritual should be preceded by several sessions of reflection with a pastor or with a small group within the church which would include family members and others involved directly in the loss experience. In this context the Christian would identify why she/he feels the loss is a resurrection experience, how God has brought her or him into a new relationship with the Christian community, and how this new relationship will find expression in ministry. This will also prepare the Christian to write a statement for use in the ritual.

This service provides the opportunity for reception back into the Christian community that both welcomes those who became less active in the community in their time of loss and recognizes that even those who remained active now participate as new persons. It may take place in a home, a hospital room, or in public worship on Sunday as part of the celebration of Christ's resurrection, following the sermon and before the celebration of communion.

Directions for standing, sitting, or kneeling have been omitted from this rite. Those planning the rite will need to be especially sensitive to limitations, physical or otherwise, of those who will participate, and should give helpful directions accordingly. Scripture references are adapted from the Revised Standard Version of the Bible unless otherwise noted.

## ORDER OF THE RITE

1. Invitation
2. Greeting
3. Introduction
4. Reading of Scripture
5. Personal Testimony
6. Act of Praise
7. Pastoral Response
8. Prayer of Intercession and Thanksgiving
9. Renewal of Baptismal Vows
10. Reception Back into the Community
11. Blessing
12. Giving of a Christian Symbol
13. Passing of the Peace
14. Benediction

*At the conclusion of the order for Christian Dying into Life, the service continues. If holy communion is not to be celebrated, the service may conclude with an offering, if one has not occurred previously. A hymn and benediction may follow the offering.*

### Invitation

*Following the sermon, the presider and others who will lead the rite may invite those who wish to gather around the participant to an area of the sanctuary closest to the worshiping community. Family members and friends may be encouraged to gather together, and one or more people are encouraged to touch the participant either by holding his or her hand, touching his or her shoulder, or using some other embrace the participant finds comfortable. The presider and other church representatives are also encouraged to touch the participant. If a Paschal candle is to be used, it may be lighted now.*

*If the rite is being performed privately, friends and family members should be invited to participate with other church representatives in leading the rite.*

### Greeting

PRESIDER:  I am the Resurrection and the Life.
PEOPLE:    Anyone who believes in me, though they die, yet shall they live.
PRESIDER:  I am the Resurrection and the Life.
PEOPLE:    And whoever lives and believes in me shall never die (John 11:25–26).

OR

PRESIDER:  Christ is Risen!
PEOPLE:    Christ is Risen, indeed! Alleluia!

*The presider may greet the congregation using the preceding words or others similar to them.*

### Introduction

*The presider may introduce this rite with these or other words.*

(Sisters and Brothers/Friends), Jesus said, "All who find their lives will lose them, and all who lose their lives for my sake will find them" (Matt. 10:39). We are gathered together to celebrate with thanksgiving _____(name)_____'s dying into life. Through his/her faith and the loss of _____(mention loss)_____, he/she has cast off his/her old self and entered into a new relationship with God and this community. We join with him/her in blessing God for the grace which has compelled him/her into new life and enabled him/her to accept this life with joy. With love we witness _____(name)_____'s renewal of his/her baptismal vows, and we reaffirm him/her as our brother/sister in faith by accepting his/her new life and the new expressions of his/her gifts to the Church. We were all buried with Christ by baptism into his death, so that as Christ was raised from the dead by God, we too might walk in newness of life (Rom. 6:4).

### Reading of Scripture

*The presider or another liturgist may read one or more of these scripture passages or may select others, in consultation with the person requesting the rite.*

Hebrew Scriptures:   Job 19:23–27;
                     Isa. 42:1–4; 42:6–8; 42:18–21; 43:8ff; or 61:1–3;
                     Pss. 23; 27:7–14; 130; 139; or 150.
Epistles:   Rom. 6:3–11; or 12:1–2;
            1 Cor. 15:12–20 or 15:36–38;
            2 Cor. 4:7–11, 16, and 5:1–5.
Gospel:   Matt. 5:3–10 or 10:38–39;
          Mark 10:46–52;
          Luke 7:18b–23 or 17:11–18;
          John 3:3–8; 9; 11:25–26; or 12:23–26.

### Personal Testimony of the Person Requesting the Rite.

*Refer to the introduction, page 156, for explanation.*

### Act of Praise

*The doxology, a psalm, or other act common in the congregation's worship life.*

### Pastoral Response

*This statement, based on the scriptures and the testimony, should be delivered from an area in the worship space from which the presider can easily be heard, but is still close to the participant. Going up into the pulpit is not recommended unless the worship space does not have another place where one can be easily be heard.*

*The pastoral response may be followed by a moment of silence for reflection and meditation.*

### Prayer of Intercession and Thanksgiving

*The Presider will lead this prayer using these or other words.*

PRESIDER:   Gentle God, Creator and Savior, Giver of all life and Forgiver of all the living, we thank you for the gift of your Son Jesus, the Christ, who suffered, died, and was raised by you so that we may know the fullness of risen life.

We give you thanks for our sister/brother _____ (name) _____ who is reborn among us. We give you thanks for who she/he once was, who she/he now is, and who she/he will become as in Christ she/he continues dying into life.

We remember that Jesus Christ lifted children into loving arms to embrace and bless them.[1] We ask you to embrace and bless _____ (name) _____ so that by grace her/his life will be brought to fullness and peace through dying and rising with Christ. Help her/him to feel your loving presence in everything around her/him and to trust in your grace as you lead her/him to eternal home.

Gentle God, we thank you for all those who ministered to _____ (name) _____ in the time of his/her great need. Continue to give them compassion, tenderness, and full use of their gifts, that they may have the blessed peace of knowing they serve you in their acts of healing and comfort. Assure them that they have done all they can as they celebrate _____ (name) _____ 's new life with you.[2] Hear us as now we pray together, with our sister/brother _____ (name) _____ :

ALL:   O God, whose days are without end and whose mercies are beyond number, awaken us to the shortness and uncertainty of human life. By your Holy Spirit, lead us in faithfulness all our days. When we have served you in our time, may we be gathered with the ones we love, having the testimony of a good conscience in communion of your holy church, in the confidence of certain faith, and in the comfort of saving hope, as we await our final resurrection.[3]

As long as we have breath, we join with _____ (name) _____ in praising you. May your great name be blessed forever and throughout eternity. May your holy name be blessed and celebrated, glorified and extolled and exalted, through Jesus, the Christ, our Lord, Amen.[4]

*If the Prayer of Our Savior has not been said elsewhere in the service, it may be said at the conclusion of this prayer.*

*Renewal of Baptismal Vows*

*The presider may introduce the renewal of baptismal vows with these or other words.*

_____(Name)_____ , God's message is near you, on your lips and in your heart—that is, the message of the faith that we preach.

If you confess that Jesus is Lord, and believe God raised him from death, you will be saved. For it is by our faith that we are put right by God; it is by our confession that we are saved (Rom. 10:8b–10 TEV).

*Questions:*

*The presider renews the vows using these or other questions. The participant should signify assent in whatever way preferred.*

Do you renounce the powers of evil and desire the freedom of new life in Christ?
    *I do.*

Do you profess Jesus Christ as Lord and Savior?
    *I do.*

Do you promise by the grace of God to be Christ's disciple, to follow in the way of our Savior, to resist evil and oppression, to show love and justice, and to witness to the work and word of Jesus Christ?
    *I do.*

Do you promise, according to the grace given you, to grow in the Christian faith and to be a faithful member of the church of Jesus Christ, celebrating Christ's presence and furthering Christ's mission in all the world?
    *I promise with the help of God.* [5]

Affirmation of Faith:

PRESIDER:   Let us unite with the one coming to Christ in affirming our baptismal faith.

*The Apostles' Creed may be used in full or in an abbreviated form, such as that which follows.*

PRESIDER to all the people:

Do you believe in God?
    *We believe in God.*

Do you believe in Jesus Christ?
    *We believe in Jesus Christ.*

Do you believe in the Holy Spirit?
  *We believe in the Holy Spirit.* [6]

*Another creed or statement may be used, according to local custom.*

### Affirmation of Baptism:

Gracious God, we give you thanks for your servant whom you have given power this day to accept the covenant of salvation. Perfect the good work which you have begun in him/her. Keep him/her always faithful that no one may take from him/her the crown of life. Grant that having continued steadfast in faith and hope to the end, he/she may be received with all the saints in the life everlasting. Amen. [7]

*This prayer may be said by the presider or in common.*
  *The presider may enact the sign of baptism by sprinkling the participant with water, making the sign of the cross, or other signs in accordance with local customs. If a sign/ action is used, the presider may say, "Remember your baptism" while making the sign.*

### Reception Back into the Community [8]

*A representative of the church may lead the reception back into the community. The liturgist may lead the prayers or they may be said in unison.*

### Question: *The presider or liturgist may read.*

By your baptism you were made one with us in the body of Christ, the church. Today we rejoice in your pilgrimage of faith which has brought you to this time and place. We give thanks for every community of faith that has been your spiritual home, and we celebrate your presence again in this household of faith.
  Do you promise to participate in the life and mission of this family of God's people, sharing regularly in the worship of God and enlisting in the work of this congregation as it serves the community and the world?
  *I promise, with the help of God.*

### Welcome and Reception:

*The congregation may say the following words of welcome to the returning member.*

PRESIDER:  Let us welcome back our brother or sister in Christ.
PEOPLE:    We welcome you back with joy as a partner in the common life of this church. We affirm our promise to you of friendship and prayers, as we share the hopes and labors of the church of Jesus Christ. By the power of the Holy Spirit, may we continue to grow together in God's knowledge and love, and be witnesses of our risen Savior.

### Touch of Christian Love:

*The presider and other liturgists may touch the participant by holding her/his hand or in some other way while saying these words.*

_____(Name)_____, in the name of Jesus Christ and on behalf of
_____(name the local church)_____, we extend to you this sign of Christian love, welcoming you back into the company of this congregation.

### Blessing

*The presider may lay hands on the head of the participant and say the following blessing.*

May God bless you and grant you the patience and love to be guided in the way of Jesus, the Christ, and the faith of the Church. _____(Name)_____, you have died and risen with Christ, you are one with the church. May your light so shine before all people that they may see your good works and give glory to God who is in heaven. God grant you strength for life's journey, the joy of faith, the freedom of love, and the hope of new life; through Jesus Christ, who makes us one. Amen.[9]

*Any elements of the participant's new life which help her/him express her/his Christian freedom may also be blessed or dedicated. These may include a dog guide, prosthetic device, or personal-care attendant.*

### Giving of a Christian Symbol

*A member of the community may present a small cross or other Christian symbol to the participant. The selection of the symbol should be done in consultation with the participant to ensure that person understands its meaning. The symbol may be presented with the following words:*

_____(Name)_____, we give you this _____(name gift)_____ as a sign of our great love for you and in celebration of your having come into new life. We promise our fidelity in your care, and we hope you will help us grow in our understanding of how you have become a new person. We give you this gift as a sign that our prayers are always with you and that you will never again be completely alone. You are our brother/sister and we rejoice that you are sharing your new life with us. We bless God for you.

*The participant may respond to the giving of the Christian symbol in any way she/he finds meaningful.*

### Passing of the Peace

*The community may greet one another with these or other words:*

The Peace of Christ be with you.
And also with you. Amen.

*Benediction*

*The presider may conclude the rite with a benediction or other words of dismissal. The service may continue with a hymn or recessional if communion is not to be celebrated.*

(VCJS)

## NOTES

1. This sentence is taken from the *Book of Worship—United Church of Christ,* United Church of Christ, Office for Church Life and Leadership (New York, 1986), 378, hereafter referred to as the UCC *Book of Worship.* All materials quoted and adapted from the UCC *Book of Worship* are used by permission of the United Church of Christ Office for Church Life and Leadership.

2. Ibid., 363–64, adapted.

3. This paragraph is adapted from the UCC *Book of Worship,* 378.

4. This paragraph draws on the Hebrew Kaddish.

5. The questions and answers for renewal of baptismal vows are taken from the UCC *Book of Worship,* 138.

6. The questions and answers for affirmation of faith are slightly adapted from the UCC *Book of Worship,* 140.

7. The prayer entitled "Affirmation of Baptism" is adapted from the Evangelical and Reformed *Book of Worship* (Cleveland: Central Publishing House, 1942), 79. It is used by permission of United Church Press.

8. Much of the section entitled "Reception Back into the Community" is quoted or adapted from the UCC *Book of Worship,* 163–64.

9. The last sentence in the blessing is adapted from the UCC *Book of Worship,* 144.

# Sentences of Celebration for Confirmation

The journey of faith is a journey through life.
We are pilgrims, travelers, making our way.
We sojourn on the pathway of the saints.
We walk the same highway
and follow the same landmarks which lead them.
But for each generation, in each place and time,
and for each seeker who travels this way
the road seems different.
Today we celebrate tomorrow's leaders,
the heroes of a history yet to be made.
We hold out our hands to them
and beckon them to join us on the journey.
As they walk beside us,
we may tell them our stories,
but we may not tell them the way.
It is a quest they must follow by themselves.
We can tell them of our questions,
but the answers must come from within their own hearts.
We celebrate a new generation of faith,
a new branch, with its leaves about to blossom.
Let us all make a place for them
and let them know that the family of Christ
is their family too,
as we all worship God together.

(JWH)

# Eucharistic Prayer for a Service of Christian Marriage

LEADER:  What has Christ promised?

PEOPLE:  Where two or three are gathered together, there the Spirit will be.

LEADER:  Are we one in the Spirit?

PEOPLE:  Alleluia. We are one.

LEADER:  O Holy One, we, the created, praise you, our Creator. Before the worlds were, before the stars exploded into birth, you intended love.

From the oneness of your will came the many forms of life.

Over the void, across chaos and its deep came your Spirit breathing light. "Let there be . . ."

And there was and is and ever shall be a new creation.

We breathe with your breath, image your likeness, share in the nature called "good."

Male and Female.

Mother. Father.

Sister. Brother.

Husband. Wife.

We long and belong together.

Like the earth, the air, the water and the fire we combine our voices in creation's chorus:

PEOPLE:  Holy, Holy, Holy, God of grace and truth,

Heaven and earth are full of your glory.

Hosanna in the highest.

Blessed is the one who comes in your name.

Hosanna in the highest.

LEADER:  Deep within us we hear your command—

"Be fruitful—"

And yet . . .

We fall from our center, deny our call.

We choose barrenness instead of beauty.

We lay waste to the fruits of our spirit.

We threaten the very life of life.

We break faith with the rest of creation.

And yet . . .

Your promise is given.

Your promise is kept.

You do not withdraw your Spirit from us.

Because you loved the world so much,

one came in your name,

one who did not despise us,

one who did not reject us.

Jesus touched and we blossomed.

Jesus spoke. We were rooted in truth.

Jesus bore our barren sins, our bitter sorrows.

Surely Jesus carried our grief to the cross.

On the night of betrayal

Jesus took the giftedness of earth into his hands,

lifted the loaf, blessed and broke it, saying,

"Take, eat, this is my body given for you."

After supper he took the cup, lifted it for blessing,

and passed it to his friends, saying,

"Drink from this, all of you.

This is the cup of the new covenant in my blood

poured out for you and many for the forgiveness of sins."

Then, as now, we taste the bread,

we touch the cup.

Now, as then, we taste and touch,

we drink and sing.

We experience Christ's presence.

We expect the triumph of God.

PEOPLE:    Christ has died.

Christ is risen.

Christ will come again.

LEADER:    O Holy One,

Gather us up.

Bond us together in your bread for the world.

Leaven us with courage, with passion, with trust.

Bless and break us open

as your child was blessed and broken.

Lift us as his cup was lifted.

Press our wills so the wine of your love overflows in our lives.

Fill us with the sweetness of a wedding,

the salt of the Gospel,
the gall of the cross.
Seal us with the new wine of creation.
Let us eat freely.
We are fed by your Word.
Let us drink deeply.
We drink from the Spirit of God.

PEOPLE: Alleluia!

(HME)

# GENERAL RESOURCES

# *Calls to Worship*

1. Come together, everyone
   and bring your stories
   and sing your songs
   and share in the Spirit.
   Let your feelings paint the sky
   like a rainbow of banners and balloons.
   Let your thought fill the air
   and come to life in bodies of sound
   ringing out like a song
   to which the whole world will be dancing.
   And let even the silence speak
   with a thousand voices
   in tribute to our loving, living God
   and in celebration of our lives—
   the priceless gift God has given us.                    (JWH)

2. Sometimes worship is a parade, a celebration,
   a gathering of people expressing their joy.
   Sometimes worship is an adventure, a quest,
   a gathering of people searching for meaning.
   Sometimes worship is a funeral, a fast,
   a gathering of people seeking comfort in their grief.
   Among us today are people who have come to march,
      people who have come to search,
      people who have come to weep . . .
   Yet we have all come to acknowledge God
   and to touch each other.
   Come with open minds, open hearts, open arms;
   that we all might find that for which we have come
   and that, as well, we all might be surprised.          (JWH)

3. We worship the God who inhabits our world
   and indwells our lives.
   We need not look up to find God,
   we need only look around:
   within ourselves, beyond ourselves,
   into the eyes of another.
   We need not listen for distant thunder to find God,
   we need only listen to the music of life,
   the words of children,
   the questions of the curious,
   the rhythm of a heartbeat.
   We worship the God who inhabits our world
   and who indwells our lives.                                                                 (JWH)

4. Come join the band,
   the sacred parade:
   a mystical fusion of ages and stages of faith . . .
   the mortal and eternal in direct encounter—
   the human soul invites the divine presence:
   the probing mind reaching out
   for a concept of the ultimate
   setting the stage for worship.                                                              (JWH)

5. LEADER:     Laugh! Children of God!
               Let tears of joy baptize your eyes and your cheeks.
               Give God thanks and celebrate!
               It's great to be alive!
   PEOPLE:     It's great to be alive!
   LEADER:     Dance! Children of God!
               Lose yourself in the choreography of the Spirit.
               Life is a dance and God is the orchestra.
               It's great to be alive!
   PEOPLE:     It's great to be alive!
   LEADER:     Embrace! Children of God!
               Open your arms and feel close to each other.
               It is in our openness where life takes on meaning.
               It's great to be alive!
   PEOPLE:     Give God thanks and celebrate!
               It's great to be alive!                                                         (JWH)

6. LEADER:     Let the festival of God's people begin
               and let the little children lead the way.
   READER:     You want the little children?

LEADER: Yes, little children, come!
For you the past is a playground
and the future is a rainbow-arched adventure.
For you there are no broken dreams—
only wishes, hopes, fantasy, and desire.
For you it is possible that giants may fall
in the face of your childlike faith.
So come, come and lead us to a new tomorrow
as we live for the God who waits beyond the sunrise.

READER: Come on, children!
The festival of God's people is about to begin
and we can lead the way! (JWH)

7. Come together, joining hands and hearts.
Let our hands be links of chain
which hold our lives together—
not a chain of bondage but a silver cord of strength,
a ribbon of love and faith and community,
giving us slack to sail the wind,
yet holding us in a mystical embrace,
that we may be alone but never lonely,
that we may be together but never lost in the crowd,
that we may be one without forfeiting uniqueness.
Come together, joining hands and hearts,
and let the spirit of God and the human spirit
flow in each one and through us all
as we gather here to share this time and space
and as we walk together on the journey. (JWH)

8. LEADER: Like empty jars, we have come to be filled.
READER: Like ornamental candles, we have come to be set ablaze.
LEADER: Like aged wine in a cask, we have come to be poured out.
READER: Like weary travelers, we have come to find rest.
LEADER: Like lovers drifted apart, we have come to be reconciled.
READER: Like little children, we have come to be surprised!
LEADER: Hear the word of God and make your reply:
"My heart has heard you say,
'Come and talk with me, O my people'!"
READER: And my heart responds, "God, I am coming!" (JWH)

9. We glory in the sea of creativity and ocean of compassion, whose flow of beauty and cresting waves of magnificence draw us to praise and prayer—the Eternal God glimpsed in creation's untiring quest, nuanced in humanity's imaginative potential,

enlivened in dynamics of love and life. Invited to joyous oneness, come, let us
worship!                                                                                                    (TEJ)

10.  As patterns of life are woven into rich textures of meaning through our
     experiences, so we enhance in worship our sensitivities and strengths. Come then,
     today, Divinity's sons and daughters, to celebrate life!                              (TEJ)

11.  LEADER:     Something awakened us this morning—perhaps day's dawning, the
                 smell of brewing coffee, the sounds of alarm on the shelf or a
                 newspaper thudding at the door.
     PEOPLE:     And now we gather with awakened spirits to worship with others the
                 Creator of this day.
     LEADER:     Something moved us this morning—we left behind a sufficiency of
                 sleep or a restless night, we engaged in feeding and dressing, we left
                 our homes for here.
     PEOPLE:     And now we gather in this place to worship the Christ who moves
                 among us and to follow the Spirit which leads us into deeds of love.
     ALL:        May ours be a faith that is both awake and moving as we serve our
                 God.                                                                                        (GER)

12.  The Christian life is not so much a destination as a journey. Even so the worship
     of God is not to be found solely in the gathering of this people of faith nor in their
     acts of worship or faithful service. But true worship is found in sharing these
     moments when we sense God's presence, and in celebrating those moments together
     with joy. Let us worship God.                                                               (MGMG)

13.  For the living of these days
     let us heed promptings of possibility,
     let us evoke creativities of compassion,
     let us be poised for flight on soaring wings of faith and love.
     O come, let us worship!                                                                      (TEJ)

14.  The presence of the divine creativity touches our living
     in the cathedral music of history,
     through designs of authentic life,
     by the poetry of pilgrimage.
     So come, receivers of the touch of trust and strength, let us worship!         (TEJ)

15.  In orchestrations of creation's bounty, we are called to celebrate the divine!
     Responding to inner promptings, we join in sounds of praise and intimacies of
     silence, remembering, "This is the day which God has made; we will rejoice and be
     glad in it."                                                                                        (TEJ)

16.  Good morning. This is the middle of Labor Day weekend! We have gathered here—apart from barbecues and sunburn and visits with family and friends. We have gathered here to worship God. And we have gathered here to remember our story within the household of God. Come let us worship; let us remember; let us sing! (CLC)

17.  We come to this service where we bring our needs and longings. Each of us has traveled different roads and conceived diverse thoughts this week. But underneath our differences lies the same basic need for love and acceptance. That's why we are here—to admit to each other our need for love. Let us celebrate in worship the most marvelous fact of the universe—God loves us and accepts us just as we are.

(PBR)

18.  LEADER: Sisters and brothers, as we gather in the welcome of God's love, as we gather in the joy of our unity in Christ, as we gather in the power of the Spirit, let us listen for the voice of God!

PEOPLE: Let us worship God, who has spoken and still speaks to those who attend to the roar or the whisper of the Holy One. Amen! (ABD)

19.  (PS. 4)

LEADER: O God, lift the light of your countenance upon us.

PEOPLE: O God, be gracious to us and hear our prayer.

LEADER: You have put more joy in our hearts than have those whose grain and wine abound.

PEOPLE: In peace shall we lie down and sleep, for you alone, O God, let us dwell in safety. (MSG)

20.  (EPH. 2:4–10)

LEADER: Let us worship God who is rich in mercy,

PEOPLE: Who makes alive when we are dead,

LEADER: Who gives new life out of great love for us:

PEOPLE: Let us worship God. (MSG)

21.  LEADER: We have encountered the Word, calling us into communion with God and with each other,

PEOPLE: And calling us into discipleship to carry on Christ's work in our world.

LEADER: So we come together here, joining hands in the great quest:

PEOPLE: To worship God, to love each other, and to serve the world. (AKJ)

22.  (DEUT. 30:14)

LEADER: The Word of God is near us.

PEOPLE:     The Reign of God is at hand.

LEADER:     Daily, daily it draws closer.

PEOPLE:     Yet its movement is very slow.

LEADER:     So slow we often lose sight of it;

PEOPLE:     Our hope falters.

LEADER:     Let us place our hope in God.

PEOPLE:     Let us commit ourselves to God's work—

Then shall we see the New Day.                              (MSG)

23. (MARK 10:13–16)

LEADER:     Deep inside us all—old and young alike—

PEOPLE:     There is a place of faith,

LEADER:     A place of trust and hope and love,

PEOPLE:     Without which there can be no peace.

LEADER:     Jesus said, "Let the children come unto me, and do not hinder them,

PEOPLE:     For to such belongs the kingdom of heaven."

LEADER:     Hear, then, O people of God:
            approach this hour as children of the Almighty,

PEOPLE:     With innocence of heart and unlimited hope,

LEADER:     With a trust that makes you vulnerable,

PEOPLE:     And with love that is easy and quick. Amen.              (RDS)

24. LEADER:     We come this morning to worship together;

PEOPLE:     Different people, different lives, different histories,

LEADER:     Yet we are all children of the same Parent,

PEOPLE:     Created lovingly by the Source of all life.

ALL:        Different people, different lives, different histories;

LEADER:     Yet we all have one Teacher,

PEOPLE:     Jesus, who is so close to God that he is said to be the living word
            that God spoke.

ALL:        Different people, different lives, different histories;

LEADER:     Yet one Lord, one faith, one baptism.

ALL:        Let us open ourselves to the word of God, which is at work in us.

(MSG)

25. To worship is to listen for the ancient song of creation and to recognize within that
song our individual songs. To worship is to share these melodies and dissonances of
our human condition. Our voices vary: some warble, some bellow, but the song is
universal. It is our ode to God, and to the God within us. Let us join hearts and
voices and worship God.                                         (MEW)

26. O great God, who are you?
O great God, where are you?

O great God, show yourself to us, in this place, at this time.
We are listening for you.
We are here because we want to know you more fully.
Let us listen and sing and pray together. (MEW)

27. Jesus said, "Follow me." We don't always know what that means. We are on a journey of discovery. We are here because we want to be God's people; we are here because we are broken and want to be whole again; we are here to celebrate our lives, and God's presence in this life. Let us worship God with great thanksgiving.
(MEW)

28. LEADER: Thanks be to Christ Jesus who has called us into service and enlisted us in a new expedition.

PEOPLE: We have been shown much mercy since we enrolled as pilgrims in the faith.

LEADER: Let us surge forward as comrades in the company of Christ; let us make preparations for a spiritual journey.

PEOPLE: We do not know just what we may encounter. The mysteries of God are many and the will of God is often hard to track.

LEADER: Shoulder your packs and gear. The Spirit will be our guide. No enemy will prevail against the Church of Jesus.

PEOPLE: We are ready to map out the uncertain terrain. We have our orders. It is enough for us to know that we start out with a perfect guide who would even give his life for us. (JWC)

# Invocations and Prayers
## of Approach

1. Invisible God,
   give us hearts to see
   the things our eyes overlook.
   Open our hearts to feel
   the things our hands can't touch.
   Open our hearts to hear
   the still, small voice
   which sounds like only silence
   to our listening ears.
   Teach us to know you for what you really are—
   not flash or thunder,
   but love, softly spoken,
   flowing like a fountain,
   bathing the soul and the skin.
   Amen.                                                    (JWH)

2. Creator God,
   It is in our lives that we become aware of your life.
   It is in the rhythms of the world
   that we hear your pulse, your breathing, your footsteps.
   We have built this house of worship
   not as a vault to contain you
   but as a reminder of the sanctuary that is the whole world you have made,
   not because this is the only place we find you,
   but because here we are reminded to look for you
   on the sidewalks we pass,
   the highways we travel,
   the rooms in which we live,
   the sky and the sea and the land which embrace us

and tickle our senses,
but even more than this
in the eyes we meet, the hands we hold,
the human stories that we hear and tell . . .
there is where we find you the nearest, the most real.
We hold a newborn child in our arms, and sense that we are embracing God.
We listen to music, and sense that we are listening to the language of heaven.
We dance, and sense that we have experienced the fullness of prayer.
It is in our lives that we know you are alive.
We thank you for the lives you have given us,
for the senses which are ours through which to experience life,
and for our human souls which reach out toward you, even now.
We thank you for your loving presence.
Amen.                                                                              (JWH)

3.  Dear Father and Mother,
    We come
    with songs aching to be sung,
    with words aching to be spoken,
    with questions aching to be answered,
    with feelings aching to be expressed,
    with hearts aching for love,
    with arms aching for embracing.

    We come
    with wounds aching to be healed,
    with emptiness aching to be filled,
    with joy aching to overflow.

    Let your love
    soak into the spirit and the skin
    like soothing salve,
    and leave a tingle where once there was an ache,
    so that all may say
    we have met with God today,
    and everyone was touched
    and no one was turned away.
    Amen.                                                                          (JWH)

4.  O God, as we worship, make yourself known to us. If we have doubts, help us not
    to fear them but, rather, help us to find your presence in the ache of our
    uncertainty. If we have questions, relieve us of the burning need always to find

answers, and help us to understand that in the darkness of things unknown it is easier to discover a flicker of light. If we have pain, help us to sense that you can always heal, though not always protect. If we have joy, help us to share it. Help us to see that joy feels best not bottled up but poured out like baptism-water on all who are here, and that in the flow of joy expressed is the flow of your spirit whom we invite, just now. Amen.                                                         (JWH)

5.  O God who is love,
    when you seem so far away from us,
    remind us to reach within
    to the fountain of feelings at the core of ourselves
    and there, let us find you.

    When you seem so unconcerned,
    so massive, so impassive,
    so insulated by your power,
    so distant by your expansiveness,
    remind us to reach out
    to the hand of a child,
    to the face of a friend,
    and there let us find you.

    And in times when we have nothing to feel
    and there is no one to touch,
    let us never close our hearts or our hands,
    but always, let us be open to you,
    and let us be open today; here and now.
    Amen.                                                         (JWH)

6.  Loving God, you molded and carved out the Universe just by speaking the words, "Let there be . . ." With one breath, you gave a lifeless lump of clay animation, and what was only an etching of earth became humanity—the image of God. Gracious God, the Gospel of John says that in Christ, your word became flesh—a living word, a touching word, an enlightening word, an empowering word, a healing word, a word which expresses love. Yet when we think of your power, we don't think first of words or of love; we think of earthquakes, and floods, violent wind, thunder, lightning, dazzle. We don't think of simple words spoken sincerely. We don't think of tender touches, whispers, glances, eyes which speak a thousand words. But maybe we should. As we worship you this morning, open our eyes to the power that shakes the world through the beat of the heart rather than with thunder. In the name of the one who is your Word and Love made flesh and dwelling among us, we say, Amen.                                                         (JWH)

7. Giver of all good gifts, we thank you for your presence deeply embedded in our lives, and for entering our lives fully in your human face: Jesus the Christ. You know our uneasiness with the claims that faith makes upon our lives, yet you linger with us in our struggle and we know we are not alone. We are thankful that you have not abandoned us and that your Spirit continues to comfort us in our search for truth. Encourage us to live the truth we find and guide us to seek the truth yet undiscovered. We are thankful for the bond of love and faith which connects us with other seekers around us and with you, as we live in this family of faith. Amen.                                                                      (JWH)

8. For Sundays When the Gospel Is Proclaimed through Music

   Touch us, O God, through the ministry of melody,
   through the sounds and senses of song,
   through the wordless wonder which fills our souls with heaven,
   through the spirit which teases our feet to dance and causes our hearts to overflow,
   that we might be absorbed
   in the mystery and magic of music,
   and that in this moment of oneness
   our lives will be bonded to each other and to you.
   AMEN!                                                                   (JWH)

9. God with us,
   we have gathered with a sense
   of the sacredness of this space,
   aware of your presence flowing from one person to another.
   We come with our wounds wide open,
   with our defenses down,
   wearing our personal needs like placards,
   calling to you as did so many who approached Jesus,
   saying, "Heal me, help me, touch me!"
   We work hard at being happy,
   at coping, at surviving, at holding on,
   but we have come here hoping to let go
   and to open ourselves to Christ's healing flow.
   Touch our lives, our God, as we worship here today,
   and cast your sunlight through our tears till rainbows rise,
   and plant dreams where wounds leave scars
   like furrows in broken ground,
   rekindling our hope,
   reviving our strength,
   refreshing our faith.
   Amen.                                                                   (JWH)

10.  As we end another busy week in our lives, we come before you, O God, knowing
     that you are always ready to receive us, shortcomings and all. We take time out to
     consider how our lives might better reflect your broad view of life, your forgiving
     spirit, your wisdom, your creativity, your patience. Today we consider what it
     means to live abundantly, like Jesus Christ, the shining light we follow. You call us
     to inspiring, difficult, and sometimes frightening missions to bring your realm into
     our midst. You challenge us to have courage in the face of possible ridicule and
     failure. We seek to be like Jesus Christ in refusing to be dead in the midst of life,
     and in refusing to ignore glaring needs and insistent cries for help. Bring us to new
     life that the spirit of the resurrection might be magnified in each of us. Amen.

                                                                                    (PBR)

11.  Creator of our lives, source and destiny of all that is, we come to you in partial
     awareness of the hallowed nature of each human life, and in need of your reviving
     Spirit for comfort and grace. In the beauty of this place set aside, in the solemn
     reverence of time set apart to hear your Word, in the strength of mutual care, in
     the silence and in the songs which attend your redeeming power, we come to
     worship you and to wait for you.
        May every bitter thought and each nagging worry about what we have done and
     what we have failed to do be washed out into the ebbing sea of your boundless
     mercy. Let every noble thought and every impulse of love be stirred anew by the
     breath of your Spirit. So lead us by your gentle inspiration to sense in each
     moment eternal depths, immeasurable goodness and the possibilities of tomorrow.
        And, in all we think or do, put upon our lips and write upon our hearts the
     Gospel of Christ Jesus, our crucified and risen Sovereign.            (APH)

12.  We have entered your chapel, O God, where there are memories of saints, messages
     of peace, imperatives of prophets; where death is overcome by resurrection and the
     pain of living turned into redemption; where sin is erased by grace, arrogance
     overcome by humility, and despair replaced with hope. We are here, and you are
     waiting for us to receive these gifts. Make it possible during our time together to
     move closer to you and your will. Amen.                               (PBR)

13.  God of love and mercy, in the quiet peace of morning we gather in this holy place
     to sing our praise to you and to be touched by your gentle Spirit. We offer grateful
     thanks for the gift of Sabbath rest and renewal. We pray that through our worship
     we may be recreated in your likeness once more. Let your cleansing Spirit enter
     our lives, that the shadows of our souls may be pierced by the brilliance of your
     Light. Let our destructive thoughts be transformed into expressions of beauty,
     reflecting your uncompromising love. We pray in the name of our Redeemer.
     Amen.                                                                 (JFDM)

14. Come into the dullness of our lives, O God, and remove the grays of stagnancy and selfishness. Fill the canvas of our lives with the color of your love, enabling our lives to burst forth and reach out to others as the blossom of the rose. Amen.

(CAT)

15. Loving God, as we worship you today let not our hearts be as hard as stone, but make us soft and pliable as clay. Let not our minds be armored as a fortress but make us as open as an archway. Let us not cling to preconceived assumptions, but relax our hands to let go of all to which we grasp. Set us free to hold whatever you might send us. May we not be like rocks, unaffected amid the current, unconnected to its source. Instead, may we flow with your Spirit as a fallen leaf floats lightly on the surface of a stream. Amen.

(JWH)

16. Graduation Prayer for a Secular Setting

Source of every human hope,
whose love and care have touched us all,
we gather here to seek fulfillment
none of us can find alone.
Open us to the deeper meanings of this moment
which is both wistful and a time of joy,
which honors our past while advancing us
on an uncertain path.
On this day of endings and beginnings
we applaud the transmission of wisdom
from one generation to the next,
yet are awed by all that remains unknown.
Encourage us always to dwell among those
   who savor beauty,
   practice truth,
   advance community,
   respond in compassion,
   are animated by wisdom not their own,
   empowered by a Spirit they do not possess,
   awed by mystery which defies comprehension,
   and wonder which claims our adoration. Amen.

(EEB)

17. Images from Hawaii

O Holy Spirit, come upon us as the kilihune [mist] fills Kalalau [a valley on the island of Kauai] at the dawning of a new day. Aliven our being with your refreshing presence so that our countenance will reveal the love and joy and caring of our Creator to those around us. Amen.

(CAT)

18.  God of our mothers and fathers,
     God of our children,
     we light our candles as we gather,
     hoping to kindle the spark of your spirit in our hearts.
     We sense your presence in the light and warmth of the altar fire,
     just as we sense your presence in the water in front of us,
     which serves to soothe the parched dry ground of our lives.
     We sing and we hear the melody of heaven in our songs.
     We pray and we hear the voice of the Holy One inside our heads.
     We touch, and feel the tingle of the Savior's hands on our skin.
     We have gathered here to fulfill our human purpose,
     to express ourselves and to find ourselves,
     to hear the truth and let the truth set us free,
     and to become all that we can be. Amen.                    (JWH)

19.  God our Mother,
     for the miracle of continuing creation
     in the conception and birth of a child,
     we give you thanks.
     For the miracle of our own birth
     and the lessons we have learned about your love
     from a mother's tenderness,
     we give you thanks.
     For the miracle of being human and being alive,
     of loving, of sharing,
     of learning and growing
     and for those who nurture us,
     we give you thanks. Amen!                                   (JWH)

20.  O thou Fount of Life, from whom flows springs of vitality and health: As we
     celebrate our worship, may our sorrows be lifted, our joys engaged, our hopes
     energized; that our living may reflect the beauties of freshness, wholeness, and love
     divine. Amen.                                               (TEJ)

21.  O God,
     as we worship you,
     lead us into life in all of its fullness.
     Help us to worship with all we are and have.
     Let our laughter and our tears
     be instruments of prayer.
     Let our loves and our delights

fly out in a sky-parade,
painting our world and our worship
with color and sound.
Make our doubt the clay from which we shape our faith.
Let our fears boil within us
until they emerge as shining hope.
And let the light of the world be born within us
until we radiate the love that is Christ.
Amen.                                                                   (JWH)

22.  God of Moses,
     our candles burn like Moses' bush.
     They burn before us while we wander
     in the wilderness of our lives,
     drawn to the Spirit
     which seems to be present within the flame.
     Our simple prayer is this:
     that we might sense your glory in the world around us,
     that we might feel the warmth of your flame,
     that we might ourselves be kindled by that Spirit.
     Thank you for hearing the cries of your people
     for their freedom,
     and thank you for following us
     when we would not or could not follow you.
     Amen.                                                              (JWH)

23.  O God,
     we need love.
     Like children,
     we need the warm arms of a mother cradling us to the breast.
     Like young lovers,
     we need the ecstasy of reciprocal desire.
     Like old friends,
     we need the comfort of the time-tested companionship
     which softly warms us like a well-worn flannel shirt.
     Like teenagers,
     we need love which expresses itself in freedom,
     and endless sky in which to test our wings.
     As we worship you today,
     let us find the love we seek.
     Let it fill our lives as wine fills a cask.

Let it overflow like water from a desert spring.
Let it glow like the noonday sun.
And let the world know that our name is Christian
because of the love we hold and share,
and the love which keeps us in your care.
Amen.               (JWH)

24. To the Lover we pray:
God of the universe,
God of the single cell,
we thank you that we have sensed your presence
in our world and in our lives.
We have felt your lure in our lives,
your tug on our emotions.
We have heard your knock at the door of our hearts.
We have sensed your desire to make your home
in the secret places of our own selves,
and we are honored to be chosen,
yet fearful,
unsure.
O Christ,
more than anything
we sense that you are love.
You are light and freedom and the hope of new creation.
Help us to know you, to feel you, to hear you,
help us to accept you as you accept each one of us,
so that you may live in us
just as we have our life in you.
Amen!              (JWH)

25. God of Life, who bears changes within our souls like the flowing of the tides, we ask your great and gracious presence with us. We your children call upon you and ask that you hear us. We, who have known hurt and healing, the agony of losses and the sheer pleasure of reunion and celebration, ask you to celebrate with us now. Help us to feel the steady rhythm of your presence from deep within us. Help us sense the gathering of your body all around us. Share your life with us, for we need you, and we know how different life can be when your Spirit fills us with your powerful love. Amen.         (SEG)

26. God, you are the source of our life.
Gather us now together, we pray.
Form us into a holy community of your own people.

Mold us by the breath of your holy spirit,
Reveal in this corporate body
the face of your anointed Christ.
Amen. (CLC)

27. Changing of Seasons

As we turn to you, O God, once again you know we have been here many times before. Too often, though, we lose interest in prayer. Let the promise of ___(the new season)___ ushered in by ____(name natural or other event)____ let loose new enthusiasm for the wonder of finding you once again. Let the images of life and the joys we receive from helping others pass through our minds and hearts. Let us recall the gratitude we felt for a kindness done for us this week. Let us be reminded of your constant presence as we focus our inner strengths to reflect on your Spirit renewed in each of us. Amen. (PBR)

28. We turn to you often, O God, as we seek through prayer to find the meaning of life. Sometimes it's a fervent prayer in the midst of serious meditation, but more often it's a fleeting prayer on the run. We pray for patience when there are too many things to be done. We pray for right answers when our children ask tough questions that we are unprepared to answer. We pray for courage when we have to set down rules we know they won't understand. We pray that you will awaken us to hear also the cries of the poor. Help us to redirect more of our resources to clothe the naked and feed the hungry. Mold us, O God, and open our hearts and minds to be willing vessels of your spirit. Amen. (PBR)

# Resources Based on
# the Psalms

## RESPONSIVE SETTINGS

### PSALM 8:1, 3–5, 9

LEADER: O God, our God, how majestic is your name in all the earth!

PEOPLE: When we look at your heavens, the work of your fingers, the moon and stars—why do you think of us?

LEADER: For you have made us with glory.
You have created us with honor and joy.

PEOPLE: O God, our God, how majestic is your name in all the earth!

ALL: In the wisdom of all ages, God gives us life with honor and glory!
We shall praise God for the works of wonder around us! (JCW)

### PSALM 30:2–5, 10–12

LEADER: We have cried to you, God of Life, and you have healed us!

PEOPLE: You have restored life to us!

LEADER: Sing praises to God, all you saints. Give thanks to God's holy name!

PEOPLE: God's favor is for a lifetime and beyond. Weeping may fill the night, but—in God—joy comes with the morning.

ALL: Hear us, O God, and be gracious! You have turned our mourning into dancing—and our grief into gladness.
We will give thanks to you for ever and ever! (JCW)

### PSALM 97:1–2, 6–7, 11–12

LEADER: Our God is the true ruler of this earth.
Let the earth rejoice in God!

PEOPLE: Peace and grace are the foundation of God's earth!
God lightens the earth so we may see!

188

LEADER:   The heavens proclaim God's glory!
          All other gods bow down before our true God!
PEOPLE:   Light dawns for the faithful!
          Joy dawns for the upright of heart!
ALL:      Rejoice in grace, saints of God!
          Give thanks to God's most holy name!
          Rejoice! Again we say, rejoice!                       (JCW)


## PSALM 104:1, 24, 28, 31, 33

LEADER:   Bless God, O my soul!
          God has great wonders for us!
PEOPLE:   The works of God are bountiful!
          The earth is full of God's creation!
LEADER:   The hands of God open—we are filled with good and wonderful life.
PEOPLE:   May we rejoice in your works, God of glory!
          You endure forever in this creation.
ALL:      Sing to God as long as we live!
          Let us rejoice in God's everlasting blessings!        (JCW)


## PSALM 111:1–4, 6–9

LEADER:   Hallelujah!
          Where the virtuous meet and the people assemble,
          I will thank God with my whole heart.
PEOPLE:   Great are God's deeds;
          they are studied by all who delight in them.
LEADER:   Every work that God does is full of glory and majesty,
          and God's righteousness can never change.
PEOPLE:   God makes those marvelous works to be remembered,
          for God is gracious and full of compassion.
LEADER:   God has shown the people the power that heaven wields
PEOPLE:   By giving them the inheritance of the nations.
LEADER:   All that God does is done in faithfulness and justice.
PEOPLE:   In all ways God's precepts are dependable:
LEADER:   Ordained to last forever and ever,
          framed in faithfulness and integrity.
ALL:      God sent redemption to God's people and commanded a divine covenant
          forever: holy and awesome is God's name!              (JWR)

## PSALM 116:5, 8–10

LEADER: Gracious is our God!
Righteous and merciful!
PEOPLE: For God has delivered our souls from death
and our feet from stumbling!
LEADER: Gracious is our God!
PEOPLE: We shall walk before our God in the land of the living. We shall keep our
faith even when we are greatly afflicted.
ALL: Gracious is our God!
Righteous and merciful!
For God has delivered us from death!                                        (JCW)

## PSALM 118:14–15, 17–19, 21, 27

LEADER: God is our strength and our song.
God has become our salvation.
PEOPLE: Hear the glad songs of God's victory!
We shall proclaim the deeds of our God!
LEADER: God has not given us over to death.
Open are the gates of life.
PEOPLE: We shall enter the gates of life
and give thanks to God!
ALL: God has answered us and has become our
salvation. We have been given light and love.
Hear the glad songs of God's victory!                                       (JCW)

## PSALM 150:2–6

LEADER: Praise our God! Praise God's wonderful deeds!
PEOPLE: Praise God with trumpet sound, with flute and harp—strings and pipe.
LEADER: Praise God with a life of dance and grace,
PEOPLE: With sounding cymbals and loud alleluias!
ALL: Let everything that breathes praise our God!
Praise to our God—all the earth!                                            (JCW)

# PSALM PRAYERS

*To follow sung or responsive psalms at morning and evening prayer or Sunday worship*

## PSALMS 42:1–2, 4; 43:3; 63:3

Refreshing God, we long for your presence. Like a deer that longs for cool water in the heat of day, we are seeking you. We want to praise you where your people gather, singing with joy; for your love is better than life itself. Guide our pilgrimage of faith, from the lonely wilderness to the crowded city, as we seek to be your people in the world. Amen.

(RCD)

## PSALM 51:1, 10, 12–13

God of compassion,
we thank you that you forgive our sins,
and blot out our transgressions.
Renew our hearts, O God,
and teach us wisdom.
Grant us the joy of your salvation,
and keep us steadfast in your service,
through the grace of Jesus Christ. Amen.

(RCD)

## PSALM 24:4, 6–7

Powerful God, we praise you for Jesus Christ,
who entered the ancient gates in peace,
whose glory was shown on the cross,
whose power was shown in love.
We come before you,
not with pure hearts,
not with clean hands,
yet we seek your blessing,
we seek your face.
Grant us your grace and your peace.
Glory be to you, O God! Amen.

(RCD)

## PSALM 84:2, 4–5

Living God,
you are the beginning of our journeys,
our guide, and our destination.
There is no joy like the joy of your presence,
in the midst of your people!
You do not deny your love to any who seek you.
You lead through times of weeping
to springs of new life and new beginnings.
Glory be to you, O God, our sun and our protection,
through Jesus Christ, in the Holy Spirit. Amen.

(RCD)

# Resources for Confession

## CALLS TO CONFESSION

### FAITH AND POLITICS

The sovereign God does not merely police our private morality; God is also concerned with the "course of human events" we know as history and politics, for in these spheres we acknowledge or fail to acknowledge God's authority for our lives. Let us confess the ways we have failed to recognize God's sovereign authority in our lives. (JTF)

### HOPE

Beloved, God does not disappoint those who come in hope, nor does God turn away those who approach in faith. Let us make our confession to God in hope and faith. (JTF)

### CARE

Care for one another, and especially care for those in desperate circumstances, has ever been a mark of those who live in communion with God. Failure to care is evidence of a breach with the unseen God and a violation of Christ's command. Let us therefore, as an appeal for pardon, confess together the ways in which we have failed to care. (JTF)

### RENEWAL

The path to authentic renewal is through repentance. In order to become more like Jesus, we must be willing to let him reveal those aspects of our lives which need to be changed. Let us accept the invitation, "Come unto me . . ." by gratefully, confidently laying our lives before Christ now. (JTF)

**GENERAL**

The confession of our sin before God and one another reminds us that as individual believers and as a community of faith, we do stray or turn from the ways of love and justice. We believe that if we confess we shall be forgiven and freed from the burden of guilt and empowered to carry on the ministry of Christ.

Therefore, with confidence in the mercy of God, let us pray together. (ABD)

# PRAYERS OF CONFESSION

*Some with Calls to Confession and Assurances of Pardon*

## SUMMER

Loving God, you are Sovereign over all our days.

When the winds of faith blow strong and our spirits are invigorated, you are with us.

When the burdens of life seem oppressive as humid hot air and our spirits become listless, you are with us.

When a sense of calm purpose moves us from the depths of our being, you are present.

And when a turbulence of confusion or pain storms within us, you are present still.

Forgive us when we neglect to acknowledge or to rely upon your steadfast love. We do so for many reasons. Sometimes we do not want to see you. At other times we try stubbornly to do without you. Sometimes we lock you in the past as if your best efforts were concluded long ago. At other times we put you off until tomorrow.

Great God, forgive us, and grant us the wisdom to trust you, the courage to serve you. Through Jesus Christ, Amen.                                          (GER)

## WHOLENESS

God our Creator, we offer our prayer as persons who often feel less than whole. We have experienced losses that have diminished us. We have found our attention to your will divided by other claims upon us. We have discovered how difficult it is to fulfill our best intentions.

God our Sustainer, we offer our prayer as a people that often feels less than whole. We have sensed an incompleteness to our unity whenever the differences between us seem more important than the one Spirit that gives us common life. We have practiced a fractional faith. We have divided our loyalties in ways that do not allow full service to you, our One and only God.

Forgive us and enable us to enjoy the fullness of your love. Strengthen us and inspire us to whole-hearted devotion. We pray with voices united in the name of Jesus Christ. Amen.                                                          (GER)

## CLUTTERED LIVES

Wise and wondrous God, we come seeking your guidance and your inspiration. Empower us to be more able bearers of hope, more dedicated doers of your Word, more resourceful enablers of others, more open channels of the faith.

We confess that sometimes our lives are more cluttered than committed; then we do not know which way to turn. Help us, when we are most lost, to find you.

What possesses us, that we act as we do? Sometimes we do not know. Forgive our misdeeds, and grant us an awareness of your will so that we might be possessed by a Spirit of freedom and grace.

Encourage us always to focus our faith and to act with purpose.

In Jesus' name we pray. Amen. (GER)

## THE CHURCH

God, bring to our remembrance the many times and many ways we have neglected to listen to you. Diagnose our sickness even today and point us to your purpose for the church. Some of us have been complacent in our appreciation of the ministry we have been privileged to share; others have chosen to heed personal preference rather than seek your will. Yet you have blessed us and given us ample signs of assurance. The problem is not with our stars, or our size, or our age, but with the depth of our conviction. Turn us, even against our hesitation, toward you and let us march as your church triumphant. Amen. (JTF)

## SUFFERING (PS. 46:1)

*Prayer of Confession*

O God of Comfort and Justice, forgive the suffering we have caused others: the malicious comment or hasty word that, once spoken, cannot be recalled, the self-indulgence that ignores real need, and the violence we wish upon our enemies. Forgive us, too, for blaming you for the evil we could have avoided or prevented. And pardon our blasphemy that uses you to explain that which we don't understand. Guide us to an understanding of you, not as source of our troubles, but as "our refuge and strength, a very present help in trouble." (JTF)

*Assurance of Pardon*

In the act of suffering, Christ absorbed our sins. In unfailing love, he forgives our heartfelt failures. In Christ's resurrection, God promises acceptance, assures pardon, and affirms eternal life. "Your sins are forgiven you," Christ says. "Go and sin no more." (JTF)

## POVERTY (LUKE 6:20; 10:30–31)

Comforter of the poor and afflicter of the proud, you are sometimes very hard to understand. Your Christ said, "Blessed are the poor," but we can find no blessing in poverty, and we surely would not stand in line to embrace it. Instead, we are afraid of the poor; we invent reasons to justify our fear; and we, like the priest and Levite of old, cross the street to avoid our fear. Often our fetters are as heavy as fetters of want. Free us from our fear; free us to befriend all people, like Jesus the Christ. Amen. (JTF)

## LITANY OF CONFESSION—COMMUNION

LEADER: As we prepare to meet Jesus Christ at table, let us confess to God our brokenness and need.

ALL: Gracious God, we come before you a people too nearly conformed to this world and its values.

GROUP 1: We fail to develop our God-given abilities, then envy those who do. Too busy for the care of our bodies or the development of our minds and spirits, we neglect the nurture of our own best selves.

GROUP 2: We serve, but sometimes with resentment, because we say "Yes" to the most insistent caller more than to you. Expecting too much of ourselves, we resent others who seem not to do their share.

GROUP 1: We waffle between weakness which allows others to walk all over us, and defensiveness which ignores the rights of others.

GROUP 2: We spend our money on that which is not bread and turn our eyes away from images of those who have no bread. Yet we ignore our own hunger and thirst for you and your righteousness.

ALL: Transform us by your Spirit and renew our minds. May we find the joy and peace that come from seeking your will, through Jesus, your faithful servant. Amen.

(RCD)

## CALL AND DELIVERANCE

LEADER: O God, you are all around us and in us.

PEOPLE: We thank you for your presence.

LEADER: From the east we hear you call us to freshness and newness of the day.

PEOPLE: Deliver us, God, from ruts and stagnant waters.

LEADER: From the west we hear you call us to the completeness and wholeness we are created to be.

PEOPLE: Deliver us, God, from our broken hearts and incompleted dreams.

LEADER: From the south we hear you call us to warmth and growth.

PEOPLE: Deliver us, God, from hard hearts and cold hands.

LEADER: From the north we hear you call us to the refreshment and peace of a cool, bubbling spring.

PEOPLE: Deliver us, God, from our boiling, destructive anger.

LEADER: From below we hear you offer us a solid foundation.

PEOPLE: Deliver us, God, from our unstable faith.

LEADER: From above we hear you call us to life beyond what we experience here.

PEOPLE: Deliver us, God, from our limited perception.

ALL: Praise be to God!

(CCC)

**SIMPLICITY**

*Prayer of Confession*

God, we have filled our lives with so many things that there is scarcely room left for each other and for you. "There's no time!" we protest. "I know you're busy," we assume. "Get ahead!" we urge our children as our lives become a dizzy flurry of distraction, deadline, and duty. Slow us down, God: forgive our busy-ness which destroys our openness, our preoccupation which leaves us unaware of the gentle breeze of your Spirit, our self-absorption which makes us ignore the cries of our brothers and sisters. And if we have not yet been possessed by your word of grace and acceptance, we pray that our ears may be opened to hear it now. Amen.                              (JTF)

## HUMOR OF CHRIST (MATT. 21:28–31)

*Call to Confession*

We laugh at God in many ways. But Jesus taught us that one of the ways in which we invite judgment upon ourselves is to promise what we believe God wants to hear while intending to do as we please. The path to righteousness is through sincere repentance which makes us new people, more inclined to obedience than deception. Let us meet God in repentance by confessing together our disbelief.

*Prayer of Confession*

Sometimes, God, we do not expect too much from you; we expect too little. Our lives are not filled with "great expectations." Sometimes your promises seem so outlandish, so unlikely as to be laughable. We are afraid that your promise, like our promises, may be broken and we are hesitant to be so vulnerable. And sometimes we are afraid they may come true and demand too much of us. Help us to cling to your promises and laugh with joy when impossibilities come true through Jesus Christ. Amen.              (JTF)

## EARTH (PS. 51:17 RSV, TEV, alludes to Gen. 1:26, 28)

*Call to Confession*

Confession is God's invitation to repentance, and authentic repentance, in turn, is the key that opens the floodgates of forgiveness. "The sacrifice acceptable to God is . . . a humble and repentant heart." Let us gladly accept the invitation to cleanse ourselves by confessing together the ways in which we have mismanaged God's gift of the earth.

*Prayer of Confession*

Creator God, we believe your word; we remember that you said, "Subdue the earth." In the beginning we had to protect civilization from nature; today we must defend vanishing reserves from a relentless onslaught of concrete. We remember that you said, "Have dominion over every living thing"; but we continue to endanger entire species and create museum exhibits of once-thriving animal populations. In the name of "progress" and "development" we have raped the countryside and plundered our brothers and sisters, until we have come to threaten life itself with extinction. We have forgotten, however, one commandment: you also said, "Replenish the earth." We cannot undo most mistakes of the past, but we can decide to become responsible and just stewards of our fragile earth. There is less time than there was yesterday but more than there will be tomorrow. Amen.                                                                                 (JTF)

## LIGHT

### Call to Confession

I invite you now to stand with me before the light of the world. Our confession may be painful at first because we will be forced to admit some things we'd rather deny and remember some things we'd rather forget. But don't become discouraged—the moment our sins and failures are recognized and offered to God they begin to lose some of their power over us, they cease to block our relationships with each other, and they become, instead of an obstacle, a bridge to the healing God offers.

### Prayer of Confession

Light of Light, Very God of Very God, you have given us Jesus, light of the world, but we choose night and cling tenaciously to behaviors that negate the brightness of your love and prevent its illumination of our society. We are afraid; your light is too bright and we resent its penetration of our private lives and secret thoughts. But we know how self-delusion harms us. Help us submit to scrutiny by the light that streams from Jesus' cross. Expose our guilt and convince us of your forgiving love. Amen.                      (JTF)

### Assurance of Pardon
### (2 Cor. 4:5; Eph. 5:8; Rom. 5:8)

Beloved, the One whose light illuminates our defects and flaws is the same One who died regardless of them. "While we were yet sinners, Christ died for us," offering forever the gift of forgiveness. It is the God who said, "Let light shine!" who makes of us what no striving, no system can. It is God's light, shining on our hearts that makes us children of light.                                                                                          (JTF)

## APARTHEID (JAMES 2:9 Brandt, *Epistles Now;* PS. 51:17)

*Call to Confession*

Our faith teaches that "when our judgment of people or our actions toward them are determined by the color of their skin we are not acting like the children . . . of God—and we ought to be ashamed of ourselves." But our God is also gracious and has provided a cure for our alienation: "a broken and contrite heart, O God, you will not despise." Let us lift our outspread hands to God.                                   (JTF)

*Prayer of Confession*
*(2 Cor. 5:18–19, Eph. 2:14)*

In your holy presence, O God, we mourn our divisions, acknowledge our fearfulness, and admit our shameful silence in the face of injustice. God, who in Christ reconciled all flesh and dismantled the divisions of race, class, and creed, forgive the smallness of our vision and our lack of concern. Spoil any pleasure we enjoy at the expense of another. Awaken within us the still small voice of Christian conscience calling us to repentance and igniting our commitment to reconciliation. Hear now our silent prayers for a swift and peaceful end to apartheid. Amen.                                   (JTF)

## INCLUSIVITY (EZEK. 37:11 NEB)

*Call to Confession*

When we are honest with ourselves, we must admit that there are times when "our bones are dry, our thread of life is snapped, and our web is severed from the loom." Let us confess together our separation from our truest selves, from our sisters and brothers, and from the Source of Life.                                   (JTF)

*Prayer of Confession*

O God, you are like a weaver in our lives. Out of the expanding energy of creation you have spun each of us into a unique, colorful strand with our own special hue and texture; you have woven us together into a single family that blankets the globe. We admit that we have rent the fabric of your design. We have allowed ourselves to be bound by the narrow contexts of race, age, sex, and ideology. Open our hearts; so that we may once again celebrate the wonder of the human fabric and dignity of all. In the name of Christ, who lived and died "that all may be one." Amen.                                   (JTF)

## AGING

O God, Ancient of Days, we live in a society that conspires against old age, not wanting to admit it exists. We esteem usefulness and devalue persons unless they are "productive." We live in a time when medical technology, nutrition, and health care can add years to our life, but not quality to our living. Forgive us, O God, for equating old with obsolete, senior with senile, age with antiquated, disabled with dispensable. Show us anew how aging can be: not a reason for despair but a basis for hope, not a slow decaying but a continual maturing, not a fate to be endured but a chance to be embraced. Amen. (JTF)

## SUMMERTIME EARTH

O God, we delight in your summers: your warming sun and your balmy night air, the first marigolds in our gardens, and the rows of new lettuce. We take pleasure in your summertime earth.

God, sometimes we use the world as if it were just another disposable product. Sometimes we ignore our debts to your planet and pretend that there will never be a day of reckoning. Sometimes we think we can get anything we need at our local discount store. Sometimes we even think the world belongs to us.

We delight in your summertime earth, God. Teach us to live in it reverently. Teach us the miracle of this place. Amen. (JJS)

## VOICE OF GOD

O God, who spoke of old to prophets and apostles, who spoke eloquently in Jesus Christ, who speaks today, we admit that we have often ignored your voice. We have heard its echo in the cries of those oppressed by apartheid, in the yearning of peoples to determine their own future, and from the land which we abuse, poison, and rape. We have heard your voice silenced by political paranoia, cultural arrogance, religious complacency, and self-interest. Voice of God, nurture our desire to be obedient and speak again to your Church assembled here in meeting. Amen. (JTF)

## IMPATIENCE

Patient God, we are a people in a hurry. We confess to you that we value *faster* more than *deeper,* and *getting there* more than *growing.* We miss the tiger lily on our way to the art museum, the wren's song on our way to the concert. God, we miss the child on the way to the adult. We only know how to wait with our fingers tapping. We hurry to do things ourselves, God, because we find your steady, deliberate slowness irritating and scary. Teach us to trust you so we can learn how to wait. (JJS)

## HUMAN VIOLENCE AND GOD'S PEACE

*Call to Confession*

What God asks of us is to remember the promise: that God will be with us and work in us. Come before God now, ready to be a part of all that is good. Let go of what keeps you from God's powerful call.

*Unison Prayer of Confession*

God, whose heart beats within creation, we confess our turning away from you. You give us life and freedom and we have traded it for convenience and greed. You celebrate at the birth of earth's children, and we have funded programs that kill your precious ones and take food out of the mouths of others. You cry out for us to follow a way of peace, and we have supported governments that tear whole countries apart in violence and war. You ask us to care for each other, and we have been preoccupied with our personal insecurities. Great God, set us free! We are tired of the slavery we have created for ourselves. Give us grace enough to follow you. Through your amazing Spirit, we pray. Amen.                                                                        (SEG)

## COMPASSION

We pray that you, O God, will bring into our hearts and minds, our plans and actions, our hopes and prayers, a greater love for all people. Break the silence of prejudice, the isolation of ignorance, the false sense of security in earthly fortresses, and erase the fear that prevents communication. Help us to come home to your love, by becoming one family on this planet we all call home. Amen.                                             (PBR)

## GIVING

O God, our Giver of Life, we confess that we have a hard time putting you first. We read the magazine ads and we hear the commercials on T.V. We want badly the clothes, the power tools, the video recorders. We like to give, God, but only when our stomachs are full and our wants are fulfilled. Forgive us, we pray. Teach us to respond to your love with generosity to the church and to the world. Help us to give to you first instead of last. Amen.                                                                                (HWW)

## STAYING ON TARGET

We confess that we have failed to concentrate on you. Our attention has wandered from you. Our hearts and minds have withdrawn from you.

We confess that our own concerns have usually taken priority over the needs of our brothers and sisters. Our comforts have seemed more important than others' poverty. Our difficulties have seemed more significant than the tragedies of others.

We confess that we have forgotten that we are created in your image. We have insulted you by treating ourselves with contempt. We have distorted our beauty with sin.

To love others, to love ourselves. Make these our targets.

Give your strength and wisdom as our bow.

Make our faith an arrow that moves us swiftly and straight to our goal of salvation.

Forgive us. Mend us. Redirect us, our Creator and God. Amen.                              (HAK)

## GENERAL

Holy God, we do not understand why you keep on loving us. We hurt our loved ones. We turn our backs on need. We seek revenge for petty wrongs in petty ways. We do not understand why you keep on loving us. Yet even as we speak these words, we know your presence and your love. We are sorry, O God, for we know that sins against one another are sins against you. Make us strong and tender, we pray, that we may live more as you would have us live. Amen.                                                     (DFC)

## PEACE

We live in the shadow of peace, O God, but too often we face the shadow and not the light. We pray for peace today because we know we are not a whole people without it. Forgive us our warring madness, our abuse of power, and our disregard of the rights of others. Lift from us the burden of the need always to be in control. Teach us the ways of mutual love for all people. Help us to give peace a chance. Amen.                     (PBR)

## PEACE

So often, God of wholeness, we are a torn people. We set ourselves apart based on differences, distinctions, judgments, and opinions. We tear ourselves from within as we strive for independence and unique individuality. We do not recognize our common longings for peace, for healing and deep meaning within life. Emerging from the heart of Christ, you come to us in reassuring love. The power of your Spirit blesses our living with hope and feeds us in joy. In the unity of that Spirit we draw together to sing and pray as your own dear renewed children. Refresh us now as we open who we are to who we may yet become. Amen.                                                     (LLK)

## SCRIPTURE

You have given us your Word, God, bound in a book. And we ignore it. Sometimes we use it to prove that we are right and our enemies wrong. Sometimes we use it to hide from our responsibility to your world. Sometimes we use it to avoid change and growth. We use it as a weapon. We use it as an excuse. We use it to avoid thinking for ourselves.

We confess that we read what we like, and pretend that the rest is not there. Worst of all, God, we think we can keep your Word bound in a dusty book, safe and harmless. We forget that you are a God who will not be bound, a God who breaks all chains.

Gracious God, forgive our narrowness and our cowardly faith. Amen.                     (JJS)

## LIMITING GOD

Holy and uncontainable God,
for trying to contain you, forgive us.
Loving and limitless God,
for trying to limit you, forgive us.
Gracious and boundless God,
for trying to bind you, forgive us.
Sometimes we are foolish enough
to believe that it is to our advantage
to reduce you to something we can comprehend.
Forgive us, Almighty God. Amen.                                             (JJS)

## FAITH AND FREEDOM

*Prayer of Confession*

Holy God, you have called us to live in faith and freedom,
but we live with tightness in our chest.
You have called us to move in a new direction,
but we cling to the path we know.
You have called us to reach outward in love,
but we draw inward for protection.
You have called us to live with abandon, in trust,
but we live carefully, in fear.
God, forgive us. Amen.                                                      (JJS)

*Assurance of Pardon*

God sent Jesus not to judge us, but to save us. God accepts both our courage and our
fears. In the name of Christ, your sins are forgiven. Dare to accept the gift of a new
beginning.                                                                  (JJS)

## LIMITED LOVING

Our lives are sometimes very lacking in love, God. We only barely love ourselves; some
days it is a struggle to love our families; and there's little energy left for loving our
neighbor.

We love you when we can, God, and *try* to believe in your inexhaustible love for us,
but the words sound hollow. When you say "I love you," we are always waiting for the
"if . . ."

Forgive us our lack of faith and limited loving. Amen.                      (JJS)

## CHOPPING THE WORLD INTO PIECES

*Prayer of Confession*

God, we have chopped ourselves, our loved ones, and our world into pieces, accepting some parts and rejecting others. We have made ourselves the judges of which hopes, which people, which nations are acceptable, forgetting that you are the only judge. We have denied, repressed, ignored, or condemned all the pieces of your world that we don't like. In our souls and on our earth we have left brokenness where you created wholeness. Merciful God, forgive us our sin. Amen.

*Assurance of Pardon*

Neither this world nor your life is so broken that God cannot restore it to wholeness. Trust and believe that, after separation, reconciliation is possible. God does show us the way home. In the name of Christ Jesus, your sin is forgiven.                                    (JJS)

## TOO BUSY TRYING

God, some days we don't even have any fun. We don't have the time for fun, or the energy. We're too busy trying. Trying to get caught up. Trying to figure out our lives. Trying to become better people.

God, show us that sometimes we try too hard. Teach us not to be scared to let go. Teach us to trust you. Teach us that it is okay to relax. Teach us to be gentle with ourselves, through your strong and gentle love. Amen.                                    (JJS)

## OFF GOD'S PATH

O mighty God, our hearts are troubled and our minds are in confusion. We have separated ourselves from your peace by attempting to shape our own path in the forest of life. But we have found that path to be lonely. We have stumbled and fallen and with humility we cry to you. Hear us, once again. Forgive us our boldness, forgive us our self-reliance. Forgive us. [Silence.] Thank you God, for allowing us yet another chance to walk the true path where the light is good and the friendship is warm. By your grace our guide awaits us. O mighty God, we remember our lonely path and we rejoice in your mercy.                                    (CSW)

## FACING THE STRUGGLE

We confess: Indeed, God, we think we've done some things right. You know, though, O God, the perpetual struggles we face—the struggle between fear and love, the struggle between safe slavery and risky freedom, the struggle between anger and love, the struggle between foolishness and wisdom, the struggle between pride and love, the struggle between disloyalty and faithfulness, the struggle between pain and love, the struggle between individualism and responsibility. We commit ourselves to carry on, but sometimes we become tired, and impatient, and angry, and scared—so we give up and give in, fail you and each other. And we're sorry. Have mercy on us, forgive us, and free us, through Jesus the Christ. Amen. (AKJ)

## CAUSING GOD PAIN

God of our grieving and of our healing, God of our comings and goings, we have abandoned you. When we might have stayed by your side as you stretched out an old hand to us, we became afraid of our own old age, and we ran away. When you looked up into our faces and asked us for food, we pitied the look and then rationalized your hunger away as if it were simply unfortunate circumstance. When you screamed out in pain because someone was beating you, we covered our ears, because the crying sounded too close to our own. God, we admit that we share responsibility for your pain. We have ignored and forgotten and declared ourselves helpless; we have done almost anything we could to avoid rising up in the name of your love. We have declared our faithfulness in church halls and in sanctuaries and then we have walked away from you on the outside, sometimes deliberately, because we were too afraid. God, forgive us. We know that you created us good; help us to be all that you made us to be. With the help of your Spirit, so be it. (SEG)

# GENERAL WORDS OF ASSURANCE

In our striving to follow Christ, God is a sure and constant presence, never coercing commitment but always inviting it. God holds before us priorities that emerge from the Word, God enlightens us when our understandings are dim, God beckons us to embody belief in deed, God strengthens us in spirit and truth. It is so that we are loved by God.

(GER)

OR

It is not to earn God's grace that we act justly; it is because God's great mercy shown in the self-giving of Jesus Christ frees us to be grateful. Filled with radiant gratitude, it becomes impossible for us knowingly to cause God pain. The experience of forgiveness makes our heart more like God's and more loving toward others. Thanks be to God!

(JTF)

# Collects and Unison Prayers

1. Eternal God, mother and father of every living creature, whose spirit of love is celebrated in our worship: Be our nurturing guide and strengthening tenderness, that we may grow and serve in ways of trust, compassion, and purposeful living. Amen. (TEJ)

2. Love Divine, whose mercies are fresh with the morning and whose grace amazes us into joy: Grant that, in our worship and in our daily living, we may be deeply aware of the strength of your mercy. Move us to share that strength in the world. Amen. (TEJ)

3. Eternal God, in birthing us into this world you have shared a great gift—life in all its dimensions. For the joys and sorrows, for the smiles and tears, for health and suffering, for belief and doubt, we praise you. May your benevolent Spirit guide us in this life, and in the life that knows no end. Amen. (JHH)

4. You have broken into our lives, O God, with the recreation of this new day. You have breathed new life into our sleeping souls and have put a song in our hearts. So we come today to offer you our thanks and praise. Pour down the blessings of your Spirit upon each one here this morning, that we may perceive your nearness once more. This we pray in the name of Jesus the Christ. Amen. (JFDM)

5. Eternal Creator and Redeemer of all, we praise your name above all others, giving you thanks for the gifts of life and love. Though we were born children of earth, you have taken us up in your arms and made us children of heaven. Let your spark of divine love glow within us once more, that through our lives others will come to know your grace, power, and love. In the name of the Christ we pray. Amen. (JFDM)

6. Thanks be to the God of the Mountain! You know our failures, yet you grace us with your presence this day. Help us to acknowledge our failures yet set them aside through your forgiveness, that we may truly share in the love you offer; through Christ Jesus, the greatest sign of your love, we pray. Amen.                    (CSW)

7. O God, we realize you do not call us to be successful in the marketplace; you call us to be faithful as disciples of Jesus. You do not call us to achievement in work, but to responsible living. You do not call us to make a great fortune, but to labor for your reign. Guide us into greater understanding of your priorities. Amen.

                                                                                                              (AKJ)

8. O God, without you, we would be terribly alone. Without your love, there would be no good life. We sense that it is through faith that we can know your presence and your love. Thank you for leading us toward faith. Amen.                    (AKJ)

9. O God, our parent, there are so many enticing things in our world which offer pleasure. There is so much to desire, so much to crave, so much to be greedy about. We seek to grow in maturity, that we might discipline our desires, control our cravings, and give up all greed. We seek to grow in wisdom, that we might discern when indulging in pleasure is a celebration of your creation and when indulging in pleasure is godless self-indulgence. We seek to know when pleasure serves life and love, and when pleasure serves death and division. Amen.    (AKJ)

10. O God, yesterday is memory. Tomorrow is the unknown. We have only today to open our hearts to others. May they find with us what we've found with you. Amen.                                                                                (AKJ)

11. Dear God, you are the author and source of our lives. You spread before us many pathways in this world of wilderness, and we are free to choose our own path. In our process of choosing, Great Spirit, lend us guidance. In our moments of despair, encourage us and broaden our perspective. In our moments of failure, empower us with strength to try again. In our moments of victory, teach us humility. Send us your loving spirit, that we may be agents of care and concern. Open our ears that we may hear each other. Warm our hearts that we may care for one another and enlighten our minds that we may be about the tasks you set before us. Amen.

                                                                                                              (CCC)

# *Prayer of Preparation*

We give thanks, O God of sacred stories, for the witness of holy scripture. Through it, you nurture our imaginations, touch our feelings, increase our awareness, and challenge our assumptions. Bless we pray, our hearing of your word this day. Speak to each of us; speak to all of us; and grant that by the power of your Spirit, we may be hearers and doers of your word. Amen.                                                    (ABD)

# Affirmations of Faith

1. An Affirmation of God's Freeing Love

   God's love frees me to be the person I am without having to become more attractive, more intelligent, more popular.

   God's love frees me to live in confidence, not needing to be self-absorbed, but ready to listen and to hear the stories of others.

   God's love frees me to take risks, to surprise even myself with courage, sometimes to fall flat on my face—but always to move onward with the knowledge that God is encouraging me.

   God's love frees me to view the world not from the standpoint of wealth gained or ambition achieved, but from the perspective of relationships lived and human love shared.

   God's love frees me to put my sins behind me, to know that no sin is too great or too small to be left open and healed by God's gentle touch.

   Thanks be to God! Amen.                                         (HWW)

2. A Glossary of Greatness
   Companion of the lonely,
   Binder of wounds,
   Seeker of lost souls,
   Friend of the poor,
   Source of all that is,
   Forgiver of sins,
   Voice of the voiceless,
   Counselor of the confused,
   Shelter from the storm,
   Creator of heaven and earth,
   we in our ways worship and adore you. Amen.                     (HWW)

3.  In faith, we acknowledge that God has acted in the past, in a holy history.

In faith, we confess that God seeks to rule our lives today.

In faith, we affirm that God continues to send prophets and speak through willing vessels to guide the course of all history toward its end.

In faith, we imagine that end to be characterized by the traits we find in Jesus Christ: compassion, justice, and love.

In faith, we long to be part of that purpose. Amen.                        (JTF)

4.  I believe it is a matter of faith to stand up for those who cannot stand up for themselves.

I believe it is a matter of faith to recognize equally and love all members of God's human family whatever their race, creed, color, gender, marital status, physical or mental capacity.

I believe God's creation is good, beautiful, sacred and therefore to condemn any portion of God's creation is to condemn a portion of God. This is sin.

I believe Jesus Christ came to us to free all people from sin and to make disciples—people willing to live Christ's discipline of love and justice for all.

I believe the Holy Spirit is that power within us that gives us courage and stamina to face the truth and to live it, even to die for it, as Jesus died.

I believe in the resurrection, the victory over death, the truth that is life for all in Jesus' name.

Glory be to God, the One in Three: Creator, Savior, and Holy power of love. Amen.

(DEW)

# *Offertory Resources*

## OFFERING INVITATION

As the days become cooler and the leaves of summer begin to wear their fall colors, we are reminded of the many ways God interacts with the world in order to meet its many needs. The cycle of life goes on and we are among the actors. But more importantly, we are stewards and caretakers of the earth because we are made in God's image. Let us now share in that responsibility as we set aside a portion of our wealth to fulfill our task as stewards of the earth.                                                                                  (PBR)

OR

God has shown us the meaning of generosity in the beautiful diversity of creation, in the overflowing love of Jesus Christ, and in the never ending gift of the Holy Spirit! God has abundantly blessed us and called us to be a community that blesses others through the sharing of our love, our talents, and our material possessions. Let us rejoice now in what we have been given and in what is ours to give as we receive our morning offering.

(ABD)

## PRAYERS OF DEDICATION

1. O God, through the offering of these gifts may we become a more open people . . .
   open-minded in hearing your Word and wisdom,
   open-hearted in healing a broken world,
   open-handed in heeding your call for charity and enacted love.
   With thanks for all good gifts, we present a portion of our substance and the whole
   of ourselves. Amen. (GER)

2. Holy One, whose heart abounds with gifts, receive this offering as sign of our
   intention to live surrounded by your mercy, inspired by your Spirit, open to the joy
   of your presence, hospitable to one another, and generous toward your world.
   Amen. (EEB)

3. O Gracious God, bless our offering that it may reach and touch those who hunger,
   who hurt, who seek new hope. As part of the global village, we care about all of
   our sisters and brothers. We pray for disarmament and world peace, for liberty to
   those oppressed, for joy to those who are weary. In honor of our Sovereign God,
   Amen. (JHH)

4. We dedicate our lives and all that we have to the work of life, of love, of peace.
   Receive our gifts and lead us in wisdom and courage. Amen. (AKJ)

# Prayers for Special Times
## in the Lives of
## Congregations

## BEFORE A BUDGET OR BUSINESS MEETING

O Sovereign God, we cannot escape aspects of the church's ministry that focus upon numbers, statistics, and projections. Bless our administrative work. Help us to discover value and goodness within reports and evaluations.

Empower with the spirit of *agape* the institutional church and its bureaucratic structures. May the gospel of Christ be felt and preached in all settings, in all places, by all people. Amen. (JHH)

## INSTALLATION OF A PASTOR

O most virtuous Spirit, may we be enjoined together this day in living out a shared ministry which emulates the life and witness of Christ. May we covenant in holy bond to love each other, to agree to disagree, to restrain from speaking unkindly of others, and to avoid all forms of unfaithfulness.

Bless our covenant as we minister together and seek to nurture harmony as pastor and congregation. May we witness your gifts in one another. May we grow together in joy and wisdom as we venture forth praising your Spirit. Amen. (JHH)

## DEDICATION OF CHURCH DOORS

LEADER: May these doors be a gateway between memory and hope.

PEOPLE: May we open our doors wide to invite, to welcome all who come seeking warmth, nourishment, and the comfort and challenge of the gospel of Jesus Christ.

LEADER: May we open our doors wide as we leave this place, empowered, surrounded by love, readied once again to live boldly and faithfully in God's world.

PEOPLE: These doors are a gateway between memory and hope. In their every opening and closing, we seek your blessing, O God. Amen. (MSG)

## FOR A CHURCH SEEKING PASTORAL LEADERSHIP

God, we pray to you for this church in this time of seeking new pastoral leadership. Guide the search committee in their deliberations; give them wisdom in the questions they ask and the choices they make. Grant our leaders wisdom in the responsibilities which they assume. Help us to identify and do the things which most need to be done. Guide us all, that we each may take our part and none be overburdened. Keep us strong as your people in this time of change; through the grace of Jesus Christ. Amen.    (RCD)

## PRAYERS FOR ANNUAL MEETING

God, be present among us today as we gather to organize our life and to join in a meal of celebration. Guide us as we deliberate together, that your Spirit might be evident among us. We have been baptized into one body and one Spirit; keep us faithful to you. Grant that the way we order our life together may enable us to be ever more effective in showing love to you and all people. For we pray in Jesus' name. Amen.    (RCD)

OR

Creator God, another year has passed in the life and ministry of our covenanted community of faith. We have sought to be a faithful and loving people. We have tried hard to live out a gospel of reconciliation and peace.

Bless our Annual Meeting that we may continue to discern your way at work within us. In all that we say and do may we be a people shaped in both values and words by a peaceful Creator. Amen.    (JHH)

## ORDER OF COMMISSIONING A SEARCH COMMITTEE

*Leadership of this liturgy may be shared by a denominational representative and an appropriate officer of the local congregation. The search committee members should be in front of the congregation, standing or sitting as they are able.*

### To the Congregation

The life of a congregation, like our individual lives, can often be best understood as a series of events that respond to the past, occur in the present, and shape the future. These events, however, are never created, developed, or completed by ourselves alone. Life is always influenced by the presence and power of God's Holy Spirit, who leads, directs, challenges, and affirms the faith and life of the people of God.

Today we celebrate a most significant event along the faith journey of this congregation—the commissioning of a committee charged with the responsibility of searching for one who will become the candidate for the position of _____(title)_____ of this congregation.

The people before you believe in Jesus of Nazareth as Lord and Savior. They are committed to the health, nurturance, and unity of this congregation. They struggle with being faithful, as you and I do. They are people very much aware of their imperfections, and knowledgeable of the grace of God. Led by the Spirit, and in response to their own faith, they have accepted the call to serve among you. They stand before you in witness to their willingness to serve.

Let us hear their words of commitment.

### To the Search Committee

It is an honor to be entrusted with responsibility in the life of the church. Having prayerfully considered the responsibilities of the position, are you prepared to serve in Christ's name for the well-being of _____ (name of church) _____ and for the glory of God? If so, answer, "I am, with God's help."

Do you promise to exercise your ministry with faith, diligence, integrity, and love in the name of Jesus Christ, our Lord? If so, answer, "I do so promise."

### To the Church Council/Consistory/Official Board

*Board members stand or sit before the congregation as they are able.*

You have heard the promise of your brothers and sisters of this congregation. Do you promise to trust their leadership, support them in the ways you are able and to extend to them the love of God in Christ? If you so desire please respond by saying, "I do so promise."

### To the Members of the Congregation

*Members of the congregation stand or sit as they are able.*

Members of _____ (name of church) _____, you have heard the promise of those called to serve on the Search Committee. You have also heard the promise of your _____ (name of board) _____. Do you promise to support the committee in the ways you are able, and to extend to them the love of God in Christ Jesus? If you so promise, please respond by saying, "I do so promise."

### Affirmation of Judicatory Support *(if a representative is present)*

As a representative of _____ (name of judicatory) _____ of the _____ (denomination) _____, I stand among you to pledge the spiritual, pastoral, and administrative resources of the _____ (name of judicatory) _____, as you search for the candidate who will most faithfully and effectively serve with you in this shared ministry of Jesus Christ.

*Prayer*

*To the Members of the Search Committee*

*spoken by a judicatory representative, if possible*

In the name of Jesus Christ, and on behalf of the members of____(name of congregation)____, I announce that you are duly installed in your office as members of the Search Committee for the position of _____(name of position)_____ of _____(name of church)_____ .

### The Hand of Christian Love

In accordance with the faith and order of this congregation and the ____(denomination)____, we extend to you the hand of Christian love, support, and affirmation.                    (DD)


## A PRAYER FOR NEW MEMBER SUNDAY

O God of Hospitality, we praise you for the opportunity to welcome new members among us today. We thank you for their life stories, their faith journeys, their diversity of gifts. May we who have been here awhile be zealous in our willingness to listen and to learn. Make us open to revised visions and new perspectives, we pray. Help us to provide a nurturing environment for these new friends as we invite them into our church and into our lives. Enable us to take time for one another as we establish a shared faith and a common history. Bless us all, O God, as we worship together and seek to be your servants in a needy world. Amen.                                    (HWW)


## SERVICE OF THANKSGIVING AND DEDICATION OF A CHURCH REBUILT AFTER A NATURAL DISASTER

*Invocation*

LEADER:   Most Compassionate God, we gather this day as we rejoice in your power for New Life!

PEOPLE:   Most compassionate God, only you could have carried us through the reign of chaos which sought to destroy us!

LEADER:   Without you, we would have crumbled in despair. Without you, any hope would have been crushed.

PEOPLE:   You gave us courage to work for your future. You gave us strength to live in unseen hope. You gave us this home so we might continue serving others in your name as you have served us.

ALL:   Gather with us today, God of love and strength!
Hear our words of joy!
Hear our prayers of thanksgiving.
Bless us with your Spirit and bless this new home to your service!        (JCW)

*Litany of Dedication*

LEADER: From chaos and death, God has saved us!

PEOPLE: Our God has never forsaken us!

LEADER: The faith God has given our lives has carried us to this time of thanksgiving.

PEOPLE: God has greatly blessed us!

LEADER: From wood and nail, brick and glass, God has given us this place of worship.

PEOPLE: From prayers and hopes, trust and love, God has given us new life for ministry.

LEADER: These walls shall begin to gather the sounds of our lives together.

PEOPLE: These rooms shall begin to hold treasured memories of growing in faith.

LEADER: In these rooms children will learn the Good News of Christ!

PEOPLE: This place will be the soil for their young ministry!

LEADER: The Spirit of God will create us anew in the times ahead.

PEOPLE: God has built us this church and we shall use it to glorify and praise God's name!

LEADER: Make these walls holy and yours!

PEOPLE: Feed us throughout the generations to come!

ALL: We dedicate this church to you, God of ages!

We dedicate this church to your glory and will throughout all generations!

(JCW)

## LITANY OF CELEBRATION FOR OPEN AND AFFIRMING CHURCHES

LEADER: Spirit of God, we thank you for all who let the light of love shine forth. And those among us who are your lesbian and gay daughters and sons, O God, are especially grateful for the brave and loving witness of churches now open to and affirming of our lives and our gifts. Most particularly at this time, we celebrate this church as it publicly welcomes all who seek to worship and serve Jesus Christ.

ALL: Thanks be to you, O God, for that inclusive love which makes our gospel "good news," our communities true reflections of your reign, and our hearts full of joy and hope!

LEADER: Even as we rejoice in the light that shines, we remember how much its brightness might be increased. There is so much yet to be done for us and by us:

ALL: So much justice yet to be established,

So much pain yet to be healed,

So much peace yet to be realized,

So much love yet to pour forth.

LEADER: O God, let the peace and power of your Spirit renew and lead us all! Touch with your sustaining presence all those in deep need of your care—those who wander homeless and hungry, those who live with AIDS and all who care for them, those who despair out of loneliness and fear, those who struggle for justice and peace. Through your Spirit and your people, come and make all things new, O God of transforming love!                                    (ABD)

# Prayers of Intercession

## LITANY FOR PUBLIC EDUCATION

LEADER: Faithful and ever-present God, we lift to you this morning our concern for public education. We raise for your blessing and guidance all who work and learn in the public schools and colleges of this state. We bring to you all our hopes and expectations.

PEOPLE: Now hear our prayer, O God.

LEADER: We pray for public schools and colleges where generations have gathered for learning, where knowledge has been advanced and individuals have grown.

PEOPLE: May they be ever strengthened and ever faithful.

LEADER: We pray for teachers, administrators, and all who work in education, where they spend long and thankless hours.

PEOPLE: May they recognize their own creativity, our thankfulness, and our caring.

LEADER: We pray for students of all ages who hope for the future yet have no assurance of what the future will bring.

PEOPLE: May they know courage, faith, and the joy of learning.

LEADER: We pray for legislators and school board members who spend long hours and receive much criticism in shaping the policy.

PEOPLE: May they seek your guidance and do your will.

LEADER: We pray for those who advocate—parents' groups and special interest groups, professional associations and student organizations.

PEOPLE: May their efforts result in responsive, effective, and diverse education.

LEADER: We pray for families who yearn for involvement but find institutions and systems distant and specialized.

PEOPLE: May they overcome that distance and fulfill their yearning.

ALL: Holy God, we ask for all of us your blessing and presence as we strive to do your will in this community. Keep us ever faithful in our caring, ready to support and challenge. Grant all these prayers in the name of Jesus Christ, that great student and teacher who came that we might have life abundant.

(DFC)

## A PRAYER FOR PEACE

Compassionate God, we bring to you our concerns for our troubled world. May the nations seek the peace based on cooperation and sharing which you offer, more than on the peace of drawn swords.

We pray for victims of senseless violence, those who are killed or wounded, those who mourn them, and those who have learned to fear.

We pray for those who labor, that they may receive just wages for their work. We pray for those who have no work, that you may encourage them in their struggle.

God, grant all people your peace. May your church remain faithful, now and forever, through the grace of Jesus Christ. Amen.                                          (RCD)


## A PRAYER FOR PEACE AND JUSTICE (JOHN 3:17)

God, we pray for our sinful world.
We thank you that you labor to renew creation,
that you seek not to judge but to save,
not to destroy but to create.
We praise you that you call the nations to peace,
and the peoples to justice.
With you we mourn that children in South Africa still fall to violence, and children in
_____(community's name)_____ still are hungry.
We pray for people everywhere
who are struggling for freedom
in the face of those who rule through terror,
who plunder the poor and imprison the just.
Save us, O God, from helplessness.
Speak to us and show us each our part to play
in your mission of recreating the earth.
Cleanse us from all that keeps us from serving you
and loving our neighbors in integrity of word and deed.
We pray to you in the strong name of Jesus Christ. Amen.                       (RCD)


## A PRAYER FOR FAMILIES

Let us pray for families:

God, in you every family on earth receives its name. Illumine the homes of this earth with the light of your love, granting courage to those who are hurt or lonely, endurance to those who care for sick family members, and wisdom to those in fearful times of change. We thank you for gifts of love we have received from mother, father, spouse, child, or companion. As we have been loved by you and by others, so may we love. Grant us your peace, through Jesus the Christ. Amen.

Let us pray for the families of violence:

We pray for the abused, that you may show them the way to safety and new life. We pray for abusers, that they may be restrained from their violence and that they, too, might discover new ways of being in the world. We pray for those who minister with victims of abuse by family members. Grant courage and healing to all who seek to build lives free from violence, through Jesus our life. Amen.

Let us pray for our world family:

God of peace, in this world so full of conflict, help us to learn from you how to strive for what is important without turning to violence. Teach all nations to turn to the ways of justice and peace, that the many peoples of this world may live as one family on earth. Amen.

(RCD)

## A PRAYER FOR THE CITY (REV. 21:1–4; LUKE 19:41–44)

God of peace, in Jesus you wept for the city,
you loved the city,
place of human greed, violence, wealth, and poverty,
but also place of hope and human gathering.
We pray for the city of _____ (name) _____, for _____ (name of your
_____ town if different) _____,
and for the metropolitan area,
that the needs of all for food, and shelter, and work,
for justice and dignity, might be met.
We pray that the diverse people living here
may join their efforts to seek the good of all.
Minister to this city through the hands of your people,
as they feed the hungry,
heal the sick, and comfort the sorrowing.
We pray for people living in cities around the world,
  who have come seeking to work and to survive.
We pray for refugees and for those who have been driven off the land.
May they too find what they need to live.
Keep alive in us that hope of the new Jerusalem,
of the city that finds its light from your presence,
and its joy in doing your will,
where tears are dried, and violence is destroyed.
Through Jesus Christ, let it be! Amen.

(RCD)

## A BIDDING PRAYER

*Based in places on Service of Word and Sacrament I and II, The Hymnal of the United Church of Christ. Also quotes the prayer over the bread from the Didache.*

Tender and Compassionate God, you ask us to pray for all people. Here we offer our prayers for our world in need, trusting in your great love.

Let us pray for the church: [*Silence*]
    Gracious God, we pray for the church of Jesus Christ around the world. As the broken bread, though once scattered as grain on the hillsides became one loaf, so may your church be one in Spirit throughout the earth, and one in witness to your saving love; through Jesus Christ we pray. Amen.

Let us pray for leaders of the church: [*Silence*]
    Gracious God, lead our leaders. Grant them your wisdom, that by their acts they may encourage the faithful and witness to the world and its people; through Jesus Christ we pray. Amen.

Let us pray for those who rule: [*Silence*]
    Eternal One, Ruler of the Universe, we pray for those who govern every land, and for the people committed to their charge. Look with grace upon the President of our country, _____(name)_____, and the legislators who guide our lives. Turn the hearts of leaders and peoples to you, that governments may seek the good of humanity and of all who suffer; through Jesus Christ we pray. Amen.

Let us pray for the homeless, the hungry, and victims of disaster: [*Silence*]
    God, you suffer with those who suffer. We pray to you for those who are denied what they need to live and those whose dreams have been shattered by war and disaster. We pray especially for _____(name recent victims of natural disaster)_____. Reach out and bring healing through the hands of your faithful people; through Jesus Christ we pray. Amen.

Let us pray for the sick and the grieving: [*Silence*]
    Holy comforter, healing Spirit, grant your peace to those who are sick and those who grieve, and especially _____(name persons from the worshiping community)_____. Radiate through their lives with the light of your presence, that renewed health and strength may be theirs; through Jesus Christ we pray. Amen.

Let us pray for our families and friends: [*Silence*]
    God in whom every family in heaven and on earth receives its name, we commend to your unfailing care all who are dear to us, that they may know you as a friend in joy and sorrow; through Jesus Christ we pray. Amen.

Let us pray for our enemies: [*Silence*]

We pray to you, God, for those whose actions offend us most and for those whom we have learned to fear and despise. Through your great love, make tender all hearts hardened by hatred and suspicion, and work your justice among us; through Jesus Christ we pray. Amen.

Let us pray for ourselves: [*Silence*]

God of hope and new life, help us to see the joy and abundant life you intend for us. Grant us your peace: peace which is not the absence of trouble, but the awareness of your guiding presence in all that we do; through Jesus Christ we pray. Amen.      (RCD)

## A PRAYER FOR MINISTRIES OF RELIGIOUS BROADCASTING

We pray to you, God, for those who minister through television and radio. Encourage those who broadcast your truth in love, comforting the lonely and challenging the faithful. Fire them with imagination as they seek to communicate stories of human faith, hope, and peace, and to praise you in new ways. Guide your people to find the resources needed for this ministry of hope. Where religious broadcasters are guided by motivations other than love for you and your people, turn their hearts to you. May Christian people grow in ability to use media wisely to open the hearts of people to you and to one other; through Jesus Christ we pray. Amen.      (RCD)

# Responsive Prayers and Readings

## PRAYER FOR THE JOURNEY

LEADER: Our lives are a journey, and the road goes ever on. It's a road that began with our birth, that winds its way through meadows and mountains, that crosses rivers and canyons.

PEOPLE: For the bread that has sustained us on our journey, and for the guides who have led us, we offer thanks and praise, O God.

LEADER: We pray for those whose journey ends mere moments after it has begun.

PEOPLE: We pray for those who do not have the strength to travel on.

LEADER: We pray for those whose path seems continually to wind back upon itself, spiraling through poverty, pain, prison of soul or mind or body,

PEOPLE: And for those whose path coils with malice until joy and power and life itself are crushed out.

LEADER: In the landscape of your abounding love we know there are paths leading into tomorrows yet unfathomed. There are days ahead when all your children shall walk upon a green and fruitful earth,

PEOPLE: Unafraid of war, unbeset by want,

LEADER: Untroubled by pain or loneliness, selfishness or uselessness.

PEOPLE: Help us to shape such a world.

LEADER: Let our paths not be narrow and self-preoccupied.

PEOPLE: Let us build broad highways, where all may walk together in beauty, tending the gardens along the way.

LEADER: As we journey on through pleasure and pain, commitment and betrayal, keep us mindful that we do not walk alone;

PEOPLE: That you are Presence in our midst;

LEADER: That in Jesus of Nazareth you came and shared our common lot;

PEOPLE: That you walk beside us and dance ahead of us into the future.

LEADER:   Deliver us, we pray, from the mire of grudges and regrets. We yearn to break away from all that, to come running to your open arms, to your arms that are spread wide with mercy and acceptance.

PEOPLE:   All these things we pray in the name of Jesus, whose story brings life to a dying world, hope to a despairing people, justice and love to a realm of strife. Amen.

(MSG)

## FROM OUR LIFE TO YOUR LIFE

LEADER:   Accept our thanks, dear God, for your gift of life. For all that you gave us in our birth; for all that you give us in the richness of our journeys, we give you thanks; and all of this we bring to you, our God,

PEOPLE:   From our life to your life, O God.

LEADER:   Accept our hopes and our promises: all of our hopes that life may yet be filled with purpose—and its purposes fulfilled; all of the promises we make to ourselves, to one another, and most certainly and inwardly to you; all these we bring to you, our God,

PEOPLE:   From our life to your life, O God.

LEADER:   All that we have been and done we bring. All that we have achieved, in which we take some childlike pride; all that we have failed to do, bringing our uncompleted lessons to you, the Teacher, to learn the answers; all arts by which we have tried and partly succeeded in fashioning sculptures of the eternal beauty; all these we bring to you, our God,

PEOPLE:   From our life to your life, O God.

LEADER:   And we bring to you the burdens of our hearts, our anxieties, our worries, our care for our loved ones, our concern for peace and prosperity, our hopes and dreams for our children; these also we bring to you, our God,

PEOPLE:   From our life to your life, O God.

LEADER:   And we bring to you our worship and our shared life in this place. This church, this altar, this caring people we bring to you, our God,

PEOPLE:   From our life to your life, O God.

(DLB)

## A LITANY OF SHALOM

LEADER:   Two things we know about the vision of *shalom*. *Shalom* is a gift to us from God. *Shalom* is our mission.

WOMEN:   *Shalom* is a personal relationship between God and all God's earthly children.

MEN:   *Shalom* is the home that we seek, the goal of our spiritual journeys, and the valley of our delight.

LAY:       *Shalom* is our sense of security, of being cared for and loved.

CLERGY:    *Shalom* is the source of our courage and strength for which we so earnestly yearn.

LEADER:    *Shalom* is the harmonious relationship with God, which then expresses itself in our thinking, feeling, and doing with ourselves, others, and God.

MEN:       *Shalom* is reconciliation: A body and soul become whole; a house once divided becomes a home again; the lion lies down with the lamb.

WOMEN:     *Shalom* is the justice for all that we so easily forget when we are in control.

CLERGY:    *Shalom* is our hope which calls us to seek liberation and justice.

LAY:       *Shalom* is our Christ, God's Holy Child, whom we crucify and bury, but who will not die.

ALL:       *Shalom* is a gift to us from God. *Shalom* is our mission.                    (CCC)


## THIRST FOR GOD (PS. 42:1–2 Brandt, *Psalms Now;* Matt. 6:33; 5:6 PHILLIPS)

LEADER:    As a desert wanderer longs for springs of cool water,

PEOPLE:    So my thirsty soul reaches out for you, O God.

LEADER:    How I long for a deeper sense of your presence,

PEOPLE:    For a faith that will embrace you without fear or doubt!

LEADER:    Set your hearts on God's goodness,

ALL:       For they will be fully satisfied!                                              (JTF)


## HOUSING (LUKE 2:7b; MATT. 3:20 RSV; MATT. 25:40 Brandt, *Jesus Now*)

LEADER:    Jesus Christ was born homeless, of transient parents.

PEOPLE:    Mary "laid him in a manger, because there was no place for them in the inn."

LEADER:    Jesus Christ knew what it meant to have no place to call his own.

PEOPLE:    "Jesus said, 'Foxes have holes and birds have nests, but I have nowhere to lay my head.'"

LEADER:    Providing adequate shelter at a reasonable price to people in need is a ministry to Christ.

PEOPLE:    "Inasmuch as you serve them, you are serving Christ."

LEADER:    The validity of our faith is demonstrated by our actions.

PEOPLE:    What can we do?

ALL:       We can reach out with our prayers, with our gifts, and with shared labor to those in need of adequate shelter, trusting God for the increase.              (JTF)


## GOD'S CALL

LEADER:    We wait for your Spirit, our God.

PEOPLE:    Like Abraham and Sarah before us, we have accepted your call to journey into unknown territory. We wait for your Spirit now to show us the way.

LEADER:   Like Moses and Miriam before us, we have accepted your call to lead your children toward freedom. We wait for your Spirit now to show us the way.

PEOPLE:   Like Ruth and Jeremiah before us, we have accepted your call to risk ourselves for your plan of hope. We wait for your Spirit to guide us.

LEADER:   Like Mary Magdalene and John the Baptist before us, we have accepted your call to bear witness to the God of life. We wait for your Spirit to lead us in word and action.

PEOPLE:   Like Paul and Priscilla before us, we have accepted your call to establish your church in this place. We wait for your Spirit to enable our ministry.

LEADER:   Guiding, empowering Spirit: we wait upon your silent breath that gives life to our faith, that makes active our love, that emboldens our commitment, and that gives direction to our work.

PEOPLE:   We wait with longing. Spirit of God, come quickly to be in us. Amen.

*The litany may be followed with a period of silence.*

(CLC)

## A PRAYER BASED ON THE TEN COMMANDMENTS (EXOD. 20:1–17)

LEADER:   I am your God; you shall have no other gods before me.

ALL:   May our lives center on you and your will for us.

LEADER:   You shall not make for yourself any graven image . . . you shall not bow down to them or serve them.

ALL:   May we be clear that you cannot be captured and made to serve us, but that we can respond to your presence by serving you.

LEADER:   You shall not take the name of your God in vain.

ALL:   May we have respect for you and invite others to respect you.

LEADER:   Remember the sabbath day, to keep it holy.

ALL:   Keep us mindful of your creative power and help us to be refreshed to enjoy life fully.

LEADER:   Honor your father and your mother.

ALL:   Enable us to care for others as you have cared for us.

LEADER:   You shall not kill.

ALL:   May we have reverence for life.

LEADER:   You shall not commit adultery.

ALL:   May we be faithful to one another and the promises we make.

LEADER:   You shall not steal.

ALL:   May we have regard for the rights of others.

LEADER:   You shall not bear false witness against your neighbor.

ALL:   May our words be truthful and may they reflect honorably on others.

LEADER:   You shall not covet anything that is your neighbor's.

ALL:   May we enjoy the blessings we receive, and share them generously with others.

(LME)

## A COVENANT PRAYER OF RECOMMITMENT TO JUSTICE

READER 1:   O God, who has created your children to be free, we attest in word and deed that you are our God and we are your people. From our earliest days as the people whom you intend to be free, O God, you have called us forth from self-seeking bondage, comfort, complacency, and complaint, to freeing and redeeming action for justice everywhere in the world.

PEOPLE:     You are our freeing God, and we would be your free and freeing people.

READER 2:   O God of the Exodus and the Burning Bush, of the Prophets and of Jesus, we hear your powerful calling to be your servants in the service of all those who are oppressed. At every turn we hear your voice in the cries of the poor, the hungry, the imprisoned, and the broken, for you have made yourself one with those who seek justice, freedom, and peace. We share a vision, a promise, and a yearning for the day of your reign, O God.

PEOPLE:     You are our servant God, and we would be your serving people.

READER 3:   O God, our Sustainer, search our hearts and reveal to us our sinfulness, all the ways that we contribute to injustice and to self-destroying bondage. Give us deep courage to find the true path of your way, ready to give our very selves as living sacrifices for your will. We have heard your calling. Hear us now as we make our pledge. [*All rise.*]

PEOPLE:     You are our God and we are your people. We pledge ourselves now to pursue relentlessly that living, breathing justice which transforms persons and peoples. To your will for justice we recommit ourselves and pledge ourselves, our funds, our actions—our selves.
            Through Christ we pray. Amen.                                    (DFC)

*Prepared for UCC General Synod, to celebrate the freeing of the Wilmington Ten*

## LITANY OF CONFESSION

LEADER:     Here, God, we are yours. Silent now, but filled with new awareness of all our possibilities. Still now, yet full of energy for your reign of justice. Prayerfully we come to hear your Word and celebrate the Gospel which makes us the new beings we are only just discovering inside ourselves. With hope we approach you in worship that we may celebrate the community we have become.
            Great and gracious God, we have known your presence in our midst through calls to personhood, to faith, to justice, and to action. We turn humbly in confession to acknowledge that we have failed you, and each other, and ourselves.

VOICE 1:    O God our Creator, we confess that we have turned away from the startling reality of our creation in your image. In fear, we have turned our backs on the dominion granted us at the beginning of time and have accepted cultural definitions of femininity and masculinity. We recognize now that by these sins we have distorted your image upon this earth. O merciful God, forgive us for failing to be with you the co-creators we were called to be.

PEOPLE: Forgive us and make us free!

VOICE 2: O God all Wisdom, confronted by injustice and the awesome powers and principalities of our day, we recoil in fear and take refuge in our powerlessness. Frozen into passivity and hiding behind complexity, we pray for others to take action at moments when our leadership is necessary. O merciful God, forgive us for forgetting that your Spirit brings wisdom to those who must step forward at times like these.

PEOPLE: Forgive us and make us bold!

VOICE 3: O God of all the universe, we confess that we have permitted the happenstance of birth to divide us not only from, but against, each other. We celebrate our differences, and yet we fail to create that unity which the gospel demands. O merciful God, forgive us for closing ourselves to your Spirit which unites and empowers us for mission.

PEOPLE: Forgive us and make us one!

VOICE 4: O God of all time, forgive us. We live in a society which wastes resources and people. We have become accustomed to such waste. We value the young and the new and the shiny. Yet you, God, promise to make all things new. O merciful God, forgive us for our willingness to be every kind of new creation but yours.

PEOPLE: Forgive us and make us new!

LEADER: Come close, God, and hear the inner yearnings of these your people who seek to be faithful, who long to live justly and to live for justice. We seek your loving forgiveness, as surely as we are a people of faith. For in this prayer, we confess not only our wrongdoing but also our faith. Come, God our Creator, who is known in Jesus the Christ. Come through your Holy Spirit and free us of these burdens.

PEOPLE: Amen!

(DFC)

*Prepared for first National Meeting of Women, UCC*

## A LITANY OF ASSURANCE (PS. 131)

LEADER: When my head is aching and my muscles are tense, you remind me of what is important and what is not.

PEOPLE: I am like a child comforted at its mother's breast.

LEADER: When fatigue confuses my thinking and clouds my perspective, you refuel my energies and assure me that sleep will be coming soon.

PEOPLE: You have calmed and quieted my soul.

LEADER:  When sickness saps my strength and pain is a frequent foe, you tell me that it will not be more than I can bear.

PEOPLE:  I am like a child comforted at its mother's breast.

LEADER:  When anger closes my throat and streams of resentment flow over me, you clear my head and help me to realize that my adversary is human too.

PEOPLE:  You have calmed and quieted my soul.

LEADER:  When sleep will not come at night and the hours crawl by amid financial worry, you let me know that you will provide for my needs.

PEOPLE:  I am like a sick child quieted at its mother's breast.

LEADER:  When my shoulders feel weighed down by the responsibility of family and work, you offer me strength to carry on.

PEOPLE:  You have calmed and quieted my soul.

ALL:  We praise you, our understanding and intimate God! Your spacious lap accommodates our frailties and your strong arms embrace and protect us. Thanks be to the God of love! Amen.                        (HWW)

# Metrical Service Music

Some congregations have been writing new words to traditional service music (the *Gloria Patri* and the Doxology) or singing parts of the service which had formerly been spoken. Here are some words which have been found, written, or adapted for this purpose.

A tune name is suggested for each text or group of texts, along with the text with which this tune has often been associated. Metrical notations are provided, in case worship leaders would like to substitute another tune for the suggested tune. Take, for example, the seasonal offering text for Advent. It can be sung to the tune OLD HUNDREDTH, which is associated with the text beginning "Praise God from Whom All Blessings Flow." If you would like to substitute another tune, consult the metrical index at the back of your hymnal and try tunes listed under "Long Meter" or "L.M." Songs listed under the same meter have the same number of poetic feet, but sometimes they accent different beats. Thus, please be sure to test the substitute tune to make sure it fits before using it in worship.

# GLORIA

*Tune: Gloria Patri ("Glory Be to the Father"), irregular meter*

Glory be to the Spirit!
To Jesus Christ! To the Eternal Source!
From the time of our beginnings,
beyond death's claim upon us:
Life, Light, and Love shall never end. Amen!

(DWY)

# DOXOLOGIES

*Tune for all texts in this section: OLD HUNDREDTH ("Praise God from Whom All Blessings Flow"), Long Meter* (L.M.)

1. Praise God from whom all blessings flow;
   Praise God, all creatures here below;
   God's praise, ye hosts on high, proclaim,
   who doth create, redeem, sustain.

   (Thomas Ken, 1692, adapted RWM)

2. Praise God the Source of life and birth.
   Praise God the Word, who came to earth.
   Praise God the Spirit, holy flame.
   All glory, honor to God's name! Amen.

   (RCD)

3. Praise God from whom all grace flows forth!
   Praise Life, all creatures here on earth!
   Praise Light who guides us on our way!
   Praise Love who forms us day by day!

   (DWY)

4. Creator God, your creatures raise
   to you and our Redeemer praise;
   we sing your Holy Spirit's power
   among us even till this hour.

   (DLB)

# SEASONAL OFFERTORY TEXTS

*Tune for all texts in this section:* OLD HUNDREDTH *("Praise God from Whom All Blessings Flow"),* L.M.

## ADVENT

Hope in the God who reigns above,
who holds us all in steadfast love;
whose spirit blows across the earth,
preparing us for second birth. (APH)

## CHRISTMAS

To God, all glorious heav'nly Light,
to Christ revealed in earthly night,
to God the Spirit now we raise
our joyful songs of thankful praise.
(Charles Coffin, 1736; trans. John Chandler, 1837, alt.)

## EPIPHANY

O God, may we who bear your name
by gentle love your grace proclaim,
Christ's gift of peace on earth declare
and your anointing Spirit share. (DAK)

## LENT

Were the whole realm of nature mine,
that were a present far too small;
love so amazing, so divine
demands my soul, my life, my all. (Isaac Watts)

## EASTER/ASCENSION

O Jesus, risen now to bless,
do thou thyself our hearts possess,
that we may give you all our days
the willing tribute of our praise!
(Latin 5th century, trans. John Neale, alt.)

OR

O thou in whom we move and live,
whose Spirit hovers like a dove;
we worship thee in Christ and give
our praises for thy steadfast love.                    (DBB)

## PENTECOST

From all who dwell beneath the skies,
let the Creator's praise arise!
Let the Redeemer's name be sung
through every land, by every tongue! (Isaac Watts)

OR

God of our lives whose call comes clear
through Jesus Christ, your presence near,
by Spirit led, your will we heed,
your grace to show in word and deed. Amen.             (DBB)

# SUNG OFFERTORY PRAYER

*Tune: AURELIA ("The Church's One Foundation") or LANCASHIRE ("Lead On, O King Eternal") 7.6.7.6.D.*

Refreshed by living waters,
renewed by living bread,
may we, your sons and daughters,
by your own hand be led.
Accept the gifts we offer;
receive the lives we owe.
Unite us in your service;
may seeds of justice grow!

(RCD)

## *SANCTUS* (FOR USE DURING COMMUNION)

*Tune:* NICAEA *("Holy, Holy, Holy") 11.12.12.10*

Holy! Holy! Holy! One God Almighty!
All your works shall praise your name
in earth and sky and sea!
Holy! Holy! Holy! Hosanna in the highest!
Blessed is Christ who comes to set us free.          (DWY, adapted from Reginald Heber)

# COMMISSIONING AND BENEDICTION SONGS

1. Tune: AMAZING GRACE, or AZMON ("O for a Thousand Tongues to Sing"), Common Meter (C.M.)

The love of God, with peace and joy,
will each of us attend,
and guide our ways through coming days,
until we meet again. (NST)

2. Tune: AMAZING GRACE (C.M.)

Depart in peace to do God's will;
walk ever in the light,
for Christ is with you evermore,
to guide you day and night. (RCD)

3. Tune: DENNIS ("Blest Be the Tie That Binds"), Short Meter (S.M.)

Until we meet again,
walk gently in the way.
Dwell in the hollow of God's hand;
rejoice, and serve, and pray! (RCD, based on an Irish Blessing)

4. Tune: AMAZING GRACE (C.M.)

Through Christ you are a child of God,
who dearly loves us all.
Go forth in peace to share God's love;
rise up to heed Christ's call. (RCD)

5. Tune: DENNIS ("Blest Be the Tie That Binds") (S.M.)

As I thy house depart,
may I be truly thine,
that those whose lives with mine may blend,
shall see thy face in mine. (DCD)

6. From the hymnal:

The first stanza of "Lord, Dismiss Us with Thy Blessing" or the second stanza of "Savior, Again to Thy Dear Name We Raise" can be used as a congregational benediction response.

# *Benedictions*

1. Glory to the Creator, who gives us life!
   Glory to Christ, the servant of love!
   Glory to the Spirit, who empowers us forward!                    (LMH)

2. Because Christ lives,
   because the Spirit flourishes,
   the headline reads: Grace, mercy, and peace are yours.
      The news is good.
   Accept it with joy and serve God gladly. Amen.                   (GER)

3. Serve your God with patience and passion.
   Be deliberate in enacting your faith.
   Be steadfast in celebrating the Spirit's power.
   And may peace be your way in the world. Amen.                    (GER)

4. Christ is the Way.
   Follow and find freedom.
   Christ is the Life.
   Receive and rejoice.
   Christ is the Truth.
   Seek, sure that those who seek find.
   All the blessings of God,
   Creator, Christ, and Spirit,
   be with you now and all your days!                               (RCD)

5. There are, in our day, so many people who
   "cannot find God."
   And I tell you:
   that God is in our future calling us;

that God is in our past forgiving us;
that God is in the present loving us.
There is no greater blessing.                                              (DLB)

6.  Like a rock,
    God is under our feet.

    Like a roof,
    God is over our heads.

    Like the horizon,
    God is beyond us.

    Like water in a pitcher,
    God is within us and
    in the pouring out of us.

    Like a pebble in the sea,
    we are in God.

    Let us go out and change our world
    as God has changed our lives.                                          (JWH)

7.  A Commissioning

    Go from here with open arms,
    with heads held high
    and with love in your hearts.
    Each one of us is beautiful and loved by God.
    No matter what happens, always remember that.
    Always believe in yourselves.
    Go out and follow your dreams,
    and if your dreams go up in smoke
    build new dreams and follow them.
    Grab hold of your future and change your world
    as Christ has changed your lives.
    Be everything you can be.
    Be at peace with your neighbor and your God,
    and be happy.                                                          (JWH)

8.  It is good to give thanks.
    It is good to offer peace, *shalom,* God's peace.
    It is good to walk in the freedom that God has obtained for you.
    Go in peace. *Shalom.*                                                 (CLC)

9. Now return to your homes, but not to stay: our pilgrimage is not complete. So come again: join us on our common journey, seeking always God's promised *shalom* and sharing it with the world. Go in peace. Come again in hope. And may God bless you. Amen. (CLC)

10. As it is a gift that we may serve God, let us now go forth, accepting the ministry to which each one is surely called, rejoicing in the blessing of our creator God, continually renewed in the life of Jesus Christ, and hoping in the presence of the spirit. Go in peace. Be led out in joy. Amen. (CLC)

11. God sends you forth from the gathered church to be ambassadors for Christ. God looks for anyone who will lift instead of lean, help instead of hinder. Go to claim a corner of the world for God and may God's Spirit go with you and abide with you. Amen. (JTF)

12. Way/Truth/Life

   The way is long, let us go together.
   The way is difficult, let us help each other.
   The way is joyful, let us share it.
   The way is Christ's, for Christ is the Way, let us follow.
   The way is open before us, let us go:
      with the love of God,
      the grace of Christ, and
      the communion of the Holy Spirit. Amen. (JTF)

13. Faith and Politics

   Let us covenant together that: We shall not rest until "God's reign of righteousness and peace is realized on earth as it is in heaven."
   We shall not seek the illusory comfort of easy answers but will do the hard work of seeking God's will with each new decision.
   We shall not succumb to the false gospel of individualism but shall pursue *shalom,* the hope of justice for all God's people.
   We shall not be seduced by the appeal of nationalism but shall consider ourselves citizens of an order ruled by Christ to whom belongs all honor and glory, authority and power, world without end. Amen. (JTF)

14. May the lonely paths of self-interest and despair lead to the broad highway of wholeness and understanding between people. Let us become builders along the access ways to God's peace. Amen. (WO)

15. Go from this place to reap the harvest of God's love. Go from this place to continue to sow seeds of justice, peace, and love. Go from this place to nourish and to be nourished, knowing that God is ever a part of our lives. Amen.          (MEW)

16. And now the service begins. Go forth into the world in the knowledge that we are God's body, that hope for a new world is in the blood of our veins, that the struggle for justice is the beat to which our hearts respond, and that God's promise is the very stuff of which our bones are wrought. Go forth to praise the God from whom all blessings flow.          (LKN)

# Miscellaneous Materials

## GUIDED MEDITATION ON LUKE 15:8-10

Begin by reading Luke 15:8–10.

Let us relax, get comfortable, take a deep breath, and reach back into that quiet space inside of us. This woman is very special. She has treasures which not all the women of her day had.

Let us imagine that we are that woman. [*Silence*] We have treasures: talents, valued relationships, abilities, memories, accomplishments, shared experiences.

In our daily life, with its emphasis on doing more and being more, we often devalue our treasures, dismissing them as insignificant, apologizing for what we perceive as their worthlessness. Let us take a moment to identify our own special treasures. [*Silence*]

We have nine coins and have lost one. God created us with great beauty, but we have lost a part of that beauty.

We light a lamp—the lamp of knowledge and wisdom—to help us perceive clearly.

We sweep out our mental house, searching for our beauty, the elusive piece of our true wholeness. We seek diligently, focusing on what is missing. What is missing is often only the *confidence,* the *belief in ourselves* to own the other parts, to say to the world simply, "I am me."

It is good that we should seek. What is the missing coin that we seek for ourselves? [*Silence*] But as we seek the missing coin, let us recognize the wealth we have in the nine. Let us see ourselves as full, rich, and complete in the love which our loving Creator has for us, in the wealth of gifts we have been given.

Then we can truly rejoice with our neighbors and friends when our searching leads us to the missing piece of truth in our lives. Let us imagine ourselves rejoicing with the special people in our lives. [*Silence*]

And then can we truly understand God's loving care for all of us, and especially those who have been lost. Let us feel God's loving care for us. [*Silence*]

God, we thank you for the special gifts you have given us. Be with us each day as we journey to wholeness. Fill us with your Spirit, that we may own our beauty and express it in our daily lives with confidence. Fill us full of a deep understanding of your loving care for us. Amen.                                                  (RA, with help from PM, MSH)

## PRAYER FOR THE WORLD

*The sections of this prayer are intended to be offered alternately with the verses of "Kumbayah." Begin with the first two verses of the song ("Kumbayah, My Lord" and "Someone's Crying, Lord")/Prayer for Those Crying. At the end of each section of the prayer people should be given an opportunity to mention names or situations to be embraced by the prayer. Then the next verse is sung.*
*Sing the first two stanzas. Then Pray:*

### *Prayer, part 1*

God of unending mercy, we pray with those who are crying. For women and men who are battered in body or spirit, for children who sleep the fitful sleep of hunger, for all who are imprisoned by walls or worries, for all who are despondent because they feel unloved. Christ, have mercy upon those who cry; Christ, have mercy on us when we turn away from the cries of others. Give us the strength of compassion, that we may not shield our eyes and hearts from the pain of our sisters and brothers, but seek to understand and to heal. Bless us with courage and arm us with hope, that we may help lessen the suffering of our world. Hear this our common prayer and those of our hearts which we offer now.

*Personal prayers*

*Sing third stanza of "Kumbayah" ("Someone's Praying"). Then pray:*

### *Prayer, part 2*

God of our tender care, we pray with those who are praying. We join the spoken and silent prayers that come to you from throughout the earth—from sanctuaries and street corners, from battle lines and prison cells, from hospital rooms and festive tables. With bowed heads or heads held high, standing boldly or kneeling quietly, we pray to you with thanks, with sorrow, with urgency. We ask your guidance; we rest in your comfort. Speak, O God, to your praying people everywhere! Hear this our common prayer and those of our hearts which we offer now.

*Personal prayers*

*Sing fourth stanza, "Someone's Singing." Then pray:*

### *Prayer, part 3*

God of overflowing joy, we pray with those who are singing! We rejoice with sunset watchers, beach-walkers, embracing lovers, playing children, new parents, old friends, and all in whom your life-giving Spirit wells up and overflows. Help us to feel it surging within us; enable us to shower it upon the world! For your steadfast love to those who have come before, your continual goodness to us, and your promised care for those who are yet to come, we give you thanks, O God! Hear this our common prayer and those of our hearts which we offer now.

*Sing last stanza, "Come by here."*

(ABD)

## INTRODUCTION TO TIME OF SILENT PRAYER

Let us take a few moments to recall in silence the events of the past week . . .

Let us remember the things we did last week . . . the things we did well . . . and the things we did not do so well . . .

Let us remember the things that happened to us . . . the things that brought us pain . . . the events that brought us joy.

In our reflection, let us mark an end to this week gone by. Let us offer it upon the altar, knowing that even with its imperfections and incompleteness it is accepted, just as each of us is accepted.

(MSG)

## TABLE PRAYER ON THE OCCASION OF A REUNION

You, God, are forever undefeated by the past, unexhausted by the present. You set us forever on new paths and open ways. Visit us now that the meaning of this occasion might be deepened. In passing years, your love and mercy have touched us all, leaving us sometimes wistful but always grateful. We ask that in meeting together we might rediscover each other and recall how sacred texts exalt such festive gatherings, women and men gathered at table to share food, drink, memories, gratitude, and joy. Amen.

(EEB)

## PASTORAL PRAYER

Loving and gracious God of the thunderstorm, God of the sun, we come before you this morning grateful for your love—not understanding it but holding fast to it.

We are awed that you love us when we do not love either ourselves or each other; that you love us not only in our pain, not only in our rejoicing, but even in our bumbling confusion.

As a father's kiss heals a wounded knee or a mother's song heals a frightened heart, so your love reaches through us and heals. We come before you and ask for healing.

We ask that your healing love come into our world which is in great need. We pray that it reach the victims of floods or terrorism, and the victims of loneliness or pain. We pray that your love touch people in all corners of the earth, people whose names we do not know, but whose lives are precious to you.

We pray for those whose names and lives we know so well: parents and children, spouses and friends. Fill them with your love.

God, we pray for ourselves, and ask your forgiveness for our inability to live fully in your loving acceptance. We are a people who fear; grant us the courage to believe in grace.

We pray in the spirit of Jesus. Amen.                                      (JJS)

## A PRAYER OF THANKSGIVING (PS. 139)

God, we cannot escape your love. We can find no place to hide. You search us out wherever we may be. Your love is like a mother's blanket, protecting us wherever we go. Your love shields us from evil. We may travel to the moon or to the depths of the ocean: your love is there. We may think ourselves to greater levels of sophistication: your love is there. We may fall into the pits of sin: your love is there.

Thank you, Mother, for steadfast mercy.

Thank you for being there, wherever there may be. Amen.             (JHD)

## A POEM

### WHEEL OF FORTUNE

Turn, turn, turn
another turn on the merry-go-round,
a spin on, a spin off of the potter's wheel
until we are molded and modeled into the creation that God has in mind for us.

The eye of God sees what we cannot know or feel,
or what we somehow sense, but are helpless to change.
The potter sees the flaw, and feels the imbalance in the dried vessel.

And so we are cracked, broken down, scattered and
splintered. Then we are brought together,
water treated and mixed with other ingredients,
and pushed, pulled, and punched
until we are pliable enough, moist enough
to be kneaded, and thrown on the wheel once more.

Becoming a piece of God's handiwork is a joy ride,
but it's painful and humiliating once dried
and readied for the kiln to find ourselves in pieces
and beginning again composed of a different mix.

How little we know, how much we need
the judgment of God
to make us into vessels fit for the fire.

Turn, turn, turn
the wheel of promise spins.
It is a wheel of necessity and good fortune
preparing vessels from which new wine shall flow.

(DLJ)

# Contributors

| | | | |
|---|---|---|---|
| ABD | Ann B. Day | JRC | J. Richard Coyle |
| APH | Allen P. Happe | JTF | James T. Fatzinger |
| AKJ | Anton K. Jacobs | JWC | Jeffrey W. Cornwell |
| CAT | Christian A. Tirre | JWH | John W. Howell |
| CJC | Carolyn J. Collins | JWR | John W. Riggs |
| CCC | Cyril C. Colonius | LKH | Lois Koester Happe |
| CLC | Caren L. Caldwell | LKN | Leslye K. Noyes |
| CSW | Cathy S. Walters | LLK | Larry L. Kleiman |
| DAK | Denise A. Karuth | LME | Linda Mines Elliot |
| DBB | David B. Bowman | LMH | Larry M. Hill |
| DCD | Donald C. Duncan | MCT | Maren C. Tirabassi |
| DD | Donnley Dutcher | MEW | M. Enid Watson |
| DEW | Diane E. Wendorf | MGMG | Margaret Gay MacKinnon Godfrey |
| DFC | Davida Foy Crabtree | MLP | Michael L. Pennanen |
| DJS | Daniel J. Schifeling | MM | Marcia Marino |
| DLB | David L. Beebe | MSG | Mary Sue Gast |
| DLJ | Doris L. Judy | MSH | M. Susan Harlow |
| DWY | David W. Yohn | NST | Natalie Smith Thistle |
| EEB | Edwin E. Beers | PBR | Paul B. Robinson |
| GER | Glen E. Rainsley | PM | Pat McCallum |
| HAK | Hilda A. Kuester | RA | Rose Amodeo |
| HME | Heather Murray Elkins | RCD | Ruth C. Duck |
| HWB | Henry W. Bruner | RDS | Roger D. Straw |
| HWW | Holly W. Whitcomb | RLA | Robert L. Anderson |
| JCW | Jann Cather Weaver | RWM | Ruth W. Martin |
| JFDM | James F. D. Martin | SEG | Sandra E. Graham |
| JHD | John H. Danner | TEJ | Terence Elwyn Johnson |
| JHH | James H. Hill | VCJS | Valerie C. Jones Stiteler |
| JJS | Janice Jean Springer | WO | William Over |

# Scripture Index

## OLD TESTAMENT